MEETING & FISHING
THE HATCHES

MEETING & FISHING THE HATCHES

by Charles R. Meck

WINCHESTER PRESS

Library of Congress Cataloging in Publication Data

Meck, Charles.
  Meeting & fishing the hatches.

  Includes index.
  1. Trout fishing. 2. Insects, Aquatic.
SH687.M35   799.1'7'55   77-5879
ISBN 0-87691-232-3

Published by Winchester Press
205 East 42nd Street
New York, N.Y. 10017

Printed in the United States of America

Book and Jacket design by Joseph P. Aschorl

WINCHESTER is a Trademark of Olin Corporation
used by Winchester Press, Inc. under authority
and control of the Trademark Proprietor.

Contents

Acknowledgments   vi

Preface   vii

I   General Rules for Meeting the Hatches   1

II   Insect Emergence   14

III   A Primer on the Hatches   44

IV   Meeting a Mayfly Hatch: the Yellow Drake   61

V   A Realistic Approach to Imitating Mayflies and Other Aquatic Insects   66

VI   Fishing the Morning Hatches (*Eastern and Midwestern*)   110

VII   Fishing the Afternoon Hatches (*Eastern and Midwestern*)   122

VIII   Fishing the Evening Hatches (*Eastern and Midwestern*)   141

IX   Fishing the Un-Hatches   154

X   Meeting the Western Hatches   158

XI   Fishing the Morning Hatches (*Western*)   164

XII   Fishing the Afternoon Hatches (*Western*)   173

XIII   Fishing the Evening Hatches (*Western*)   178

XIV   A Plea to All Fisherman   186

Index   189

Acknowledgments

I have seen many well-intentioned fly fishermen over these many years anxiously identify emerging mayflies. Sure, many of these cursory observations might be accurate, but the only certain method of identification is by a skilled entomologist examining a male spinner in the laboratory. In preparing this book I have relied heavily on these experts who are adept at mayfly identification. I have been fortunate to have the complete cooperation of one of these experts, R. Wills Flowers of Florida A&M University. Wills has identified some of the Eastern and many of the Western species, and has suggested several changes in Chapters III and IV. Without his assistance, especially in identifying troublesome mayfly species, this book might never have been completed.

Charlie Brooks of West Yellowstone, Montana, has contributed by reviewing, commenting, and suggesting changes in the Western hatches. Without Charlie's help the Western stories and hatches would have been much more difficult to complete.

In Pennsylvania I have had assistance from Greg Hoover, who is a graduate student at the Pennsylvania State University, and is presently doing research on the Green Drake. His aid and encouragement have been invaluable in the preparation of this text.

Dennis Bender, also with Penn State University, has assisted by sketching most of the mayfly drawings in Chapter III (Figs. 4, 5, 6, and 7).

There are many others who have also helped – to all who have assisted I say thanks.

C. R. M.

Preface

With the advent of the energy famine, fishermen will feel the pinch in their travel plans to their favorite fishing spots. However, with better planning to fish the hatches, fly fishermen, at least, can enjoy those less frequent trips with more success.

The purpose of this book is to provide North American fly fishermen with information on some of the most important mayflies, stoneflies, and caddis flies and their probable emergence times. Even though your trips may be fewer, your chances of success should be greater. The inexperienced fly fisherman especially needs guidelines to aid him in his pursuit of a new sport. This book will not tell you how to fly-fish, but it will tell you what fly to use, when to use it, and why you're using it.

All too often we do little or no advance planning when hatches of insects appear on the water, and when trout feed voraciously on naturals. Do you want to increase your chances of success? Then plan ahead – schedule your trips to meet the hatches. Be prepared to fish while the hatch is in progress with an artificial that imitates the actual insect. The answer to meeting and fishing the hatches is planning, planning, and more planning. This book will help you in planning, organizing, and scheduling you future fishing trips. Then you too can enjoy the success usually associated with fly fishing when insects appear on the surface.

Admittedly, insect hatches are not the only complexity that troubles many new fishermen. Fly fishing has an intimidating mystique. Many of us would like to try fly fishing as a new skill, but when we observe the "expert" displaying his adroitness, we give up without even trying it. This is a pity, for fly fishing isn't really difficult. The techniques of presentation can be acquired by anyone – and without a book. Presentation and casting are skills, and, as with most skills, can best be learned through practice.

However, meeting and fishing the hatches is not a skill but a body of knowledge, and can be learned from a book. This book doesn't deal with the mystique of fly fishing. Rather, it attempts to simplify the subject by pinpointing one specific but troublesome aspect – the imitation.

Another aspect of fly fishing that I do not discuss is its history and the texts associated with it. The evolution of fly fishing is an entertaining subject, and an understanding of it can even help the angler astream, but it has been presented many times by many authors and need not divert us from our topic.

As you read this book, you'll almost immediately note a strong personal bias on my part. I find that enticing a trout to the surface with a lifelike dry fly is much more enjoyable, rewarding, and challenging than any other type of fishing.

Granted, an expert nymph fisherman will take more and larger trout day after day, year after year, than any angler relying solely on dry flies. But when fishing a weighted nymph you lose the same thrill you forfeit when using "garden hackle" or spinner, you lose the ultimate thrill: that split-second sensation when trout meets fly in full view. However, if you're a wet-fly fisherman and converting you to the dry fly is out of the question, then you can tie all the patterns discussed in the following chapters as downwinged wet-fly versions.

You'll note too as you read through the chapters that I have included some new, untried recommendations and virtually untested hypotheses. There is other material which, although not new, is presented in a new way. Dividing the hatches into morning, afternoon, and evening is a new approach to the problem of meeting and fishing the hatches. Chapter IX is devoted to meeting the "unhatches" and suggests possible flies you might use during this period.

Thus I have done my best not only to cover the subject but to contribute to it. I hope that the next time you find yourself in the midst of a hatch of emerging insects, and with the appropriate imitation on your tippet, it will be this book – not just good luck – that has put you there. And, of course, I wish you good luck too.

MEETING & FISHING
THE HATCHES

Chapter I

General Rules for Meeting the Hatches

Has the following series of events ever happened to you?

You're on the most productive pool of your favorite stream, and a hatch appears. The mayfly resembles a Pale Evening Dun, so you check your fly box for an appropriate imitation. The closest artificial you have is a size 12 Light Cahill – the mayfly would more appropriately be imitated by a size 16 Pale Evening Dun. You hurriedly cast in the direction of five rising trout. The first two trout rise to the imitation, but refuse it. Finally, you hook a trout! Many more casts over rising trout – but no more success. You decide you'll quit for the day, angry at yourself for not being better prepared with proper dry flies.

Sure you fished while a hatch developed – but were you prepared for it? Suppose you had planned to meet this specific hatch, and suppose you had some prior, basic knowledge of hatches.

Let's look at the same hatch with some planning on your part. You've looked forward to this trip for a long time. You've planned the trip to be on your favorite stream when the Pale Evening Dun appears. You're prepared for the hatch with plenty of size 14, 16, and 18 Pale Evening Dun imitations. A half-hour after you arrive at the pool, the expectant mayfly emerges. Several trout feed in front of you on sluggish naturals, and you begin casting in their direction. After twenty minutes you've hooked and released four heavy brown trout. You move downstream toward several other feeding fish, and experience the same success there.

This latter example clearly depicts meeting and fishing the hatches – scheduling your trip at a certain time and date for an anticipated hatch. If you follow the rules for fishing the hatches later in this chapter, you too might experience the latter series of events more often.

Meeting and fishing the hatches offers fishermen many advantages. First, it should increase the number of fish you catch. With some knowledge of the hatches you'll be prepared with an imitation resembling the emerging dun or mating spinner. Furthermore, during this anticipated hatch trout are more apt to be feeding.

Secondly, fishing the hatch is extremely important for the novice fisherman. I know of no better way for a beginner to get "hooked" on fly fishing than to have him experience a fantastic insect emergence and the concomitant success of matching the hatch.

As a novice, watching several hatches progress encouraged me the first few times I met them.

Many years ago, before I knew what words like "hatch," "dun," "spinner," and even "mayfly" meant, I encountered the Green Drake (*Ephemera guttulata*) on Penn's Creek. It was only an accident that I decided to fish a pool near the town of Coburn. When I arrived at the stream I saw twenty cars parked near the stream, so I assumed the state had recently released trout. As I collected my gear out of the car I noticed that not one of the more than two dozen fishermen were actively casting – all of them were resting near the bank. The anglers huddled in clusters of twos and threes, apparently discussing strategy. This really prodded my curiosity, so I stopped and talked to a couple "locals."

"Why isn't anybody fishing?" I said.

"Gotta wait until the shadfly gets thicker," one man near me said.

I didn't want to appear stupid, so I stood back and carefully surveyed the stream. Five to ten large dark insects flew toward trees on the far shore. Only an occasional trout rose for these large morsels. At 8:00 all hell broke loose – hundreds of these insects now rested on the surface and thirty to forty trout actively fed on the laggards.

"They're working, they're working," shouted several fishermen above and below me. They all immediately jumped to their feet and started casting toward rising fish.

Since this was my introduction to fishing the hatches, I was unprepared. But I was impressed, so I decided to stay and observe the show that evening.

I was fortunate enough during the hatch to be near a true expert fly fisherman. This man cast a Green Drake imitation flawlessly over one rising trout after another. He caught more trout that evening than I would normally catch in an entire year. He promptly released most of these trout back into the water to fight another time, to rise during another hatch. He kept only one huge dark brown trout that weighed close to 4 pounds.

Through more than two hours of light, half-light, and darkness, I observed and conversed with the adept fly fisherman. I was curious to discover his success. I knew it took time to learn to cast as faultlessly as he did, but there seemed to be much more.

"You have to be at the right place at the right time and fish the hatches," he said, as he disassembled his fly rod in front of his car lights.

"That's easy to say," I said, "but how do you know when, where, and what hatches will appear?"

"Well, that's where experience helps," he said. "You should familiarize yourself with some of the common hatches, and when and where they'll appear."

These astute words fell on deaf ears, and within a week I was back to my normal fishing with spinning rod in hand.

It took another so-called coincidence or another accident rather than knowledge before I became a true convert to the when and where of a common hatch.

This next fortuitous event occurred almost one year later, again in June. I had coaxed a friend, Lloyd Williams, to resume fly fishing after a hiatus of twelve years. Tom Taylor also accompanied us to a small mountain stream in north-central Pennsylvania, Hoaglands Branch. As usual I used my spinning rod with a Mepps spinner and had a few trout flash at the lure, but I didn't hook any. About 6:00 p.m. we decided to travel downstream to a large open pool formed by the confluence of Hoaglands Branch and Elk Creek. Here we sat and chatted, mostly about our lack of success that day. Lloyd said that if that afternoon was any sample of the fishing to come, it would probably be twelve more years before he purchased another license.

About 7:00 p.m. some large cream duns started emerging – I didn't know what they were at the time, but they were probably *Stenonema* subimagos. The hatch became heavy, and by chance we had Light Cahills to match the hatch effectively.

When several trout started surface-feeding, all three of us moved toward the stream and cast to the rising fish. All of us netted and creeled trout after trout, until we ran out of imitations. We began the hatch with five dry flies – now all had been mutilated beyond recognition. However, before our abortive finish, I caught my limit of eight trout. This was a momentous evening for all of us, but especially for me. I have never cast my spinning rod over trout since I experienced that hatch all those many years ago.

After the second accidental meeting-and-fishing-the-hatch episode with the Light Cahill, I recalled and reviewed the advice the expert had given me a year earlier on Penn's Creek. His suggestion, that I should familiarize myself with some of the common hatches and when and where they'll appear, evolved into four rules, which I follow rigidly when I want to meet and fish a specific hatch: (1) *select a common species of mayfly or caddis fly;* (2) *choose a probable date the common species emerges;* (3) *look for the hatch on a good stream; and* (4) *fish the stream at the proper time.* All four rules are equally important to follow; if you miss one you'll likely miss the hatch, if you execute all you very well may meet the hatch.

Let's look at each of the rules in some detail:

1. When attempting to fish the hatch, *select a common and fishable species of mayfly, caddis fly, or stonefly.* Some mayflies, caddis flies, and stoneflies inhabit more streams than other species. Why? There are probably many limiting characteristics; the following are just a few:

   a. Nymphs of many species have exacting habitat requirements. Nymphs of *Hexagenia*, *Ephemera*, and other genera in the Family Ephemeridae seek out bottoms of mud, silt, or other similar material to burrow. These species will be found in numbers only in those streams that meet their requirements. When conditions are right, however, hatches of this family can be truly phenomenal.

      Other genera like *Baetis* and *Isonychia* have no such habitat reqirements and swim about freely on the bottom. These latter two genera should be found in a wider range of waters than the burrowers – though of course they too have requirements, like the need for fast water.

A common mayfly species is the *Ephemerella subvaria* female dun (Hendrickson), common on many Eastern and Midwestern streams.

The *Ephemerella inermis* male dun (Pale Morning Dun) is found on many Western waters from Alaska to California.

Other nymphs like those of the Family Heptageniidae usually cling to rocks in fast to moderate water. If these features are missing or minimal, then hatches will be lacking or unimportant.

b. Some species can apparently withstand pollution more readily than other species. *Epeorus* species are common only in cold, rapid, and highly pure waters. Conversely, both *Stenacron canadense* (Light Cahill) and *Ephemerella invaria* (Pale Evening Dun) appear to be able to withstand some pollution – or at least they return more quickly to a stream just emerging from pollution. This comes from no scientific study, but rather from my own personal observations. These two species produce heavy hatches on two Central Pennsylvania streams – Spring Creek and the Little Juniata River – that are just returning from extensive periods of severe pollution.

c. Finally, some mayflies develop on large rivers usually too warm to be permanent trout streams, and not the typical water to which we are accustomed. Still other species are found mainly on slow water, and on ponds and lakes – again not on waters we often fly-fish for trout. Then there are others (most of those listed in Chapter III in the Emergence Chart) that we often find on typical trout streams.

But there's the question: Why is a species of mayfly found on one stream and not on another when both are in close proximity and similar in characteristics? This apparent inconsistency has bothered me on many occasions – but let me cite one. There are two Bald Eagle Creeks in the Bald Eagle Valley in Central Pennsylvania – one flows northeast (NE), while the other flows southwest (SW). Although the two flow in opposite directions, both begin in the same swampy area near Port Matilda. In late August, 8 miles downstream from its source, the Bald Eagle Creek (NE) has an impressive hatch of the huge *Hexagenia atrocaudata* (Big Slate Drake). No such hatch apparently occurs on the other Bald Eagle Creek (SW). I have observed the latter stream night after night between 6:00 and 7:00 p.m. and have not sighted one spinner of the species. Here are two streams, approximately the same size, both beginning in the area, and having similar characteristics – but one has a good hatch of *Hexagenia atrocaudata*, while the species is probably lacking on the other stream.

But a species must be not only common, but fishable. That is, the species must be slow enough in its takeoff from the water's surface to encourage trout to surface-feed. What's the use of imitating a species with a dry fly when trout rarely get an opportunity to observe the dun on the surface, let alone seize the natural? Several years ago a friend wanted to show me a fantastic hatch on a local stream in late August. I decided to go because it was the last week of the season and I was curious about the hatch. Around 7:30 p.m. thousands of duns from all sections of the stream emerged – but not one trout showed. Why? It was a *Heptagenia* species, and like most *Heptagenia* species, it rose rapidly from the surface, rarely if ever pausing to rest before flying. Here's a classic case where a nymphal pattern takes precedence over the dry fly.

I've seen many hatches like this over the years – fantastic, indescribable, prolific emergences, but *not fishable*. If you plan to use dry flies, then the dun's ability to escape from the water's surface is an important aspect to consider. In Chapter II we rate duns (and spinners) subjectively, according to their speed of takeoff from the water. Usually the slower the takeoff the more fishable the hatch.

A summary for Rule 1: Choose a *common* and *fishable* mayfly or caddis fly species which can be found on most streams; or at least choose one which might be common to the stream you plan to fish.

2. *Choose a probable date* the common species emerges. Nature works in orderly ways. As the forsythia begins blooming in late April in central Pennsylvania, so then does the Hendrickson begin its annual appearance. When the locust tree is full of fragrant, white blossoms, the Green Drake is leaving its muddy aquatic habitat and emerging on the surface. Many plants and animals, including mayflies, caddis flies, and stoneflies, appear with some scheduled regularity year after year.

However, emergence does vary to a limited extent for the same species in different locations, and in fact it may deviate from year to year even on the same stream.

Emergence of the same species can vary considerably in different locations – especially as you travel north or south. The Hendrickson (*Ephemerella subvaria*) commonly begins emerging in central and northeastern Pennsylvania about April 28. But as you travel north this species consistently appears later and later. Conversely, as you travel south, the same dun is apt to emerge earlier than April 28. The Emergence Map in Chapter II is a rough guide to compensate for north-south emergence variations.

There are even discrepancies in beginning emergence dates from year to year on the same stream. A colder-than-average March or April might cause hatches to be later than normal. Warmer-than-average temperatures these two months might produce premature appearances.

Species affected most by variations in temperature, and therefore most difficult to predict accurately, are usually the earliest ones like the Quill Gordon and the Hendrickson. Hatches after June (except for the Green Drake and a few others) don't appear to be affected as much by weather variations.

Not only does a species appear later in the season as you travel north, sometimes it emerges later in the season as you move upstream. The Green Drake presents a good illustration of this on Penn's Creek. The Drake first appears on the lower stretch near the town of Weikert around June 1 (plus or minus seven days). Within seven to ten days the hatch travels 15 miles upstream to Coburn. Usually about the time the Drake has ended on Penn's Creek, it just begins on one of its tributaries, Elk Creek. Also, when the hatch has ended on Penn's Creek, it usually just begins on Big Fishing Creek in nearby Clinton County.

I state these examples to show you that emergence of the same species does vary considerably even on the same stream, in the same year – and it varies even more on different streams. However, you can utilize this information to your advantage. When fishing the Green Drake, or for that matter any common hatch, if you don't know ahead of time where the hatch is on a specific date, start at the lower end of the stream. Here you can check the trees carefully for resting duns and recently matured spinners. You can also query local fly fishermen to ascertain exactly where the hatch presently is. If the hatch has not yet begun, you can remain on the lower stretch, hoping that particular night will be the beginning of a big hatch.

Buss Grove and his friends, with their many years of experience in fishing the Green Drake, use this knowledge to their advantage. They begin their fly fishing near Weikert on Penn's Creek, fish the hatch upstream for the next week or two, then move to Big Fishing Creek for that Green Drake hatch. When the emergence wanes on Big Fishing Creek, Buss travels to Pine Creek to fish over the same species there.

With a little knowledge, therefore, you can meet and fish short emergence species for a relatively long period by moving with the hatch – first upstream, then to another stream where the species appears later.

I tried this method of meeting and fishing while the Green Drake emerged this past year. My first meeting with the Drake occurred on Spruce Creek on May 27. That evening, hundreds of spinners reappeared for their final flight, and at about the same time an equal number of duns appeared on the water's surface. Five days later, again in central Pennsylvania, I met the Green Drake on a small mountain creek called Big Fill Run. I was surprised to see the Drake on these fast waters, but especially amazed to observe a heavy hatch at 1:00 in the afternoon. I caught and released more than fifteen trout during those warm daylight hours on a size 10 Green Drake imitation. Several of the trout were in the 12- to 16-inch category.

I next met the hatch, and by far the heaviest, on Penn's Creek on June 4. Duns emerged and spinners fell in numbers difficult to comprehend unless you have actually experienced such an event.

By far the most productive hatch occurred on Mountain Pool of the Beaver-kill on June 8. Hundreds of duns emerged and thirty to forty fish actively fed during the hatch on this Catskill stream.

A summary for Rule 2: Emergence dates for many mayflies are predictable if you *select a good average date for a particular stream*. Always be prepared with other artificials in case the species you plan to fish is not emerging. And always remember: *Emergence dates are only rough guides and never should be adhered to rigidly.*

3. Look for the hatch on a *good stream*. The opening story about the Green Drake is a good example of the importance of stream selection – had I been on most other streams, I would not have found this species. A good stream has varying characteristics to hold a large variety of species. It has fast, moderate, and slow stretches of water, in addition to a bottom containing rocks and mud for a diversity of nymphal life. Some of our so-called trout streams are at best marginal for nymphs, because they're polluted. Don't expect sizable hatches on these questionable waters. Rather, when you plan to fish a hatch, try to be on a fertile, unpolluted stream. *Even a "good stream" doesn't contain all species.* What you should do is to learn which waters contain which hatches and record the information for future trips.

I've had some fishermen tell me that using emergence dates to fish the

Big Fishing Creek near Lamar in central Pennsylvania is an example of a good
stream. On the stretch pictured, good hatches of *Ephemera guttulata* (Green
Drake), *Litobrancha recurvata* (Brown Drake), *Ephemerella subvaria* (Hendrickson), *Paraleptophlebia guttata* (Dark Blue Quill), and many more appear.

hatches is futile. They were on a good stream at what they thought was the
proper time and date, but they didn't see a specific insect appear. Remember,
not all mayflies and caddis flies emerge on all streams. Remember too that
hatches vary greatly in intensity from stream to stream.

Find out from other fishermen which mayflies and caddis flies prevail on
your favorite streams. Then plan your trips to those streams for those hatches.
Also, after a couple years of observation, you'll be aware of which waters contain which hatches.

When hatches occur in June, July, and August, a "good stream" is not only
one which has a large variety of hatches, but also one which is cool enough to

encourage trout to surface-feed during those hot summer months. If a species occurs on your favorite stream, but the water is too warm for trout, look for the species on a colder one. The experience with the Yellow Drake in Chapter IV depicts this incident readily. What good is a tremendous hatch if water temperatures are too high to produce a good response?

A summary for Rule 3: *Select your stream carefully* for a specific mayfly and choose one which has a variety of hatches.

4. Fish at the *proper time* for a specific hatch. Sure you can be on an ideal stream at a good date expecting a common hatch and still not meet the mayfly. Why? You might be there at the wrong time of day. If I had been on Penn's Creek in the opening story at noon, I probably would not have experienced the enormous hatch of Green Drake duns that I saw at 8:00 p.m. Or look for a great hatch of Yellow Drakes at any time other than 8:00 to 9:30 p.m. and you'll probably not see any, or at best only a few.

Because many fly fishermen are creatures of habit, "proper time" may be difficult to heed. They're creatures of habit because they customarily fish the same time each day. One fishing friend I know fishes only Saturday mornings, and another fishes only evenings. Although both are excellent fly fishermen, because of their fishing habits, they'll miss some of the good hatches throughout the season. To fish the hatches, you must be willing to alter your time to that of the hatch time of the species you wish to meet.

Let me cite an example:

One early-August evening several years ago, I appeared on Big Fishing Creek near Lock Haven. It's unusual to meet another fly fisherman that time of year, so when I saw one nearby, I approached him to find out how he was doing. He complained that most of the fly hatches had ended, and that this would probably be his last time out this year. After about a half-hour's discussion, I asked him to fish one more time, and to meet me next morning on the stream at 7:00 a.m.

That morning was preceded by a late-evening thunderstorm, and when we met the next morning, the water was a bit discolored. By 7:30 a.m. we saw a few Blue Quills (*Paraleptophlebia guttulata*) and Pale Olive Duns (*Tricorythodes stygiatus*) emerging. A half-hour later, emergence of the latter species was in full swing, and hundreds of spinners had already moved upstream, just above the surface.

It was now 8:30 a.m. and we hadn't yet cast a line. Soon female *Tricorythodes*, spent after laying their eggs, floated past us by the hundreds. Now several trout started feeding on the spent imagos. Jim quickly tied on one of the female spinner imitations, the Reverse Jenny Spinner, and cast three or four times to the nearest rising trout and caught it. Ten minutes later he hooked another, just as the fall subsided.

"I guess we can leave now," Jim said.

"No, let's wait another hour or so."

"Why? The spinners are gone and the trout have quit feeding."

"There should be another mayfly species hatch around 11:00 a.m.," I said.

"I guess we might as well stay," Jim said as he scratched his head in doubt.

We then moved upstream to a fast shallow riffle where I had seen a large hatch of Blue-Winged Olives (*Ephemerella cornuta*) emerging the past couple days, and we sat and chatted.

By 10:45, a few duns had appeared, and within fifteen minutes, a second major hatch had occurred. Only a couple trout rose to take the escaping duns, however, since the subimagos of this species depart rapidly from the water's surface. Jim earlier had tied on a size 14 Blue-Winged Olive, and now started casting. Another half-hour and the emergence dissipated, but only after he had caught and released two more trout.

I state this story mainly to convey to you that the time of day is extremely important when fishing the hatches. Here was a good fly fisherman who, because he fished at inappropriate times in early August, diminished his chances of success *by not fishing* over trout rising to a specific hatch.

A summary for Rule 4 is: *Fish the time of day a specific mayfly or caddis fly is most likely to emerge.* Remember, on dark, cloudy days, evening hatches may occur during the day.

Are these the only rules you need to fish the hatches? No, there are others, although not as important as the four just discussed. For instance, many mayflies emerge on fast, moderate, or slow stretches only. You should know this so that you can be at the proper place on a stream.

We've discussed, in some depth, the four rules of meeting and fishing the hatches. But do they really work? Can they aid you in catching more fish? The only way you'll know is by trying the method several times. Let's take a sample hatch and follow it through the four rules.

For our example we'll select the Hendrickson (as the female dun is known) or the Red Quill (the male dun of *Ephemerella subvaria*). First and foremost, this species conforms with the requirements of Rule 1 – that is, it is *common* and *fishable*.

Fish small streams or large streams in early spring and you're likely to encounter this hatch. Not only is it common on many trout waters, but it is fishable on most occasions (see Chapter III). Since the species appears on many cool spring afternoons, many of the duns ride the water for long distances before taking flight. Trout seem to sense that this is the harbinger of things to come and eagerly devour duns, even in the chilled waters of April. Another asset when meeting and fishing while this hatch appears is that it usually emerges in large numbers. Furthermore, the hatch can occur on any given day for an hour or more.

Rule 2 suggests we select a good average *emergence date* for the Hendrickson. Selecting a good emergence date for this species is risky at best, since the hatch appears on any selected stream for at most two to three weeks in late April and early May. Also, atypical spring temperatures might delay or antedate the hatch.

I've seen Hendricksons appear on Cedar Run in northern Pennsylvania as early as April 21 and as late as May 8. However, selecting a date as early as April 21 is hazardous. The Emergence Chart in Chapter II suggests April 26 as the average beginning emergence date. We'll opt for April 28 (for climates similar to central and northern Pennsylvania), since at this later date the hatch might have appeared the past couple days and trout have become accustomed to the insect.

Rule 3 recommends that we look for the hatch on a *good stream*. Better than hoping the hatch occurs is to know ahead that it does appear on the stream you plan to fish. You might be able to discover this information ahead of time by quizzing local fishermen. The Hendrickson appears on many small, mid-sized, and large streams. For our example we'll select the Loyalsock Creek in north-central Pennsylvania. The "Sock" has a fantastic hatch of Hendricksons, and in each of the past three years, in late April, I have encountered a sizable emergence on each occasion.

Finally, Rule 4 suggests that you select an optimum *time of day* the species might appear on April 28 on the Loyalsock. Although some duns appear as early as 10:00 or 11:00 a.m., most appear from 2:00 to 4:00 p.m. (EST). To be prepared, we'll plan to be on the stream by 1:00 p.m.

If we've followed all four rules, we should meet a hatch of *Ephemerella subvaria*. But more important, we'll be prepared with proper imitations to fish while the hatch occurs. Cold weather, rain, high murky water, and cloudy skies – any of these or a combination can alter the predicted emergence and create a wipeout.

You can meet spinner falls too. In fact, many spinner falls can be more productive than dun emergences. They can be more productive since imagos often mate and lay eggs in a short, concentrated period. However, females of many species drop their eggs from several feet above the water, and are not accessible as food.

For our example we'll select the Ginger Quill Spinner (*Stenonema fuscum*). Again, we have chosen this species because the spinners fall in great numbers in a short period and often die spent on the water. *Stenonema fuscum* is probably one of the most common mayflies in the Northeast. Duns usually emerge sporadically throughout the day and evening. Spinners fall at dusk and provide plenty of food for trout. Therefore, the spinner is *common and fishable*, and conforms to Rule 1. We'll choose to meet the spinner on May 30 (Rule 2), at the Bald Eagle Creek (Rule 3), and be on the stream at 8:00 p.m. (Rule 4). Again, if all four variables go as planned, we'll be on the stream prepared to fish while a spinner fall occurs.

What about other species? Can you utilize the four rules to meet them? Here are two suggestions which should help. First, use the Insect Emergence Chart in Chapter II for three of the four rules (emergence date, common and fishable species, and emergence time). The fourth rule, selecting a good stream, is up to you. Second, keep a record of all insect activity on your favorite stream.

RECORDING THE HATCHES

Up to now we've discussed, rather thoroughly, the four rules for meeting and fishing the hatches. But what about some of your locally significant hatches which we have not listed? Furthermore, when do species listed here emerge in your locality? You can increase your knowledge immensely by keeping records of all fishing trips and the mayflies, caddis flies, and stoneflies you encounter.

But immediately another problem crops up: "How in the world do I know what species is emerging?" If you feel the hatch is an important one, you might capture a male dun and attempt to identify it by using the procedure in Chapter III, or better yet, have it identified by an entomologist. If you can't do either of the above, describe the coloration of the hatch and list a pattern which imitates it. Keep records habitually and record every pertinent piece of information you feel is necessary so you can meet and fish the hatch annually.

Recording relevant information worked for me on a troublesome hatch I first met several years ago. Five years ago I recorded a large *Hexagenia* species on the Cherry Run section of Penn's Creek. I carefully noted all the information about this unusual spinner. This species is unusual because it appears late in the season, and also because the spinner appears above the water at 6:15 p.m. and just as abruptly disappears at 6:45 p.m. I meticulously noted all necessary information in my diary on that first meeting night. Since I didn't capture any of the male imagos, I couldn't have the species identified.

Now, in the summer of 1973, I returned to the same spot on the same day, August 25, determined to snare some of the large male spinners, if they appeared. I arrived at Johnson's Camp at 5:30 p.m. and scanned the air above the water for any large mayflies – no *Hexagenia* spinners had yet appeared. By 6:16 p.m. and not much before, several dark reddish-brown spinners appeared from their resting areas on giant oaks, high above the stream, and headed for the pool.

By 6:30 p.m. thousands of these huge spinners saturated the air, carrying out their predestined mating flight. I busily swung an insect net at some of the lower imagos, determined to capture several for positive identification. For what seemed like hours I was oblivious to signs of trout rising to the spent female spinners. However, trout must have fed on the spinners upstream, because I heard gulping and splashing sounds most assuredly coming from rising fish. Finally, I caught several of the giant *Hexagenia* males and secured them in a killing solution. I looked at my watch. It was now 6:45 p.m., and only a dozen or so males remained in the air. All the females apparently had completed their reproduction cycle and died. The few remaining male spinners now headed toward trees on the far shore.

Here was a spinner I hadn't seen in five years – but because I had recorded the important information on its emergence when I first saw it, I was able to observe it again. More important, I saw the mating display five years later on the same day at the same time. By the way, the species has been identified as *Hexagenia atrocaudata*, and it can provide some great late-season fly fishing on our larger streams.

Yes, meeting and fishing the hatches does work – and it can be even more successful if you keep a record of the hatches. To record pertinent information, I use a Keuffel and Esser Weatherproof Level Book. Following is a suggested format for the diary:

Date	Time	Stream	Imitation	No. of fish caught
April 28	2 p.m.	Loyalsock	Hendrickson	5

Insects seen	Water temp.	Air temp.	Weather
Ephemerella subvaria	52	60	clear
Epeorus pleuralis			

Chapter II

Insect Emergence

Much of a trout's diet consists of three orders of insects – Ephemeroptera, or mayflies; Tricoptera, or caddis flies; and Plecoptera, or stoneflies. The percentage of the three food sources varies considerably among the different species of trout. Paul Needham, in *Trout Streams*, indicates that brown trout appear to prefer mayflies (including nymphs and adults), whereas brook trout, in the same stream, prefer caddis flies. Rainbow trout, in studies, select mayflies slightly more than caddis flies. Needham's figures are:

	Mayflies Nymphs and adults	Caddis Flies Larvae and adults
Brook Trout	19%	43%
Brown Trout	79%	9.5%
Rainbow Trout	37%	19%

We can see that mayflies make up a large portion of a trout's diet. Since trout eagerly take both nymph and adult, it's important to understand the life cycle of the average mayfly (Figure 1).

The female mayfly spinner, or mature mayfly (scientists call the spinner an imago), mates with the male spinner, usually over fast stretches of a stream and most often in the evening. The male appears over the stream first, waiting for the female spinner. The female, after mating, deposits her fertilized eggs by one of three methods: (1) flying just above the surface, (2) sitting or dipping on the surface, or (3) diving underwater. After the egglaying is completed, many females fall onto the water, usually with wings spent (flat on the surface). Later in this chapter we rate many of the spinners according to their availability as a source of food for trout. This is an important concept, because when trout feed on natural spinners, they will often take artificials imitating the dead imagos.

Nymphs hatch from the fertilized eggs in a couple weeks. The nymph spends approximately a year (there are exceptions in the Family Ephemeridae) in slow, medium, or fast stretches on rocky or muddy bottoms – many species are specific in their habitat. After almost a year of growing and shedding its outer covering many times, the nymph is ready to emerge.

After several false dashes, the nymph reaches the surface. Here it sheds its nymphal skin dorsally (a few do this on the bottom of the stream), and becomes a dun (often called a subimago). Many of these duns, including the Quill Gordon

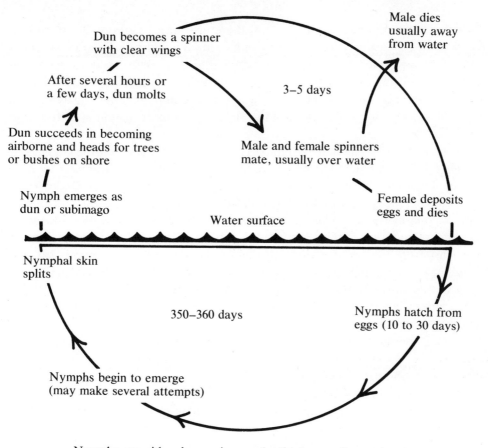

Figure 1. Life cycle of a typical mayfly.

(*Epeorus pleuralis*), Yellow Drake (*Ephemera varia*), Green Drake (*Ephemera guttulata*), and others, have difficulty leaving the water and ride the surface for some distance before taking flight. These duns are especially important to imitate with dry-fly patterns.

When the dun finally becomes airborne, it usually heads for the nearest tree or bush close to the stream. Duns emerging early in the season sometimes rest on sun-warmed rocks or debris next to the water to protect themselves from early-season freezes.

Although a few genera (*Tricorythodes*, *Caenis*, and *Ephoron*) change from dun to spinner in an hour or less, and a few never change (*Ephoron* female), in most genera the transformation requires one or two days. With a final molt, the dun shucks its outer covering and reappears over the water as a more brightly colored mayfly with clear glassy wings. These spinners then meet and mate to complete the life cycle.

As you can note from the life cycle, there are three stages of the mayfly on which trout can actively feed – the nymph, dun, and spinner. Trout discriminate little, and take either male or female nymph and dun. With the third phase, the spinner or imago, the female is devoured more often than the male. In many species, the female dies spent on the water after completing her egglaying task. The male, conversely, often leaves the stream area after mating and frequently dies over land.

The longer the mayfly dun or spinner is on the water, the better the chances for surface-feeding by trout. This length of time on the water is critical if we're using floating imitations. With some species such as the Dark Green Drake (*Litobrancha recurvata*) and the Big Slate Drake (*Hexagenia atrocaudata*), the dun escapes so rapidly that few trout feed on them. The Green Drake (*Ephemera guttulata*) and many other species are just the opposite. These latter mayflies take off sluggishly from the surface, often resting on the water for quite some distance. These laggards are important to imitate with dry-fly artificials. We'll discuss time spent on the water in more detail later in this chapter.

The emergence of many duns is sporadic – that is, they do not appear in concentrated numbers, and few trout rise to the naturals. However, many spinners of these same sporadic species often fall in large enough numbers in a short period to create rises. Yes, often the spinner falls of sporadic species are concentrated, occurring for an hour or less in the evening.

We mentioned several times before that fishing some hatches can be unpredictable – you might be late for the peak of the subimago by a couple days. In these instances, being prepared with imitations of the imago of the species can turn a frustrating experience into a successful one.

Two years ago, several of us met at Penn's Creek during the Green Drake hatch. As often happens with this species, we arrived a couple days too late to experience a major emergence – only a few duns appeared that evening. However, around 8:30 p.m. Lloyd Williams pointed to thousands of white-bodied spinners moving toward the stream. By 9:00 p.m. there were literally thousands of spinners, now slowly, methodically moving upstream, 10 to 15 feet above the surface. Can you imagine so many spinners on wing that you could actually hear a humming sound?

Within fifteen minutes after mating, spent females floated past us in unbelievable numbers. Scarcely a square inch of water was not now covered with these dead spinners. I could hear trout gulping loudly, taking in two, three, even four naturals on each rise. It was difficult to catch these trout now because it was totally dark. Besides, how can a trout select your imitation in the midst of thousands of naturals in the same area?

This story is a good case in point: When fishing the hatches, have imitations handy of both dun and spinner. As with the dun, we rate the spinner according to its importance as a source of food later in this chapter.

THE CADDIS FLY'S LIFE CYCLE

Up to this point we have mentioned little about caddis flies. As streams become polluted, caddis flies take on added importance. This order might be able to withstand a greater degree of pollution than some other orders of aquatic insects, especially mayflies.

Unlike the mayfly, the caddis goes through a complete metamorphosis. It has a pupal stage which lasts a couple weeks. After the male and female mate, the female dives underwater and deposits the eggs. Some species drop the fertilized eggs in flight like many mayflies, while others actually swim underwater to place them. The eggs develop in a few weeks, and the newly hatched larvae build cases to protect their fragile bodies. Unlike the mayfly nymph, which has a hard outer covering called an exoskeleton, the caddis larva has only a thin integument covering the greater part of the body. Only the legs and head of the larva are heavily protected (sclerotized), and these parts usually extrude from the case.

To construct a covering, the larva uses sand, pebbles, stone, or any number of things found in a stream. Each genus is usually specific in selecting building materials. In some genera, however, the larva moves about freely and has no case. An example of the latter is the Green Caddis (*Rhyacophila lobifera*); imitations of this larva usually work well.

Most species, however, do build cases. The Grannom (*Brachycentrus fuliginosus*) builds its case of sticks and is usually found in backwater areas of streams. Another important caddis, the Dark Blue Sedge (*Psilotreta frontalis*), found most often in fast water, builds its case of sand and pebbles. Several genera, like *Hydropsyche* and *Chimarra*, are called net spinners, and build small fibrous nets which serve to collect food.

As the larva feeds and grows, it adds to its case. About two weeks before it emerges as an adult, it goes into a pupal stage. In this stage, the case (in this stage called a cocoon) is almost completely closed except for a small hole which allows some water to enter. During this stage the adult develops. After about two weeks the pupa, encased in a protective membrane, swims to the surface. At the surface it breaks the covering membrane and flies to the shore.

Adults usually live longer than mayfly adults, perhaps a week or more. Since emerging adults are capable of mating, no change occurs from dun to spinner as it does in mayflies. At the time of emergence and during the egglaying process, trout seize adults eagerly. Since the wings of the adult are folded back over the body in a tentlike fashion, the wings of your imitations, whether wet or dry, should be shaped similarly.

TERRESTRIALS

There are many insects that don't live in water, but at some time are found near or on the water. Terrestrials, as these forms are called, can be especially plentiful on warm blustery summer days. Beetles, ants, crickets, grasshoppers, two-winged flies, and leafhoppers take on added importance as a source of food during days such as these. Gusty winds sometimes transport terrestrials to strange aquatic environs.

The grasshopper and cricket are visitors to trout waters, but usually only in limited numbers. However, ants, especially the winged varieties, and beetles occasionally land on the surface in large enough numbers to produce a typical hatching situation. Imitations of ants and beetles are often difficult to follow on the water, but can be extremely effective. Needham, in *Trout Streams*, indicated that beetles, ants, grasshoppers, leafhoppers, and two-winged flies make up 85 percent of the total true terrestrial food (this does not include adult mayflies, caddis flies, or stoneflies) taken by brook trout.

A few years ago I journeyed to the fly-fishing area of Bowman's Creek in northeastern Pennsylvania. The creek was a foot above its late-summer flow from an early-morning shower. During the last few trips to this spot, I had seen many Japanese beetles on bushes and weeds near the stream, especially on the far shore. Now, many of these low plants were partially submerged by increased runoff from the precipitation. After looking over the situation, I decided to try a beetle imitation – besides, there were no mayflies or caddis flies on the water or in the air. I tried to place the artificial as close to the far shore as possible. The first attempt landed on a low-lying bush on the far shore. I was able to disentangle the fly from the branch, and the artificial alighted gently on the water, barely 6 inches from the far side. The beetle floated 2 feet under an overhanging bush, and I noticed an almost imperceptible dimple. I set the hook immediately, and the heavy trout headed for the center of the stream. When I finally netted the rainbow, I saw it had almost swallowed the imitation. Even with the long-nosed pliers that I always carry with me it took quite a while to dislodge the hook. I was about to release the trout when it began to bleed profusely, so I decided to dispatch it. I was curious to validate the theory that these fish had been feeding on beetles, so I cut open the stomach immediately, and dozens of partially digested beetles popped out.

Ants also make up a portion of the trout's diet, particularly around the end of August. This is the time when dark-brown winged varieties are common on many streams. A few years ago I traveled to the Cherry Run section of Penn's Creek on August 25 to meet and fish an exciting hatch that we discussed earlier – *Hexagenia atrocaudata*. When I arrived at the long quiet pool, I saw literally thousands of winged ants on the water. The water temperature was about 73 degrees that late afternoon, and only four or five trout fed on the displaced terrestrials. I selected a dark-brown winged imitation, but caught only one small brown trout that afternoon. As I say, ant imitations are often extremely difficult for the fisherman to detect on the water.

AQUATIC BEETLES

Usinger, in *Aquatic Insects of California*, indicates that there are 5,000 species of aquatic beetles (order Coleoptera). This number does not include the terrestrial beetles we just discussed, which only occasionally wander onto the water. In this number we include only species that spend at least part of their life cycle underwater. If aquatic beetles are so widespread, then it should make sense that they are underrated as a source of trout food.

Two effective terrestrials are the beetle (left) and the ant (right).

The life cycle begins when the female deposits her eggs beneath the surface. The eggs hatch into larvae shortly. Most of these larvae have gill filaments and respire like mayfly nymphs. However, the next two stages, the pupa and adult, depend on atmospheric air for respiration. The pupa usually crawls out of the water, but remains nearby for this resting stage. Many adults spend their complete life cycle underwater, coming to the surface only to capture needed air under their wings. Other adults spend their final stage completely out of water.

Various stages of the beetle become available as potentially important sources of trout food – the larvae, the pupae, and the adults provide nourishment. Up to now not much has been written about this order of insects and its significance to trout fishermen. More will probably be mentioned in the future. However, if you want to be innovative, here's an area where there's a need for some creative patterns. For example, we find *Psephenus* species larvae or "water pennies" in numbers on the undersides of rocks in many of the fertile limestone streams in central Pennsylvania. Bob Murphy first brought this unusual creature to my attention. Bob caught several large trout on those streams, and their stomachs contained many of these larvae. His problem was to tie a good imitation of the larval stage. Since the larva is flat and round, it is difficult to tie with conventional methods. This example illustrates the diversity of possible imitations for aquatic beetles.

NOTES ABOUT THE INSECT
EMERGENCE CHART (EASTERN)

The Insect Emergence Chart should be of special interest to you when attempting to meet and fish the hatches. You'll note that most of the species listed are mayflies, although there are a few stoneflies and caddis flies. An explanation of the chart's column heads follows.

Scientific and Common Names

Most mayflies, stoneflies, and caddis flies have common names that refer to the coloration of the insect. Some, but not as many, are named for their creators or for well-known fishermen. Still other common names have come, intact, from England. This latter type of acquisition has created, along with incorrect nomenclature, a weird conglomeration of artificials. These artificials appropriately match species on English waters, but do little for us on our streams. However, even with this lack of consistency, most common names will suggest a pattern for the emerging dun or spent spinner.

Emergence Date

Those dates listed in the chart are *approximate* beginning emergence dates for the duns in central Pennsylvania. Spinner falls usually occur one to three days after the dates listed for the duns. Remember, beginning emergence dates, even on the same stream, can vary from year to year by as much as two weeks. (Caution: The dates, times, and body colorations that are listed in the next few chapters can be extremely variable. Dates and times are provided only to suggest to you crude estimates.)

The map (Figure 2) will suggest possible emergence dates for your area. The map is included for your use as a very rough guide and is not meant to be a scientific tool to follow rigidly. The lines used in the map correspond to degree-days. Each line represents a difference of approximately 500 degree-days per year. Degree-days are determined by taking average daily temperatures, and if that average is below 65, by accumulating that number for a 365-day span. It stands to reason that an area having more degree-days (colder) should have later hatches of a species.

You can plot degree-days in your area. The U.S. Department of Commerce has issued, state by state, "Decennial Census of the United States Climate – Heating Degree Day Normals." You can most likely obtain a copy for your state from

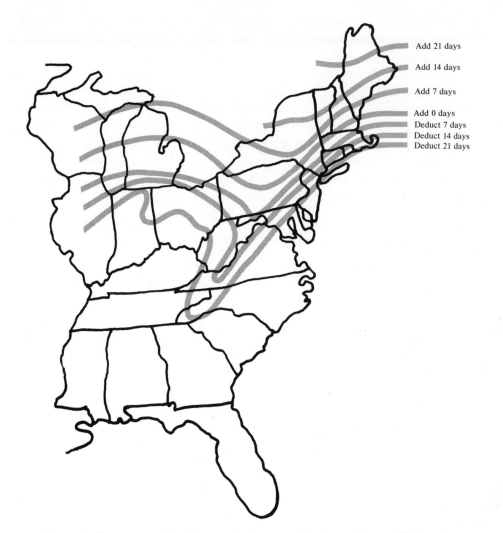

Add 21 days

Add 14 days

Add 7 days

Add 0 days
Deduct 7 days
Deduct 14 days
Deduct 21 days

Figure 2. Emergence Map for aquatic insects. Number of days added or deducted at various locations cannot be precise; they are just a very rough guide.

your local Weather Bureau Office. The number of degree-days for central Pennsylvania (our zero point) is approximately 6,500 (or an average of 18 degrees per day per year). Of course, most degree-days occur from November through April.

Time of Day the Largest Hatches Emerge (Duns) or Flights Take Place (Spinners)

Because of Daylight Saving Time, all times listed are in that reference. Time of day can vary considerably, especially on overcast days. Some species are specific in their emergence time, whereas others appear over a long period of time – that is, are sporadic. Species like *Epeorus pleuralis* (Quill Gordon), *Ephemerella sub-*

varia (Hendrickson and Red Quill), and *Ephemera varia* (Yellow Drake) usually emerge for a short, consistent period. This short period is usually two hours or less, and seldom varies in its beginning and ending time.

Other species, although they vary in timing, do emerge in numbers large enough to be called a hatch (sometimes a fantastic hatch). Examples of the latter are *Ephemera guttulata* (Green Drake), *Stenocron canadense* (Light Cahill), and *Stenonema fuscum* (Gray Fox), and there are many, many other species. The Light Cahill and Gray Fox might begin emerging at 3:00 or 4:00 p.m. in numbers and on another day they may not appear until later. Some caddis flies too fall in this variable category. The Green Caddis (*Rhyacophila lobifera*) and Grannom (*Brachycentrus fuliginosus*) too can fluctuate in their appearance from day to day.

Nymph Is Found in Fast, Medium, Slow, or All Types of Water

This column indicates in what part of the stream you can find the emerging duns. If you're looking for a hatch of *Tricorythodes stygiatus*, you wouldn't go to a fast mountain stream. Conversely, if you're searching for the Gray Fox or American March Brown, you wouldn't fish a slow meandering stream void of any fast stretches. As mentioned before, it's not only important to plan the time of day and time of year, but also to find a type of stream which will provide a suitable habitat for that species.

Nymph Burrows in Mud, Clings to Rocks, or Swims Freely

This column is fairly self-explanatory. Some nymphs live on rocks (like those in the Family Heptageniidae), some burrow in mud, silt, or sand (most of those in the Family Ephemeridae), still others spend most of their nymphal life swimming about freely (the Family Baetidae). You might say at this point, "So what? How will this information help?" Well, if you're looking for the Green or Yellow Drake (Family Ephemeridae), you should search for water which contains some mud on its bottom. If you're trying to locate a *Stenonema* species, look for fast or moderate, rocky stretches of a stream.

Hook Size

Size of imitations can be very important when duplicating mayflies. It's always a good idea to have several sizes of an imitation available, since size of naturals of the same species may vary from stream to stream. The Green Drake, American March Brown, and Pale Evening Dun appear to vary in size according to the fertility and/or size of the stream. On Penn's Creek, the Green Drake is usually 18–22 mm long; whereas the same species on White Deer Creek, a much smaller stream, is only 16–18 mm long. To imitate the Drake on Penn's Creek calls for a size 8 artificial, while a size 10 would do well on White Deer Creek.

Emergence Type

If you've been meeting and fishing the hatches for some time, then you've noticed that some of the mayflies and caddis flies appear over a longer part of the season than others. Some *Tricorythodes* species emerge from late July until mid-October, with heavy, fishable hatches each morning they appear. Then there are others, like the Hendrickson, which appear for a much shorter time; heaviest hatches emerge from late April through early May (in central Pennsylvania), and fishable hatches usually occur for less than two weeks on any stream.

The following classifications, geared to emergence length, are very arbitrary, since one stream's major hatch might be another's minor hatch. Also, a species might emerge for a longer period on one stream than on another. Too many of our marginal waters, which are polluted to varying degrees, will have sparse or no hatches of many species. Even though there are great variations, the emergence types might aid you in selecting species to meet and fish.

Type 1 – *Short duration, heavy emergence*
Emergence of these species occurs usually at a highly specific time for two weeks or less on the same stream. Each day this type appears, it does so usually in large numbers.

Type 2 – *Short duration, sparse emergence*
These insects never appear plentiful, and emerge for only a couple weeks. The stonefly *Isoperla signata* (Light Stonefly) is an example of this type.

Type 3 – *Medium duration, heavy emergence for two to four weeks,*
then a short period of sparse emergence
These individuals emerge in heavy numbers for two to four weeks. This is preceded and followed by a period of sparse emergence which lasts a couple weeks.

Type 4 – *Medium duration, sparse emergence throughout*
These insects appear for two to four weeks, but never in great numbers.

Type 5 – *Long duration, heavy emergence for four or more weeks,*
then a sparse emergence for several additional weeks
Emergence in this group is heaviest for more than four weeks, and is preceded and followed by a long period of sparse emergence.

Type 6 – *Long emergence, heavy emergence throughout*
Emergence occurs daily for more than five weeks with heavy hatches on almost every appearance. *Tricorythodes stygiatus* is a good example of this type with hatches occurring daily for six or more weeks.

Type 7 – *Long duration, sparse emergence throughout*
Hatches of this type may occur daily for many weeks, but in very limited numbers. Many of these hatches appear for six or more weeks. Some *Baetis* and *Callibaetis* species are examples of this type.

Following are some of the ways the emergence type classification can be used:
Easiest category to meet: Type 6.
Most important groups to imitate: Types 1, 3, 5, and 6.
Most difficult types to predict accurately: Types 1 and 2.
Least important categories to imitate: Types 2, 4, and 7.

Sporadic and concentrated

We indicated before that some species appear in a short, concentrated hatch. Other species, however, may emerge throughout the day (or evening), and not at any predictable time; that is, they are sporadic. The most important duns to imitate (if their rating is low) are those that appear at a concentrated, scheduled time.

Immediately following the type number of each dun is the letter S (sporadic), C (concentrated), or S & C (sporadic and concentrated). The last designation indicates that the dun sometimes appears sporadically and other times as a concentrated hatch.

Rating

Duns and spinners are rated from 1 to 10. Duns are rated depending on their characteristic takeoff from the water's surface. Those species that have a rating from 1 to 5 are important to imitate in the dun or subimago stage. Those with a rating of 6 to 10 are less important, since they rarely, if ever, pause on the surface before taking flight. Although the duns of a species might be of questionable importance, the spinner or imago stage of the same species might be rated lower, and therefore be important to copy. Species toward the high end of this very subjective scale might better be matched by nymphs than by dry flies.

As already indicated, this rating system is subjective because it's based on my own observations and not on any concise scientific study.

Spinners are also rated from 1 to 10, but by different criteria. Even though emergence of a species (dun) may be sporadic, and appear in small numbers throughout the day, the spinner fall can be concentrated into an hour or two (most often in the evening). After the female mates with the male, it typically deposits its eggs in one of several methods. Many species of a genus deposit eggs in the same manner. Following are some of the methods by which females deposit eggs:

1. Female intermittently lands on the surface for a couple seconds, extrudes some eggs, takes off, then repeats the process (some *Stenonema* species, *Heptagenia* species, and some *Epeorus* species).
2. Female intermittently dips or touches the surface and immediately takes off (*Leptophlebia* species, some *Stenonema* species, and some *Epeorus* species).
3. Female carries an egg sac and drops it from just above or on the surface (some *Stenonema* species, some *Tricorythodes* species, and *Ephemerella* species).
4. Female usually rides the surface until all eggs are extruded (*Ephemera* and *Hexagenia* species).
5. Female dives beneath the surface to deposit eggs (*Baetis* species).

6. Female drops eggs from several feet above the water (*Paraleptophlebia* species and *Isonychia* species).

As with the dun, the importance of the spinner varies greatly from species to species. Probably the main group to imitate, according to their method of depositing eggs, is category 4. Least significant would be those species that drop their eggs several feet above the water, category 6 (still, many of these females find their way to the water's surface).

We have rated spinners too according to their importance as a source of food for trout. This rating is based, to some extent, on their method of depositing eggs. Again, those rated from 1 to 5 are the most important species to imitate.

Even though two species deposit eggs in the same manner, they may be rated differently. Females of one species might die spent on the surface, whereas females of another species might die over land. Furthermore, *Stenonema luteum* will never be as important as *Stenonema fuscum* because the latter usually falls in enormous numbers, whereas the former does so in restricted numbers.

Most caddis flies escape rather rapidly from the surface. Adult stoneflies too are often not readily available to surface feeding trout since they emerge on rocks, emergent logs, bridge abutments, etc. Therefore, we have rated few of these aquatic orders in the Insect Emergence Chart. As we have indicated, however, when many of these insects return for their egg-laying phase they can be important to meet.

NOTES ABOUT THE INSECT
EMERGENCE CHART (WESTERN)

If emergence dates can vary by two, three, and even four weeks in the East and Midwest, then the dates listed for Western species can be off by five or more weeks. What I am saying is that *emergence dates for Western species are only crude guides and should never be adhered to rigidly*. Because of water-temperature differences a species might have completed its annual hatch on a relatively warm Western stream, whereas on a colder river the hatch might not occur for another month. Moreover, these two streams might be only a few air miles apart. The Upper Madison River and the Gallatin River are excellent examples of this latter diversity.

You'll note in the Emergence Chart (Western) that I've included temperature and elevation ranges for most of the Western species. These ranges, as well as the emergence dates and times, are very crude. However, all variables do aid the fisherman in meeting and fishing the hatches by helping him pinpoint streams, locations, and approximate days and times for many species.

Most of the column heads are similar to those in the Emergence Chart (Eastern). Those that are different or that require further explanation are discussed below. Emergence types are not listed at all, because of the extreme variability of many Western hatches.

1. Emergence Date

Emergence dates listed for Western species are usually the earliest dates that hatches of a given species appear. In several cases where I have not determined the beginning date I indicate this in a footnote. A few hatches will begin before the dates listed in the chart (in addition to those listed with an asterisk). But most hatches, if not all, will continue to appear well past the date listed.

The Gray Drake (*Siphlonurus occidentalis*) and Gray Fox (*Heptagenia solitaria*) are excellent examples of the latter statement. The Gray Drake begins its annual emergence around July 5. Of course a few emerge before that date, but the majority won't appear until early August. Another example is the Gray Fox. I have suggested a beginning date as July 5. However, hatches of this species may occur as late as early September on some streams. Moreover, the hatches and spinner falls encountered of *Heptagenia solitaria* are extremely heavy in late summer.

Approximate Elevation

The elevation of a stream has an effect on which species it contains. Much of the basic information on elevation, and for that matter water temperature also, has been adapted from Steven Jensen's *The Mayflies of Idaho*, and modified from my personal observations. As with emergence dates, elevation ranges listed in the chart are imperfect and will be modified with further observations.

Following is a breakdown of the elevation ranges:

High (H): Mayfly species is often found on streams with elevations of more than 7,000 feet.

Moderate (M): Mayfly species is often found on streams with elevations ranging from 4,000 to 7,000 feet.

Low (L): Mayfly species is often found on streams with an altitude lower than 4,000 feet.

All (A): Mayfly species is often found on streams at all elevations.

To reiterate, even though we have listed a species as one that appears on streams at high elevations, the species could well appear on streams at moderate elevations. In fact, this same species might also emerge on streams at all elevations. Remember, too, that some Western streams range in elevation from high (above 7,000) in their upper reaches to low (lower than 4,000) in their lower sections. The Yellowstone River is a good example.

Approximate Water Temperature

Water temperature also affects which streams a species inhabits and when this species will emerge (emergence date). Again, the temperature ranges for species listed in the chart will be modified with future observations.

When I refer to water temperatures I am of course referring to temperatures at the time a species emerges. Water temperatures will rise above or fall below those listed on the river that a particular species inhabits.

Following is a breakdown of the water-temperature ranges for the various mayfly species:

Warm (W): Mayfly species often emerges in water at temperatures higher than 65 degrees.

Moderate (M): Mayfly species often emerges in water at temperatures between 55 and 65 degrees.

Cold (C): Mayfly species often emerges in water at temperatures lower than 55 degrees.

Nothing is sacred about the elevation or temperature ranges used. Many species will emerge in two ranges of temperature, and two elevation classifications. Those species that do emerge in a wide range of elevations and water temperatures are usually among the more common species.

Look at *Ephemerella inermis* as an example of a very common species. The Pale Morning Dun inhabits streams at all (A) elevations with water temperatures *below* 65 degrees (C&M). On almost every occasion that I have fished Western waters after mid-June I have fished while a hatch, even though sometimes sparse, emerged. I have encountered this mayfly on Clark Fork below Missoula (elevation, 2,900 feet; water temperature, 57 degrees); on the Bitterroot (elevation, 3,400 feet; water temperature, 54 degrees); and on Henry's Fork (elevation, 6,100 feet; water temperature, 60 degrees). Of course, we take for granted that we're on the stream from late morning until early evening in late June or July (possibly earlier and later).

Rating

Rating the value of duns and spinners is even more subjective with Western species than it is with Eastern and Midwestern species. Again, using *Ephemerella inermis* as an example, the dun of this species would have a rating of 2 on the Railroad Ranch of Henry's Fork. However, on the Bitterroot, the same species has a rating of 3.

If I have observed a species in only limited numbers or not at all, I have not attempted to suggest a numerical rating for the species. In those cases the space is left blank.

INSEX EMERGENCE CHART (*Eastern*)

Scientific and Common Name M = *Mayfly* C = *Caddis fly* S = *Stonefly*	Emergence Date *(dates are only rough guides and should not be followed rigidly)*	Time of Day Largest Hatches Emerge (Duns) *or* Flights Take Place (Spinners)
Baetis vagans (M) Dun: Little Blue Dun Spinner: Rusty Spinner	April 1	10:00 a.m.–6:00 p.m.
Taeniopteryx faciata (S) Early Brown Stonefly	April 10	Afternoon
Paraleptophlebia adoptiva (M) Dun: Dark Blue Quill Spinner: Dark Brown Spinner	April 15	11:00 a.m.–4:00 p.m. Heaviest: 2:00–4:00 p.m. Spinner: 4:00–7:00 p.m.
Epeorus pleuralis (M) Dun: Quill Gordon Spinner: Red Quill Spinner	April 18	1:00–3:00 p.m. Spinner: 11:30 a.m.–2:00 p.m.
Chimarra atterima (C) Little Black Caddis	April 26	11:00 a.m.–6:00 p.m.
Ephemerella subvaria (M) Male dun: Red Quill Female dun: Hendrickson Spinner: Red Quill	April 26	2:00–4:00 p.m. Spinner: 3:00–8:00 p.m.
Leptophlebia cupida (M) Dun: Black Quill Spinner: Early Brown Spinner	April 27	2:00–4:00 p.m. Spinner: 1:00–6:00 p.m.
Isoperla signata (S) Light Stonefly	May 8	Afternoon
Ephemerella rotunda (M) Dun: Pale Evening Dun Spinner: Pale Evening Spinner	May 8	2:00–8:00 p.m. Spinner: 6:00–8:00 p.m.
Pseudocloeon species (M) Dun: Blue Dun Spinner: Rusty Spinner	May 10	Afternoon and evening
Rhyacophila lobifera (C) Green Caddis	May 10	4:00–9:00 p.m.; caddis fly appears later (around dusk) in June and July
Brachycentrus fuliginosus (C) Grannom	May 10[1]	3:00–7:00 p.m.
Stenonema fuscum (M) Dun: Gray Fox Spinner: Ginger Quill Spinner	May 15	Dun emerges sporadically throughout; chance of heaviest hatches 4:00–8:30 p.m. Spinner: 7:00–8:30 p.m.
Ephemerella septentrionalis (M) Dun: Pale Evening Dun Spinner: Pale Evening Dun[3]	May 18[1]	8:00 p.m.

mph Is Found in st (F), Medium (M), w (S), or All (A) pes of Water	Nymph Burrows in Silt or Gravel (M), Clings to Rocks (R), or Swims Freely (F)	Hook Size	Emergence Type; Sporadic (S) or Concentrated (C)	Rating Dun	Spinner
A	F	18	3 (S&C)	3	5
F	R	14	4 (S)		
A	F	18	3 (S&C)	2	4
F	R	12	1 (C)	2	8
F	R	16	1 (C)		
A	F	12 or 14	1 (C)	2	4
S	F	12	4 (S)	9	4
F	R	12 or 14	4 (S)		
A	F	14 or 16	3 (C)	3	7
S&M	F	20	3 (S&C)	2	
F		14	5 (S&C)		
F		12	1 (C)		
F&M	R	12	3 (S&C)	4	2
F&M	F	14 or 16	1 (C)	5	7

Scientific and Common Name M = Mayfly C = Caddis fly S = Stonefly	Emergence Date (dates are only rough guides and should not be followed rigidly)	Time of Day Largest Hatches Emerge (Duns) or Flights Take Place (Spinners)

Heptagenia aphrodite (M)
  Dun: Pale Evening Dun
  Spinner: Pale Evening Dun[2]
	May 18[1]	8:00 p.m.

Ephemerella invaria (M)
  Dun: Pale Evening Dun
  Spinner: Pale Evening Spinner
	May 20[1]	3:00–8:00 p.m.
		Spinner: 7:00–8:30 p.m.

Stenonema vicarium (M)
  Dun: American March Brown
  Spinner: Great Red Spinner
	May 20	10:00 a.m.–7:00 p.m.
		Spinner: 8:00 p.m.

Hydropsyche slossanae (C) Spotted Sedge	May 23	1:00–6:00 p.m.

Ephemerella bicolor (M)
  Dun: Chocolate Dun
  Spinner: Chocolate Spinner
	May 25	Late morning and early afternoon

Stenonema ithaca (M)
  Dun: Light Cahill
  Spinner: Light Cahill
	May 25	Evening

Isonychia sadleri (M)
  Dun: Slate Drake
  Spinner: White-Gloved Howdy
	May 25	Evening

Epeorus vitreus (M)
  Male Dun: Light Cahill
  Female Dun: Pink Cahill
  Spinner: Salmon Spinner
	May 25	Evening

Stenacron interpunctatum (M)
  Dun: Light Cahill
  Spinner: Light Cahill
	May 25	Evening

Stenacron canadense[4] (M)
  Dun: Light Cahill
  Spinner: Light Cahill[3]
	May 25	Sporadic during day but mainly 6:00–8:30 p.m.
		Spinner: 7:00–9:00 p.m.

Litobrancha recurvata[4] (M)
  Dun: Dark Green Drake
  Spinner: Brown Drake
	May 25	1:00–8:00 p.m.
		Spinner: 7:00 p.m.

Ephemera simulans (M)
  Dun: Brown Drake
  Spinner: Brown Drake
	May 25	8:00 p.m.

Ephemera guttulata (M)
  Dun: Green Drake
  Spinner: Coffin Fly
	May 25	8:00 p.m.

Nymph Is Found in Fast (F), Medium (M), Slow (S), or All (A) types of Water	Nymph Burrows in Silt or Gravel (M), Clings to Rocks (R), or Swims Freely (F)	Hook Size	Emergence Type; Sporadic (S) or Concentrated (C)	Rating	
				Dun	Spinner
F	R	16	1 (C)	5	7
A	F	16	5 (S&C)	3	5
F&M	R	12	3 (S)	3	6
F	R	14 or 16	1 (C)		
M	F	16	3 (S&C)	4	4
M&F	R	12	3 (S&C)	5	
M&F	F	12	5 (S&C)	5	5
M&F	R	14	4 (S)	6	
M&F	R	14	3 (S&C)	4	
F&M	R	12	3 (S&C)	3	3
S	M	8 or 10	4 (S&C)	7	3
S&M	M	10 or 12	1 (C)	4	2
A	M	8 or 10	1 (C)	1	1

Scientific and Common Name M = *Mayfly* C = *Caddis fly* S = *Stonefly*	Emergence Date (dates are only rough guides and should not be followed rigidly)	Time of Day Largest Hatches Emerge (Duns) or Flights Take Place (Spinners)
Ephemerella species (M) Dun: Blue-Winged Olive Dun Spinner: Dark Olive Spinner	May 26[1]	Sporadic during day with a possible spurt 11:00–12:00 noon Spinner: 7:00–9:00 p.m.
Isonychia bicolor (M) Dun: Slate Drake Spinner: White-Gloved Howdy	May 30	Sporadic, but mainly 7:00 p.m. Spinner: 8:00 p.m.
Ephemerella needhami (M) Dun: Chocolate Dun Spinner: Chocolate Spinner	May 30[1]	Afternoon (early) and morning (late) Spinner: afternoon and evening
Ephemerella dorothea (M) Dun: Pale Evening Dun Spinner: Pale Evening Dun[3]	June 1[1]	8:00 p.m.
Paraleptophlebia mollis (M) Dun: Dark Blue Quill Male spinner: Jenny Spinner Female spinner: Dark Brown Spinner	June 3[1]	10:00 a.m.–4:00 p.m.
Paraleptophlebia strigula (M) Dun: Dark Blue Quill Male spinner: Jenny Spinner Female spinner: Dark Brown Spinner	June 5	Early morning to mid-afternoon
Ephemerella attenuata (M) Dun: Blue-Winged Olive Dun Spinner: Dark Olive Spinner	June 5[1]	Sporadic during day Spinner: evening
Psilotreta frontalis (C) Dark Blue Sedge	June 8	8:00 p.m.
Leptophlebia johnsoni (M) Dun: Iron Blue Dun Male spinner: Jenny Spinner Female spinner: Blue Quill Spinner	June 9[1]	11:00 a.m. Spinner: evening
Stenacron areion[4] (M) Dun: Light Cahill Spinner: Light Cahill[1]	June 10	7:00 p.m.
Stenacron heterotarsale (M) Dun: Light Cahill Spinner: Light Cahill	June 15[1]	Evening
Stenonema luteum (M) Dun: Light Cahill Spinner: Olive Cahill Spinner	June 15[2]	8:00 p.m.
Stenonema species, *pullchellum* group (M) Dun: Cream Cahill Spinner: Cream Cahill Spinner	June 15[2]	Sporadic, around midday Spinner: evening

ymph Is Found in st (F), Medium (M), ow (S), or All (A) pes of Water	Nymph Burrows in Silt or Gravel (M), Clings to Rocks (R), or Swims Freely (F)	Hook Size	Emergence Type; Sporadic (S) or Concentrated (C)	Rating	
				Dun	Spinner
A	F	14	1 (C&S)	3	5
F	F	12	5 (C&S)	5	8
A	F	14 or 16	1 (S&C)	4	5
A	F	16 or 18	5 (C)	5	8
A	F	18	3 (C)	1	7
A	F	18 or 20	3 (S&C)	2	5
A	F	14 or 16	3 (S&C)	5	7
F		12	1 (C)		
A	F	14 or 16	3 (C)	5	8
F	S	14	2 (C)	5	3
M&F	R	14	7 (S&C)	4	
F&M	R	12	7 (S)	9	3
F&M	R	12	7 (S)	8	5

Scientific and Common Name M = *Mayfly* C = *Caddis fly* S = *Stonefly*	Emergence Date *(dates are only rough guides and should not be followed rigidly)*	Time of Day Largest Hatches Emerge (Duns) *or Flights Take Place* (Spinners)
Ephemera varia (M) Dun: Yellow Drake Spinner: Yellow Drake	June 22[2]	8:00–9:15 p.m.
Heptagenia hebe (M) Dun: Pale Evening Dun Spinner: Pale Evening Dun	June 22[1,2]	8:00 p.m.
Paraleptophlebia guttata (M) Dun: Dark Blue Quill Male spinner: Jenny Spinner Female spinner: Dark Brown Spinner	June 25[1,2]	Sporadic during day Spinner: morning and afternoon
Potamanthus distinctus (M) Dun: Golden Drake Spinner: Golden Spinner	June 28	9:00 p.m.
Ephemerella cornuta (M) Dun: Blue-Winged Olive Dun Spinner: Dark Olive Spinner	June 25	Sporadic during day, but mainly 11:00 a.m Spinner: 7:00–9:00 p.m.
Baetis species (M) Dun: Little Blue Dun Spinner: Rusty Spinner	July 5[1]	Sporadic during afternoon and early evening
Isonychia harperi (M) Dun: Slate Drake Spinner: White-Gloved Howdy	July 20[1,2]	Sporadic during day, but mainly 7:00 p.m.
Tricorythodes stygiatus (M) Dun: Pale Olive Dun Female spinner: Reverse Jenny Spinner Male spinner: Dark Brown Spinner	July 23[2]	7:00–9:00 a.m. Spinner: 8:00–11:00 a.m.
Tricorythodes attratus (M) Dun: Pale Olive Dun Male spinner: Dark Brown Spinner Female spinner: Reverse Jenny Spinner	July 23[2]	7:00–9:00 a.m. Spinner: 8:00 a.m.
Ephoron leukon (M) Dun: White Mayfly Spinner: White Mayfly	August 15	7:00 p.m.
Hexagenia atrocaudata (M) Dun: Big Slate Drake Spinner: Dark Rusty Spinner	August 18	8:00 p.m. Spinner: 6:00–7:00 p.m.

[1] Beginning emergence date might vary from the listed date considerably.
[2] Hatches occur for a long period after the date listed.
[3] Most appropriate imitation.
[4] Recent change in name of genus.

Nymph Is Found in Fast (F), Medium (M), Slow (S), or All (A) Types of Water	Nymph Burrows in Silt or Gravel (M), Clings to Rocks (R), or Swims Freely (F)	Hook Size	Emergence Type; Sporadic (S) or Concentrated (C)	Rating	
				Dun	Spinner
M&S	M	10 or 12	5 (C)	3	5
A	R	16	6 (C)	9	4
A	F	18	5 (C)	4	8
S&M	M (does not burrow)	12	3 (C)	5	5
A (mainly in shallow riffles)	F	14	5 (S&C)	5	5
A	F	20	3 (C)	3	7
F	F	12	5 (S&C)	5	8
S	F	24 or 26	6 (C)	3	1
S	F	24 or 26	6 (C)	3	1
S&M	M	12 or 14	3 (C)	5	3
S	M	6 or 8	3 (S&C)	9	5

INSECT EMERGENCE CHART (*Western*)

Scientific and Common Name M = *Mayfly* C = *Caddis fly* S = *Stonefly*	Emergence Date (dates are extremely variable)	Time of Day Largest Hatches Emerge (Duns) *or Flights Take Place* (Spinners)
Baetis tricaudatus (M) Dun: Little Blue Dun[2] Spinner: Light Rusty Spinner	April through October	Morning and afternoon[1] Spinner: early morning and evening
Baetis intermedius (M) Dun: Little Blue Dun Spinner: Dark Rusty Spinner	April through October	Morning and afternoon Spinner: early morning and evening
Ephemera simulans (M) Dun: Brown Drake Spinner: Brown Drake	May 25[3]	Evening
Ephemerella inermis (M) Dun: Pale Morning Dun[5] Spinner: Pale Morning Spinner[5]	May 25[4]	Morning, afternoon, and evening Spinner: morning and evening
Pteronarcys californica (S) Salmon Fly	May through July	Emergence often occurs in the morning; egglaying can occur almost any time of the day or evening
Brachycentrus species (C) Dark Gray Caddis; Dark Brown Caddis	April through October	Egglaying can occur almost any time of day – sometimes in the morning on colder streams, but often in the evening on many streams
Rhyacophila species (C) Green Caddis	May through October	Variable
Baetis bicaudatus (M) Dun: Pale Olive Dun Spinner: Light Rusty Spinner	June through October	Morning and afternoon Spinner: morning and evening
Acroneuria pacifica (S) Willow Fly	June and July	Variable
Callibaetis nigritus (M)	June through September	Late morning
Paraleptophlebia heteronea (M) Dun: Dark Blue Quill Spinner: Dark Brown Spinner	June 1	Morning and afternoon
Cinygmula ramaleyi (M) Dun: Dark Red Quill Spinner: Red Quill Spinner	Late May and early June	Late morning Spinner: midday
Ephemerella grandis (M) Dun: Western Green Drake Spinner: Great Red Spinner	June 5	Late morning and afternoon Spinner: evening

ymph Is Found in ast (F), Medium (M), ow (S), or All (A) pes of Water	Nymph Burrows in Silt or Gravel (M), Clings to Rocks (R), or Swims Freely (F)	Approximate Elevation at Which Hatch Occurs: High (H), Moderate (M), Low (L), or All (A)	Approximate Water Temperature When Hatch Occurs: All (A), Cold (C), Moderate (M), or Warm (W)	Hook Size	Rating	
					Dun	Spinner
M&F	F	A	A	18	3	7
M&F	F	M&H	A	18 or 20	3	7
S&M	B	M	M&W	10	2	2
A	F	A	C&M	16 or 18	3	6
F	R			4	8[6]	2[7]
M&F	F	A	C&M	20	2	6
F	R			6	8[8]	2
S	F	A	M&W	14	3	3
M&F	F	M&H	A	16	3	
M	R	M	C&M	16 or 18		
M	F	L&M	C&M	10 or 12	2	

Scientific and Common Name M = *Mayfly* C = *Caddis fly* S = *Stonefly*	Emergence Date (dates are extremely variable)	Time of Day Largest Hatches Emerge (Duns) *or Flights Take Place* (Spinners)
Ephemerella tibialis (M) Dun: Red Quill Spinner: White-Gloved Howdy[10]	June 5	Midday Spinner: evening
Hexagenia limbata (M[11]) Dun: Michigan Caddis Spinner: Michigan Spinner	June 12	Dusk and later
Callibaetis coloradensis (M) Dun: Speckle-Winged Dun Spinner: Speckle-Winged Spinner	June 12	Late morning and early afternoon
Epeorus longimanus (M) Dun: Quill Gordon Spinner: Red Quill Spinner	June 12	Late morning and afternoon
Ephemerella doddsi (M) Dun: Western Green Drake Spinner: Great Red Spinner	June 15	Late morning and afternoon
Ephemerella flavilinea (M) Dun: Blue-Winged Olive Dun Spinner: Dark Olive Spinner	June 15	Morning and evening (heaviest hatches seem to appear in the evening)
Heptagenia elegantula (M) Dun: Pale Evening Dun Spinner: Pale Evening Spinner	June 20[12]	Late afternoon and evening Spinner: evening
Baetis parvus (M) Dun: Dark Brown Dun Spinner: Dark Brown Spinner	June 20	Late morning, afternoon, and early evening Spinner: early morning and evening
Ephemerella infrequens (M[13]) Dun: Pale Morning Dun[14] Spinner: Rusty Spinner[14]	July 1	Late morning and afternoon Spinner: morning and evening
Paraleptophlebia memorialis (M) Dun: Dark Blue Quill Spinner: Dark Brown Spinner	July 1	Morning and afternoon
Rhithrogena futilis (M) Dun: Quill Gordon Spinner: Quill Gordon	July 1[15]	Late morning and afternoon Spinner: evening
Cinygmula reticulata (M) Dun: Pale Brown Dun Spinner: Dark Rusty Spinner	July 5[15]	Late morning and afternoon Spinner: early morning

Nymph Is Found in Fast (F), Medium (M), Slow (S), or All (A) Types of Water	Nymph Burrows in Silt or Gravel (M), Clings to Rocks (R), or Swims Freely (F)	Approximate Elevation at Which Hatch Occurs: High (H), Moderate (M), Low (L), or All (A)	Approximate Water Temperature When Hatch Occurs: All (A), Cold (C), Moderate (M), or Warm (W)	Hook Size	Rating Dun	Rating Spinner
M&F	F	M&H	C&M	16 or 18	3	
S	M	L&M	M	8	2	2
S	F	M&H	C&M	16	3	3
M&F	R	M&H	C&M	12 or 14		
M&F	F	A	C&M	10	2	
S&M	F	M&H	C&M	14 or 16	2	4
S&M	R	L&M	M&W	14	4	5
M	F	L&M	C&M	20	1	
M	F	L&M	C&M	18	3	5
S&M	F	A	C&M	18	3	5
M	R	L&M	C&M	12	3	4
M&F	R	M&H	C&M	14	7	4

Scientific and Common Name M = Mayfly C = Caddis fly S = Stonefly	Emergence Date (dates are extremely variable)	Time of Day Largest Hatches Emerge (Duns) or Flights Take Place (Spinners)

Paraleptophlebia vaciva (M)
  Dun: Dark Blue Quill
  Spinner: Dark Brown Spinner
	July 5	Morning and afternoon

Heptagenia solitaria (M)
  Dun: Gray Fox
  Spinner: Ginger Quill Spinner
	July 5[16]	Late afternoon and evening
		Spinner: late morning and evening

Epeorus albertae (M)
  Dun: Pink Lady[17]
  Spinner: Salmon Spinner[17]
	July 5	Evening

Paraleptophlebia debilis (M)
  Dun: Dark Blue Quill
  Spinner: Dark Brown Spinner
	July 5[18]	Morning and afternoon

Siphlonurus occidentalis (M)
  Dun: Gray Drake
  Spinner: Brown Quill Spinner
	July 5[19]	Late morning and afternoon; heaviest
		  hatches seem to appear around 3:00 p.m
		Spinner: morning and evening;
		  evening seems to be heavier

Cinygma dimicki (M)
  Dun: Light Cahill
  Spinner: Light Cahill
	July 5[15]	Evening

Ephemerella hecuba (M)
  Dun: Great Red Quill
  Spinner: Great Brown Spinner
	July 5	Evening[20]

Rhithrogena hageni (M)
  Dun: Pale Brown Dun
  Spinner: Dark Tan Spinner
	July 10	Late morning and afternoon
		Spinner: morning and evening

Ameletus cooki (M)
  Dun: Dark Brown Dun
  Spinner: Dark Brown Spinner
	July 10[15]	Late morning and afternoon
		Spinner: early afternoon

Rhithrogena undulata (M)
  Dun: Quill Gordon
  Spinner: Red Quill or Dark Red Quill[13]
	July 10[15]	Morning and afternoon
		Spinner: afternoon and evening

Tricorythodes minutus (M)
  Dun: Pale Olive Dun
  Male spinner: Reverse Jenny Spinner
  Female spinner: Dark Brown Spinner
	July 15	Morning

Ephemerella coloradensis (M)
  Dun: Dark Olive Dun
  Spinner: Dark Brown Spinner
	August 1	Midday
		Spinner: evening

Nymph Is Found in Fast (F), Medium (M), Slow (S), or All (A) Types of Water	Nymph Burrows in Silt or Gravel (M), Clings to Rocks (R), or Swims Freely (F)	Approximate Elevation at Which Hatch Occurs: High (H), Moderate (M), Low (L), or All (A)	Approximate Water Temperature When Hatch Occurs: All (A), Cold (C), Moderate (M), or Warm (W)	Hook Size	Rating	
					Dun	Spinner
A	F	A	M	18	3	
M	R	M&H	C&M	12 or 14	4	2
M	R	L&M	A	12	5	4
S&M	F	L&M	M	18	2	
S	F	A	C&M	10 or 12	3	5
S&M	R	A	M	12	5	3
M	F	L&M	M&W	10	3	
M&F	R	M&H	C&M	12 or 14	5	
A	F	A	M	14	6	3
M	R	L&M	C&M	12	5	3
S	F	A	M&W	24	3	2
M&F	F	M&H	C&M	12	3	

Scientific and Common Name M = *Mayfly* C = *Caddis fly* S = *Stonefly*	Emergence Date (*dates are extremely variable*)	Time of Day Largest Hatches Emerge (Duns) *or Flights Take Place* (Spinners)
Ephoron album (M) Dun: White Mayfly Spinner: White Mayfly	August 15	Evening
Paraleptophlebia bicornuta (M) Dun: Dark Blue Quill Spinner: Dark Brown Spinner	September 10	Morning and afternoon

[1] Heaviest hatches of many Western *Baetis* species occur in the afternoon; spinner falls are usually heaviest in the evening.
[2] Little Brown Dun might be a more appropriate name.
[3] Appears on Henry's Fork in late June.
[4] Species may appear for many days.
[5] Since color varies tremendously, there might be more appropriate local names.
[6] Rated at emergence time.
[7] Rated at egglaying time.
[8] Refers to emergence; spinner refers to egglaying.
[9] Species most often appears on Henry's Fork and the Madison from middle to late June.
[10] Common name taken from the Eastern *Isonychia* spinner.
[11] Important species in the Midwest; only locally significant in the East and West.
[12] Species appears in heaviest numbers in August and continues emerging into September.
[13] Color of species varies considerably.
[14] Since color varies from stream to stream, patterns may not be appropriate for your stream.
[15] Hatches may occur before date listed.
[16] Species emerges in heavy numbers into September.
[17] Pattern refers to female of species.
[18] Hatch continues into October.
[19] Heavy hatches occur in August.
[20] Species may appear at another time of day in heavier numbers.

nph Is Found in st (M), Medium (M), w (S), or All (A) es of Water	Nymph Burrows in Silt or Gravel (M), Clings to Rocks (R), or Swims Freely (F)	Approximate Elevation at Which Hatch Occurs: High (H), Moderate (M), Low (L), or All (A)	Approximate Water Temperature When Hatch Occurs: All (A), Cold (C), Moderate (M), or Warm (W)	Hook Size	Rating	
					Dun	Spinner
S	M	L&M	M&H	12	4	3
S&M	F	L&M	M&H	18	3	3

Chapter III

A Primer on the Hatches

Why should you worry about scientific names for mayflies? All you want to do is enjoy yourself with a great leisure-time activity – fly fishing. Besides, it's hard work to learn those names.

I'm certain that this is the opinion of many fly fishermen – but let me cite an incident that occurred recently, which reiterates the need for at least a basic knowledge of insect classification.

I had heard for years that Pine Creek in north-central Pennsylvania had an unbelievable hatch of Green Drakes, and that few fly fishermen actually fished while this hatch appeared. The night before, I had fished the same hatch on Penn's Creek. On a 2-mile stretch of that latter stream, I had counted over two hundred fishermen. I enjoy fishing, but I detest crowded conditions. I was determined that I would fish on a different and far less crowded stream tonight – Pine Creek, for example.

Jim Heltzel and I traveled to Pine Creek that evening. We stopped at a local store near Cedar Run and inquired about the fishing.

"The Green Drake's on heavy – you'll have a good night tonight," one local fisherman reported.

Great! We were well prepared for the expected hatch – I had tied a dozen imitations of the Green Drake and the Coffin Fly Spinner just the night before. Now all we had to do was wait until 8:00 p.m. or a little later, and then we'd meet and fish the hatch.

Pine Creek is a massive river, even larger than the Beaverkill. We stared at a section of the stream from the high bridge crossing Cedar Run. How in the world would we ever successfully fish this water?

Since there was no action on Pine Creek we moved up Cedar Run to explore it. This fantastic freestone water, loaded with stream-bred browns, has incredible hatches of many mayfly species. As we arrived at the first pool 100 yards upstream from Pine, we noted thousands of Ginger Quill Spinners already high over a fast-water section preparing for their final ritual before death.

Trout rose to a variety of insects on that first pool, but we wanted to investigate this fertile stream more fully, so we moved upstream several hundred yards beyond the pool. Here, in the fast water, and about 5 to 10 feet above the surface, we saw clouds of Dark Olive Spinners (*Ephemerella* species). Trout rose throughout the 200-yard stretch above us, and we caught trout after trout on the Dark Olive Spinner.

The sun set behind the huge canyonlike wall to the west, and now the water chilled the early June air. As I looked up toward the cliff on the far side I saw a few large dark brown spinners now positioning themselves 30 feet above the stream.

As Jim and I retraced our steps back downstream to Pine Creek we noted that these dark brown spinners became more numerous. These huge imagos began to puzzle me as we arrived on Pine Creek. Were they Great Red Spinners (*Stenonema vicarium*)? Where were the Green Drakes? It was now past 8:00 p.m. These brown spinners became more numerous – thousands and thousands flew 20 to 30 feet above the river. Shortly, spent females landed on the surface – first a few, and then many. Large trout sensed the almost unending food supply and fed freely on the spent spinners.

I still didn't know to which species these imagos belonged, but I hurriedly tied on one representing *S. vicarium* (similar to the Great Red Spinner). Besides, I was in a hurry to fish the spinner fall, even though I still didn't know what spinner it was. Now fifty large trout surfaced freely in front of Jim and me. I fruitlessly cast the dry fly toward the largest of these trout, and after ten minutes, I finally caught a heavy brown about 16 inches long. Eight other trout seized our imitations that evening before dusk and darkness finally ended our fishing.

Just before we left the stream I was able to capture one male and one female spinner. I was amazed, puzzled, curious, and frustrated at the spinner fall and our inability to do well while it occurred. When we got back to the car, I carefully examined the spent spinners. They were Drakes, but they were imagos of *Ephemera simulans* – Brown Drakes, not Green Drakes. Now I knew why we hadn't caught more trout. We had been casting dark-brown-bodied dry flies over those educated trout, while they captured naturals with tannish yellow bodies.

On our way back home we stopped in the same local store that we had before the hatch that evening. Some of the locals talked freely about the great "Green Drake" spinner fall they had just experienced. Green Drake? Yes, that's how some of the local fishermen refer to the Brown Drake on Pine Creek.

If only one of those fishermen who told me about the hatch had also indicated which species it was. If only fishermen would use scientific names, especially in cases where one common name describes, many times inadequately, several species. Because of the frequent inaccuracy of common names, and for many other reasons, you should learn the scientific names of the more important species, especially those capable of producing fishable hatches in your locality.

To start with, you should understand the relationship of aquatic insects to the total fauna. Mayflies, caddis flies, and stoneflies are members of the Class Insecta. Class Insecta belongs to the Phylum Arthropoda, and all phyla are components of the Animal Kingdom.

If we look at the Brown Drake (*Ephemera simulans*, to be precise) as an example, we should be able to see more clearly just how it is that mayflies fit into the scheme of things.

An *Ephemera simulans* female dun (Brown Drake). On Pine Creek, this species is sometimes incorrectly called the Green Drake.

A female dun of *Ephemera guttulata* (Green Drake).

KINGDOM: Animal (includes all animals from one celled to man)

PHYLUM: Arthropoda (animals which have outer skeletons called exoskel-
etons)

CLASS: Insecta (these are the true insects with three pairs of legs and one pair
of antennae)

ORDER: Ephemeroptera (all mayflies)

FAMILY: Ephemeridae (nymphs usually are burrowers; in adults longitudinal
vein M_2 is bent sharply toward Cu at its base)

GENUS: *Ephemera* (fore wing darkened or heavily spotted)

SPECIES: *simulans* (differentiated by the coloration of various body parts and
the shape of the penis – the Brown Drake)

The subdivisions become more specific as we descend the hierarchy, less specific as we ascend. Each part of the hierarchy contains a degree of relationships.
The affiliation at the top is very general, but as one progresses from kingdom to
species the relationship becomes highly specific.

The basic unit in the classification system is species. A species is sometimes
divided into subspecies. When this occurs the subspecies is listed as *Ephemerella
grandis grandis*, with the last of the three names referring to the subspecies.
Usually only members of the same species can mate and have offspring. Usually
several species (sometimes only one) belong to the same genus. In our sample
genus, *Ephemera*, we also have *Ephemera varia* (Yellow Drake), *Ephemera guttulata* (Green Drake), and others. The genus of a mayfly is much easier to determine than is the species, and more difficult to ascertain than family.

The next rung up the ladder is the family. The family of a mayfly is easier to determine than is the genus. In our example, the genus *Ephemera* belongs to the
Family Ephemeridae, or the true burrowers. In addition to *Ephemera*, other
genera, such as *Hexagenia* and *Litobrancha*, belong to the Family Ephemeridae.

Ephemeridae is one of at least seventeen families of the Order Ephemeroptera
(mayflies) found in the United States. Below are some of the more common families and genera, along with some of the characteristics of each. I have attempted,
under each genus, to list those species which are most common. This is by no
means a complete list, and many others can and do produce fishable hatches. I
also have tried to indicate where these hatches are found – E for those species
found in the East; M for those found in the Midwest; and W for those found in the
West. A word of caution: Even though the species is supposed to be common in
your area, there's a good possibility that it might not exist in any numbers on your
favorite stream.

A. Family Ephemeridae

Most members of this family inhabit slow to moderate stretches of streams
and lakes and ponds. Most nymphs burrow in mud, silt, or fine gravel. Duns
usually appear, and spinners fall at dusk or later from late May until mid-
September. This family contains many of the largest mayflies in North

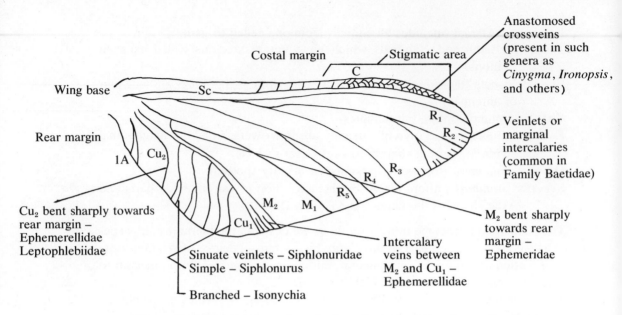

Figure 3. Composite fore wing of a hypothetical adult male mayfly showing identifying features of some of the families and genera of the Order Ephemeroptera.

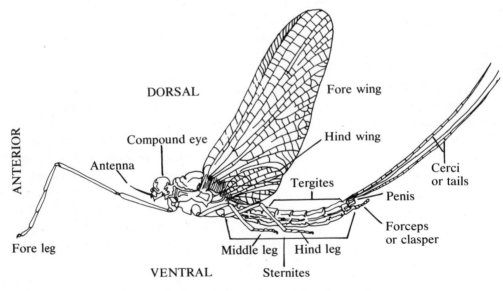

Figure 4. Lateral view of an adult male mayfly.

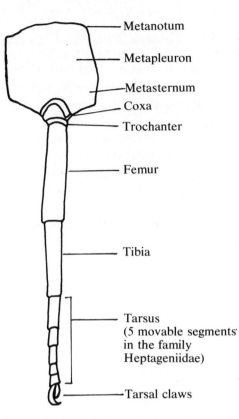

— Metanotum

— Metapleuron

—Metasternum

— Coxa

— Trochanter

— Femur

— Tibia

— Tarsus
(5 movable segments
in the family
Heptageniidae)

—Tarsal claws

Figure 5. Hypothetical hind leg of an adult
mayfly male of the Family Heptageniidae.

America. Ephemeridae species are separated from other families by the bent
path of vein M_2 in the fore wing (Figure 3).

1. Genus *Ephemera*

   This genus contains moderate to large (10–25 mm) gravel-burrowing
   nymphs. Most species emerge and fall (spinners) at dusk, and many continue well past dark. Wings on duns and spinners are heavily spotted, and
   all adults have three tails—unlike members of the genus *Hexagenia*, which
   have no spotting and only two tails. Sternites (underside of abdomen) vary
   in color from pale cream for *Ephemera guttulata* to tannish yellow for *E.
   simulans*. This latter species, *Ephemera simulans*, is extremely widespread
   and is found in Pennsylvania, Montana, Wyoming, Colorado, and Michigan, as well as many other states, and Canada. *Ephemera* contains the
   well-known Drake hatches (Green, Yellow, and Brown) and is an
   extremely important genus to meet and fish.

      Following are some *Ephemera* species that you might encounter:

   Ephemera compar (W)   *Ephemera simulans* (E, M, & W)
   Ephemera guttulata (E)   *Ephemera varia* (E & M)

2. Genus *Hexagenia*

These are large mayflies (14–30 mm). The nymph usually inhabits slow stretches of streams and lakes, or ponds, where it burrows in silt. Dun emergence and spinner fall often occur at dusk or later, and continue well past that time. Wings of the duns are heavily barred, and the veins of the spinners' wings are often dark reddish brown. In all species the middle tail is reduced to a barely visible vestige, and only two tails are prominent. *Hexagenia recurvata* is now placed in a new genus, *Litobrancha*. Although members are large, I have seen only *H. limbata*, *H. atrocaudata*, and *L. recurvata* produce fishable hatches (or spinner falls).

Following are some of the *Hexagenia* (and *Litobrancha*) species that might appear:

Hexagenia atrocaudata (E & M) *Hexagenia munda* (E & M)
Hexagenia limbata (E, M, & W) *Litobrancha recurvata* (E & M)

B. Family Polymitarcidae

This resurrected family includes mayflies with nonfunctional legs. Until recently these species were included in the Family Ephemeridae.

1. Genus *Ephoron*

These medium-sized (6–12 mm) burrowers frequent large and medium-sized streams. Duns of these species emerge most abundantly in July, August, or September in the evening. The female never molts, but emerges, mates, and lays eggs as a subimago – all in the same evening. Legs of both sexes (front legs of the male are an exception) are atrophied in the adult stage. The number of tails differs with the sex of the individual – the female has three and the male two. Tails in the male (spinner) are longer and better developed than in the female (dun).

Most adults appear almost totally white, sometimes with a gray cast. The White Wulff is an effective imitation during an *Ephoron* hatch. Although these mayflies aren't as common as many other species, they appear late in the season when few other true hatches occur, and are therefore important to meet and fish.

Following are the common *Ephoron* species:

Ephoron album (M & W)
Ephoron leukon (E & M)

C. Family Potamanthidae

Until recently *Potamanthus* species also were included in the Family Ephemeridae. However, *Potamanthus* nymphs are not true burrowers, and adults can be separated from the true burrowers by the branching of the first anal vein in these species. Only one genus is presently in this family.

1. Genus *Potamanthus*

These moderate-sized (9–16 mm) nymphs are sprawlers rather than burrowers, although they inhabit the same areas of a stream as the true bur-

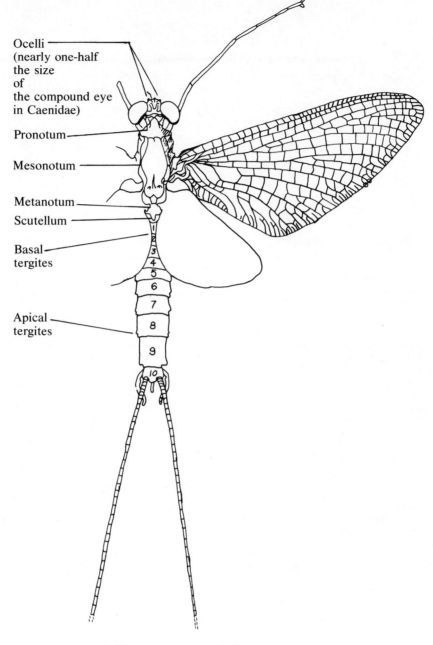

Ocelli
(nearly one-half
the size
of
the compound eye
in Caenidae)

Pronotum

Mesonotum

Metanotum

Scutellum

Basal
tergites

Apical
tergites

Figure 6. Dorsal view of an adult male
mayfly (after Leonard and Leonard and
Burks).

rowers (Ephemeridae). Duns emerge and spinners fall at dusk or shortly thereafter, and all have white, cream, or creamish yellow bodies and wings, sometimes with tan shading on the abdomen.

Fishermen commonly call mayflies of this genus Golden or Cream Drakes. Wing venation and body shading is important in separating species.

Following are some of the *Potamanthus* species that might produce fishable hatches:

Potamanthus distinctus (E)
Potamanthus rufous (E & M)
Potamanthus verticus (E & M)

D. Family Caenidae

Members of this family are often found in quiet water, where the nymphs move about freely in debris, trash, or silt. These diminutive mayflies rarely exceed 6 mm. Dun emergence and spinner fall occur at dark, before morning appears, or in the early morning hours. Most species appear after June. Members of this family are separated from other families by the size of the ocelli (simple eyes located between the compound eyes); these ocelli are at least half the size of the compound eyes (Figure 6).

1. Genus *Caenis*

These tiny mayflies are rarely longer than 5 mm and inhabit lakes, ponds, and slow stretches of streams. Adults are white, cream, or buff-colored, and usually appear at or shortly before dark. Duns change to spinners shortly after they emerge, and these imagos meet at dark, or in the early morning hours, and mate. Spinners are strongly attracted to light, and thousands can be seen near lighted areas at night.

Following are *Caenis* species that you may encounter:
Caenis anceps (E & M)
Caenis simulans (E, M, & W)

I have seen *Caenis anceps* emerge by the thousands in late July and August on Spruce Creek. However, to imitate this mayfly one would have to use a size 28 or 30 hook. This size is almost impossible to use effectively.

E. Family Tricorythidae

Until recently members of this family were included in Caenidae; however, *Tricorythodes* adults have claspers with three distinct segments (parts), compared to one in *Brachycersus* and *Caenis*.

1. Genus *Tricorythodes*

We find these tiny (3–5 mm) but important species on small streams like Falling Springs in south-central Pennsylvania, and on large ones like the Beaverkill and the Loyalsock in the East, and on the Colorado in the West. Duns often emerge in the morning, molt to spinners almost immediately, and mate within a couple hours. Male and female spinners often fall spent to the water, so it's important to have imitations of both sexes on hand. All species have three tails.

Some *Tricorythodes* species that seem to be common and can produce fishable hatches are:

Tricorythodes attratus (E & M)
Tricorythodes minutus (E & W)
Tricorythodes stygiatus (E & M)

F. Family Ephemerellidae

This family contains one genus, *Ephemerella*. Members are separated from other families by the few cross veins adults have in their fore wings, by the two long intercalary veins between M_2 and Cu_1, and by the bent path of vein Cu_2 (Figure 3). The three tails are often extremely weak (fragile) on the subimago.

1. Genus *Ephemerella*

Moderate-sized mayflies (5–20 mm), the nymphs of which swim freely among gravel in rapids, and amid aquatic plants in moderate and slow stretches. Many subimagos possess chocolate brown, brownish-olive, olive, olive creamish, tannish olive, or cream bodies. Fishermen call many members of these species Blue-Winged Olive Duns, because of their familiar dark bluish black wings and olive bodies. Many other species of this genus contain cream, yellow, or pale-olive bodies and are dubbed Pale Evening Duns (East and Midwest) or Pale Morning Duns (West). A third large group important for the fisherman are those imitated by the Chocolate Dun. Several species of the *bicolor* group of this genus are effectively imitated by the Chocolate Dun. To date this group of species and the proposed imitation have been overlooked by fly fishermen.

As a very general rule the olive, brown, and black species emerge during daylight hours (morning and afternoon) and the lighter species emerge in the evening. Of course there are many exceptions, especially in the West with species like *Ephemerella infrequens,* etc.

This genus contains some of the most important hatches of the season in the East, Midwest, and West. Who hasn't heard and probably experienced an emergence of the likes of the Hendrickson (*E. subvaria*), or the Pale Evening Dun (*E. invaria*) in the East or Midwest? The West has its share of *Ephemerella* species with Pale Morning Duns (*E. inermis* and *E. infrequens*) and Western Green Drakes (*E. doddsi* and *E. grandis*).

Following is only a partial list of some of the *Ephemerella* species that may produce fishable hatches:

Ephemerella attenuata (E & M)   *Ephemerella funeralis* (E & M)
Ephemerella coloradensis (W)   *Ephemerella grandis* (W)
Ephemerella cornuta (E & M)   *Ephemerella inermis* (W)
Ephemerella deficiens (E & M)   *Ephemerella infrequens* (W)
Ephemerella doddsi (W)   *Ephemerella invaria* (E & M)
Ephemerella dorothea (E & M)   *Ephemerella lata* (E & M)
Ephemerella flavilinea (W)   *Ephemerella longicornis* (E)

Ephemerella margarita (E & W)   *Ephemerella subvaria* (E & M)
Ephemerella needhami (E & M)   *Ephemerella tibialis* (W)
Ephemerella rotunda (E & M)   *Ephemerella walkeri* (E & M)
Ephemerella septentrionalis (E)

G. Family Leptophlebiidae

These small-to-moderate sized (6–14 mm) nymphs prefer lakes or ponds, or slow-to-moderate stretches of streams. Subimagos of most species appear dark brown or dark grayish brown, and most imagos are dark brown or reddish brown. Fishermen call the male imagos of many species of this family Jenny Spinners – these males have an abdomen of white or amber with the last few segments dark brown.

The family is separated from others by the bent path of vein Cu_2 in the fore wing (Figure 3).

1. Genus *Leptophlebia*

Many duns of these species appear around noon or shortly thereafter. Both dun and spinner have three tails; however, the middle tail of the male is almost always only one-third to two-thirds as long as the outer ones. Dark-brown or black imitations (Early Brown Spinner and Black Quill) work well when a hatch or fall of this genus occurs.

Some of the more common *Leptophlebia* species are:
Leptophlebia cupida (E & M)   *Leptophlebia johnsoni* (E)
Leptophlebia gravestella (W)   *Leptophlebia nebulosa* (E, M, & W)

2. Genus *Paraleptophlebia*

These small to moderate (5–9 mm) nymphs can tolerate much more current than *Leptophlebia*, and are therefore more common on trout streams and seem abundant on many smaller streams. Fly fishermen match the dun effectively with the Blue Quill or Dark Blue Quill and the female spinner with the Dark Brown Spinner.

The dark-grayish-brown duns often appear during the morning or early afternoon. Male spinners have a characteristic undulating mating flight and are active from morning until early evening.

The genus *Paraleptophlebia* contains many species that on occasion can produce fishable hatches. Among some of the more common examples of these species are the following:
Paraleptophlebia adoptiva (E & M)   *Paraleptophlebia memorialis* (W)
Paraleptophlebia bicornuta (W)   *Paraleptophlebia mollis* (E & M)
Paraleptophlebia debilis (E, M, & W)   *Paraleptophlebia packii* (W)
Paraleptophlebia guttata (E & M)   *Paraleptophlebia strigula* (E)
Paraleptophlebia heteronea (W)   *Paraleptophlebia vaciva* (W)

H. Family Baetidae

Nymphs are free-swimming, highly streamlined, and range in size from 3 mm in species like *Pseudocloeon* to 10 mm in *Callibaetis*. Nymphs vary in their

The successful meeting and
fishing of mayfly hatches
depends largely upon recogniz-
ing and then duplicating the
species that is emerging.
The assortment of mayflies
included here is intended to
assist the fisherman in
this process.

Ephemera varia,
male spinner

Ephemera guttulata,
female spinner

Ephemera simulans,
female spinner

Ephemerella infrequens,
male dun

Cinygma dimicki,
female dun

Ephemera simulans,
female dun

Callibaetis nigritus,
female spinner

Ephemerella bicolor,
female dun

Baetis vagans,
male dun

Ephemerella flavilinea,
female dun

Ephemerella grandis,
male dun

Cinymula reticulata,
male dun

The fish's view of a floating mayfly is, of course, from underneath. What it sees is the abdomen. As a result, matching the color of the abdomen of the emerging insect is paramount if fishing is to be successful. Here are included a group of unusual closeup shots of some representative mayfly abdomens.

Ephemera varia,
  female spinner

Ephemera guttulata,
female spinner

Litobrancha recurvata,
male spinner

Stenacron canadense,
female dun

Ephemerella bicolor,
female dun

Stenonema vicarium,
male dun

Leptophlebia cupida,
female spinner

Isonychia harperi,
female dun

Ephemerella septentrionalis,
female dun

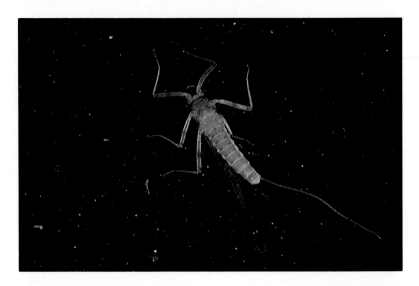

Stenonema fuscum,
female dun

Ephemerella cornuta,
female dun

Paraleptophlebia guttata,
female spinner

habitat from ponds and slow-water stretches, where we find species like *Calli-baetis*, to fast water, where several species of *Baetis* live. This family is separated from others by veinlets (small free veins) on the margins or the fore wing, which is characteristic of the genus *Baetis*. Some members of the family (*Cloeon* and *Pseudocloeon*) lack hind wings.

1. Genus *Pseudocloeon*

   These are small mayflies, but sometimes extremely important to match. Species of this genus can be separated from *Baetis* by the absence of the hind wing, and from *Cloeon* by the two veinlets between the longitudinal veins (*Cloeon* has one).

   Duns emerge on Eastern and Midwestern waters on many cold May afternoons and evenings. Fishermen can match many of these species with a Blue Dun (size 20–24) for the subimago, and a Rusty Spinner for the spinner.

   Some of the more common *Pseudocloeon* species are:

Pseudocloeon anoka (M)	*Pseudocloeon edmundsi* (W)
Pseudocloeon carolina (E)	*Pseudocloeon futile* (W)
Pseudocloeon cingulatum (E)	*Pseudocloeon parvulum* (E & M)
Pseudocloeon dubium (E & M)	

2. Genus *Baetis*

   These small (3–7 mm) nymphs often inhabit shallow-water areas of streams. Many duns of this genus rest for protracted periods before taking flight. Therefore, even though they're extremely small, many of these species are important for the fly fisherman to imitate. Furthermore, many of these species, including *Baetis parvus*, a common Western species, emerge on midsummer afternoons – a period often void of other mayfly species.

   Duns usually have dark gray, dark brown, or tan bodies, often with an olive cast, contrasted to the rusty brown or dark brown bodies of the imagos. The Blue Dun, Blue Upright, or Blue-Winged Olive Dun are used to match the subimago. Many male spinners resemble some of the *Paraleptophlebia* species, and have abdomens with the middle segments almost colorless (hyaline). *Baetis* species are difficult to separate. The venation of the hind wing and the presence of projections on that wing are important factors to consider in determining species.

   Some common species are:

Baetis bicaudatus (W)	*Baetis quebecensis* (*cingulatus*)
Baetis intermedius (W)	(E & M)
Baetis levitans (E & M)	*Baetis tricaudatus* (M & W)
Baetis parvus (W)	*Baetis vagans* (E & M)

3. Genus *Callibaetis*

   The free-swimming nymphs of this genus dwell in still water of permanent ponds and lakes, or sluggish areas of streams. Many species develop from egg to adult in five to six weeks, and consequently appear throughout the summer. Adult females live a week or more after mating. When eggs are finally deposited in still water, the young hatch out almost immediately.

Adults range in size from 5–10 mm. The female spinner has wings washed heavily with gray flecks. All species have two tails.

Following are some *Callibaetis* species that you might encounter:

Callibaetis coloradensis (M & W)   *Callibaetis fluctuans* (E & M)
Callibaetis ferrugineus (E & M)   *Callibaetis nigritus* (W)

I. **Family Siphlonuridae**

Members of this family until recently were included in the Family Baetidae. It is now separated because all members have four segments on the hind tarsi (Baetidae members have three), and by the path of M_2 in the fore wing (this vein is detached in Baetidae).

Siphlonurus and *Isonychia* can be separated by the sinuate veinlets in the fore wing – single in *Siphlonurus* and branched in *Isonychia* (Figure 3).

1. Genus *Isonychia*

These large, streamlined nymphs prefer rapid water. Nymphs, when emerging, often swim to shallow rapids, crawl onto an exposed rock, break their nymphal skin, and escape to a nearby tree.

Adults usually have dark forelegs and creamish hind legs. All have two tails. Duns often have slate-colored bodies, while spinners are dark maroon or dark rusty brown in color. The Slate Drake effectively imitates many species of this genus.

Some common *Isonychia* species are:

Isonychia bicolor (E & M)
Isonychia harperi (E & M)
Isonychia sadleri (E & M)

2. Genus *Siphlonurus*

These moderate-sized (9–14 mm) mayflies are often called Gray Drakes by fishermen. Emergence for different species occurs throughout the season. *Siphlonurus quebecensis* appears near the end of May in the East and Midwest, *S. alternatus* emerges around the end of June in the same areas, and *S. occidentalis* appears on Western waters from mid-July into August. Species often emerge in the afternoon sporadically.

Legs, wings, tails, and bodies of many species are dark gray, with the bodies ribbed slightly lighter.

Some of the more common *Siphlonurus* species are:

Siphlonurus alternatus (E & M)   *Siphlonurus quebecensis* (E & M)
Siphlonurus occidentalis (M & W)   *Siphlonurus rapidus* (E & M)

3. Genus *Ameletus*

Duns and spinners of these moderate-sized mayflies are usually brown or yellowish brown in general coloration. Some species of this genus are locally important in the West. I have noted only one species that appeared in fishable numbers in the West. That species, *Ameletus cooki*, can be important to imitate.

J. Family Heptageniidae

Nymphs of this rock-clinging family often dwell in moderate and fast water. All individuals have two tails. The tarsi on the hind legs have five movable parts – a distinguishing feature of this family (Figure 5).

1. Genus *Stenonema*

   Many species of this genus spend much of their nymphal life attached to rocks in moderate and fast water. Adults vary in size from 8–16 mm, and most have cream, yellow, or tan bodies. Legs of duns and spinners are cream or yellow with characteristic darker banding. Male and female of the same species often vary considerably in color, sometimes necessitating two patterns. Few *Stenonema* species are found in the West.

   Species previously listed in the *interpunctatum* group of this genus are now placed in a new genus, *Stenacron*.

   Some of the more common *Stenonema* species are:
   Stenonema fuscum (E & M)
   Stenonema ithaca (E)
   Stenonema luteum (E & M)
   Stenonema pulchellum (E & M)
   Stenonema vicarium (E & M)

   Some of the more common *Stenacron* species are:
   Stenacron interpunctatum canadense (E & M)
   Stenacron interpunctatum heterotarsale (E & M)
   Stenacron interpunctatum interpunctatum (E & M)

   Although we consistently refer to many *Stenacron* species throughout the text as *Stenacron canadense*, *Stenacron heterotarsale*, etc., the proper nomenclature should be as we have indicated above. These mayflies, plus others, are considered as subspecies of *Stenacron interpunctatum*.

2. Genus *Heptagenia*

   Duns of this genus often escape rapidly from the surface when emerging, and therefore many duns are of questionable value to the angler. Spinners sometimes take on more importance because they characteristically rest on the surface while depositing eggs. Duns and spinners usually have bodies of cream, pale yellow, or tan, often with an olive cast. Some Western species like *Heptagenia solitaria* are more important than their Eastern counterparts because of their size and type of emergence. Fishermen imitate many species of this genus with the Pale Evening Dun or Gray Fox.

   Some of the more common *Heptagenia* species are:
   Heptagenia aphrodite (E)   *Heptagenia pulla* (M)
   Heptagenia diabusia (M)   *Heptagenia solitaria* (W)
   Heptagenia elegantula (W)   *Heptagenia walshi* (E)
   Heptagenia hebe (E & M)

3. Genus *Epeorus*

These nymphs often inhabit fast, shallow sections of pure, cool water. Duns, when emerging, shuck their nymphal skin on the bottom of the stream or river rather than near or on the surface. Wet flies work well during emergence activity of these species. Many species (*Epeorus vitreus* and *E. albertae* are exceptions) have bodies of pale to dark gray. Species are most important in fast-flowing trout streams of the East and West.

Some common *Epeorus* species are:

Epeorus albertae (W)   *Epeorus longimanus* (W)
Epeorus deceptivus (W)   *Epeorus nitidus* (W)
Epeorus grandis (W)   *Epeorus vitreus* (E & M)
Epeorus pleuralis (E)

4. Genus *Rhithrogena*

Nymphs of these species usually cling to gravel in fairly fast current. Adults are often dark tan, dark gray, or dark brown. Species can be locally important, especially on Western waters. The fore wings of spinners are anastomosed (netlike) in the stigmatic area.

Some common *Rhithrogena* species are:

Rhithrogena futilis (W)
Rhithrogena hageni (W)
Rhithrogena undulata (M & W)

5. Genus *Cinygma*

Another genus of some importance on Western streams. The cross veins in the stigmatic area are also anastomosed, but the veins in that area are divided into two fairly even rows (*Rhithrogena* is not divided). *Cinygma dimicki*, which outwardly resembles *Stenonema fuscum*, is important on some Western streams.

6. Genus *Cinygmula*

Species of this genus are often in moderate to small streams that are relatively cool. Wings of most members have a decided gray or yellow coat. Wings of the spinners are not anastomosed, in contrast to *Cinygma* and *Rhithrogena*.

Some common *Cinygmula* species are:

Cinygmula ramaleyi (W)
Cinygmula reticulata (W)

MAYFLY IDENTIFICATION

When attempting to identify species, genera, and families of mayflies, entomologists use keys. When utilizing these keys, it's important to remember significant features of the adult male that differentiate it from other species. Following are some of the body parts of the adult that are important in identification.

1. Wings
    a. Fore wing
        1. Color and shading of the parts.
        2. Path of veins – branching of longitudinal veins.
        3. Veinlets or intercalaries present or absent and number.
        4. Stigmatic area – anastomosed – shaded.
    b. Hind wing
        1. Present or absent.
        2. Shading and coloration of veins.
        3. Costal projections present.
        4. General venation.
2. Legs
        1. General coloration and markings; tarsal claws similar or dissimilar; number and size of tarsal segments; length of leg parts, especially fore legs; color of coxae and trochanters.
3. Abdomen
    a. General coloration or shading; color and shading of each tergite; are spiracular dots present or absent, and what is the shape of these dots; markings, including dots and shading of ganglionic areas; shading around the pleural fold.
    b. When working with the parts of the abdomen, it's important to know locations to which keys often refer. Such terms as lateral, posterior, anterior, mesal, dorsal, ventral, apical, and basal, among others, are especially important.
4. Tails
    a. Number, general coloration, length, and color at joinings.
5. Thorax
    a. Coloration and shading of top (notum), sides (pleuron), and bottom (sternum). Color pattern of scutellum.
6. Head
    a. Size of ocelli; shape and general color of the eyes; size of eyes. Coloration and shading of head and antennae.
7. Genitalia
    a. Forceps – number of segments, shape, and color.
    b. Shape of penis; presence and location of spines; general coloration; any projections present.

The number of tails a mayfly species has is helpful in identifying it. All mayflies have two or three tails, and although there are a few exceptions (*Ephoron*), all species of a genus have the same number of tails. Here is a list of mayfly genera according to the number of tails each has:

Two Tails			
Baetis	*Cinygmula*	*Heptagenia*	*Pseudocloeon*
Callibaetis	*Cloeon*	*Hexagenia*	*Siphlonurus*
Cinygma	*Epeorus*	*Isonychia*	*Stenacron*
	Ephoron (male)	*Litobrancha*	*Stenonema*

Three Tails	*Leptophlebia*
Caenis	*Paraleptophlebia*
Ephemera	*Potomanthus*
Ephemerella	*Tricorythodes*
Ephoron (female)	

Tails are extremely fragile – make certain when examining mayflies that none of the tails are broken.

Chapter IV

Meeting a Mayfly Hatch:
the Yellow Drake

Up to this point we've discussed emergence and hatches as if you were completely familiar with these phenomena. This chapter is intended to clarify any question you might have about hatches. In it we'll examine the emergence characteristics of one species, the Yellow Drake.

Mayflies appear annually. Members of a species appear for a few days, a week, two weeks, or much longer. During this annual emergence period many species appear in greater numbers on certain days, and in reduced numbers on other days. We'll call this period of heavy emergence the peak. Probably the best time to meet and fish a hatch is at its peak. This peak emergence can occur for a short, medium, or long period. The peak dates may vary for a species from year to year, but will often be of the same duration on the same stream. Also, the peak is usually preceded and followed by periods of sparser hatches. It is probably less important to meet and fish the hatch on these days. However, with some species, the period immediately after the peak, when the number of a species is waning, can be exceedingly productive.

The following study should place the whole concept of emergence in the proper perspective. A few years ago I visited the Bald Eagle Creek in central Pennsylvania almost daily to determine the peak period and emergence characteristics of *Ephemera varia*, commonly called the Yellow Drake by fishermen. I marked off a 200-foot slow to moderate stretch of stream, and spent evening after evening carefully counting the number of *Ephemera varia* subimagos (duns) emerging within that stretch.

Why did I select this species for this experiment? First and foremost, the Yellow Drake is large (13 to 17 mm) and fairly easy to identify in the air because of its pale yellow wings and body. Even in the half-light after 9:00 p.m. this pale yellow mayfly is relatively easy to see. Second, this species often concentrates its daily appearance from 8:30 to 9:15 p.m. This time might vary east or west of central Pennsylvania because of an earlier or later sunset.

Not only did I count the number of duns emerging during the observation period, but I also scanned the surface for signs of feeding trout. High water temperatures adversely affected this part of the study, since temperature readings from 68 to 75 degrees were common on the Bald Eagle Creek in late June and July.

The Yellow Drake was selected because it is large, and fairly easy to identify – even in the air. Pictured here is an *Ephemera varia* female dun.

When the water temperature rises to the mid-70s, trout usually seek out cooler environs. We discussed this point earlier when we talked about selecting a good stream. What good is a dense hatch if high water temperatures discourage trout from feeding?

Figure 7 shows the number of duns appearing and the dates they emerged. I recorded seeing duns as early as June 16 and as late as August 6. However, duns probably appeared earlier and later than the observations indicate. The peak of the annual emergence for that year occurred from June 23 to July 5. Determining the length of a peak is somewhat subjective. Furthermore, many species probably don't display the drastic decline that the Yellow Drake did between July 5 and July 8. Peaks for some species may be much more difficult to determine. Other species might well be erratic, showing an increase after a decrease. A point worth noting is that the Yellow Drake has a longer emergence peak on Fishing Creek in northeastern Pennsylvania. On this latter stream good hatches appear for two or more weeks.

Several evenings during the observation period it rained. On most of these occasions I noted only a few rain-soaked duns emerging. The highest number on any day was recorded on June 23, with seventy-two duns appearing in the 200-foot area. After the peak, for about three to four weeks, ten to fifteen duns emerged almost every evening. This latter phase, where only ten or so duns appeared, encompassed the last three weeks in July. Finally, a period of even fewer numbers occurred during early August, when only a few duns emerged nightly.

But the reason for the study is to determine how trout react to the emergence, especially the peak. As early as June 18 I observed one large trout feeding on the lethargic duns. On June 23, the beginning of the peak, I noted only three trout taking duns on the surface. Remember, I commented earlier about the warm water

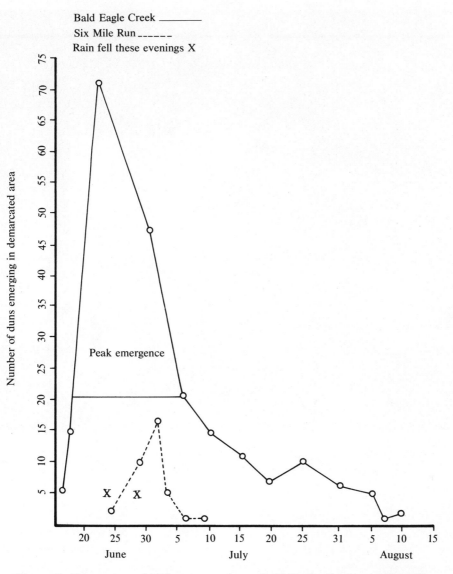

Figure 7. Emergence of *Ephemera varia* on Bald Eagle Creek and Six Mile Run in 1974. If observation were made every evening, the lines would probably be more erratic and less linear.

temperatures and how these probably discouraged other trout from seizing duns on the surface. After the peak, in mid-July, I saw only one trout rise to the now-reduced hatch.

The same year I also counted duns of the same species on Six Mile Run on alternate nights and later in the season. This is a small, extremely cold mountain stream in central Pennsylvania just 15 miles north of the Bald Eagle Creek. But

The study site for the Yellow Drake on the Bald Eagle Creek. Note the branch in the foreground. This marks the end of the site.

the elevation on the Bald Eagle Creek at the study site is 850 feet, whereas the altitude at the Six Mile Run study area is 1,790 feet – a difference of almost 1,000 feet. Six Mile Run is substantially slowed in its downstream movement by numerous beaver dams and other natural and man-made obstructions. These impoundments evidently slow this water enough so it can harbor a fair-sized *Ephemera varia* population. As it does on the Bald Eagle Creek, the Yellow Drake appears on Six Mile Run most often from 8:30 to 9:15 p.m. You'll note in Figure 7 that the peak emergence occurred about a week later on this latter stream.

Although the water temperature never rose above 66 degrees in the study area on Six Mile Run, I saw only three trout rise for escaping duns during the peak. I presume this happened because of the relatively small number of emerging duns (seventeen was the highest number).

Time of emergence for this species is interesting. Most duns appear (in central Pennsylvania) between 8:45 and 9:15 – a few before and some later – but the majority emerge in that half-hour. It's intriguing because the last swallow and flycatcher leave the stream near 8:45, and the first insect-eating bat appears on the stream around 9:15. A biological clock has instinctively alerted the majority of these slow-moving, easy-to-capture subimagos to emerge during that half-hour each night when the air is relatively free of winged predators.

Spinners too provide an important source of food for trout. The duns emerging last night and the night before become tonight's spinners. Imagos of some species are more readily available as food for trout than others. *Ephemera varia* exudes its eggs while riding on the surface, and therefore is potential food for trout. In addition to counting duns each evening, I also tried to approximate the number of spinners above and on the water in the study area. The peak of the spinner fall occurred the evening of June 25.

A word of caution: Emergence times can and do vary. I've seen our sample hatch on occasion appear in the morning. The time of emergence (and time of the spinner fall) can deviate considerably from the times listed in the Insect Emergence Chart. *Ephemera varia*, and for that matter most other species, may emerge earlier or later in your locality because of light differences between your stream and those in central Pennsylvania.

Peaks vary tremendously from species to species – even from stream to stream for the same species. Nonetheless, trout activity (surface feeding) is usually at its best during the peak of a hatch. The emergence dates listed in Chapter II are rough estimates of the earliest dates you might expect a peak to occur.

Chapter V

A Realistic Approach to Imitating
Mayflies and Other Aquatic Insects

I first attempted fly fishing on a local, marginal stream in eastern Pennsylvania in the early fifties. Some prodding by several angler friends, and stories of success with artificials they used, motivated me into purchasing an initial selection of two March Browns. I chose the March Brown wet fly because one of the locals indicated that he had limited out the day before on the same stream with that pattern. These imitations had a brown partridge hackle, tannish body, brown tail, and dark-brown wings.

As luck would have it, I came home that day with three heavy trout, all caught on the March Brown. I lost the first artificial on an early cast, and caught all three fish on the second and last imitation I had. That latter wet fly was badly mutilated after a couple hours of fishing, so I decided to obtain a couple March Browns at another store on my way home.

"Do you have any March Brown wet flies?" I asked the owner.

"Yes," he said, and he opened a large box of patterns and pointed to some imitations with very dark brown bodies.

"No, I want a March Brown with a tannish body."

"Only ones I have are these dark ones," the owner said.

In desperation I looked for any artificial that roughly matched my original March Brown. Finally, I selected several patterns the owner listed as Brown Mallards, because they did look a bit like the March Browns I had purchased before.

I've been dismayed these more than twenty years by the tremendous number of artificials available to fishermen – but more than that, dismayed by the variation of patterns with the same name.

Want to be utterly frustrated sometime? Then try this experiment next time you purchase artificials. Visit two sporting-goods stores and order the same pattern at each. If the patterns are not supplied by the same tier or company, you'll probably note some differences in the "same" dry fly. Of course, the Light Cahill, Dark Cahill, Quill Gordon, and many, many other common patterns will vary little. But procure two March Browns, Gray Foxes, Slate Drakes (I bet they don't have this one), or Yellow Drakes (they probably won't have this one either), and you'll notice that the patterns are probably not similar.

66

Purchasing a good caddis-fly or stonefly imitation is even more difficult. Ask for an imitation of the Grannom, or the Little Black Caddis – they probably won't have either. The same comment goes for the Early Brown Stonefly. Yet all of these, plus many others, work well during the hatches they match. All of these artificials should have wings folded down over the body like the natural.

Suppose you tie your own imitations. Where do you look for information on the suggested pattern? You might check Donald DuBois' book, *The Fisherman's Handbook of Trout Flies*. This excellent work codes fly patterns according to common names. Examine this volume for patterns of the American March Brown and March Brown and you'll find sixteen separate patterns for the first and sixty-four separate patterns for the second. Thus for two common names we have eighty different patterns from which to choose. Moreover, check five other texts or articles on fly tying or fly fishing and you'll probably come up with five additional March Brown patterns. Granted, the differences may be slight, but they're still differences.

Let's look at one more pattern in DuBois' book – the Green Drake. He has sixty-seven imitations listed for this mayfly, with body materials ranging from white floss to green floss to yellow floss to brown raffia. Hackles in these patterns range from brown to ginger to green. It appears that one man's Green Drake is another man's March Brown.

With this myriad of patterns available, how can we find appropriate patterns to imitate emerging naturals? Most writers on the subject depend on past recommendations for fly patterns. This is good to some extent – we can't knock success – and most of the patterns have been productive for years. But that doesn't say we can't refine patterns to be even more productive.

If we're going to duplicate the natural, then let's look at the natural, and copy it as closely as possible. A problem immediately arises: The *Stenonema fuscum* (Gray Fox) hatch is long gone in January when you're tying a new supply of artificials for the coming season. Moreover, you don't dare be without an imitation of the Fox the first evening the hatch appears next year.

If you've recorded the information on size and coloration of the Gray Fox as I suggested earlier, you're well on your way. Even a greater aid would be a photograph of the natural that you could refer to from time to time during those long winter months. With recent developments in photographic equipment such as the macro lens, we're able to make crisp, clear closeups of mayflies. Through these enlargements we're better able to discern color and form of the various naturals. However, most photos I've seen show top or side views of the insect – rarely the ventral or underside. Why is this oversight important to correct? Many times the dorsal (top) and lateral (side) views are entirely different in color from the ventral (bottom) view. The Gray Fox, Green Drake, and American March Brown are examples of this. Observe any of these from above and below and you'll see significant variations. From above the Gray Fox has a yellowish cream body, ribbed heavily with brown. From the bottom this same insect has a yellowish cream body with little or no ribbing. The Green Drake has a dark dorsal abdomen, but the belly is a consistent pale cream. If you plan to imitate the underside, which is the view most often seen by fish, then the coloration of the belly and not the back is what you should use. If you ever see duns riding on their wings on the surface, then it's time to use a pattern copying the dorsal view.

Copy the natural as carefully as possible in every detail, and as realistic as the pattern might appear, it will not always work. Sometimes what seems like an exact imitation doesn't work during a hatch of naturals that the imitation seemingly duplicates. Recently, Bill Kimmel of the State College and I traveled to Falling Springs near Chambersburg to meet and fish while a *Tricorythodes* species appeared. Clouds of spinners saturated the air, and many spent females were already drifting on the water. I tied on a spent-female imitation, hook size 24, and cast over twenty or twenty-five actively feeding trout. Cast after cast, for two hours, we fished over these trout until the spinner fall subsided – and we caught only two fish. I became so frustrated I grabbed one of the female spinners floating past me and placed it next to my imitation. Although the natural was infinitesimally smaller, the color and the appearance were very similar. Was it the tapered leader? I was using a 6X leader with a tippet diameter of .042. Would another pattern have been more effective? Maybe. I'd rather think that the trout that Bill and I were attempting to catch that day had been "fished over" by hundreds of other fly fishermen. For two months this particular *Tricorythodes* species had appeared faithfully daily, along with fly fishermen matching it. After all those imitations cast over them, the trout had become highly selective. Besides, this is a "no kill" stream and probably most of the trout had been hooked and released several times. Well, anyway, you can't blame me for trying to rationalize!

PATTERNS

If the Green Drake artificial is supposed to imitate the *Ephemera guttulata* dun, why do imitations with the same name vary so greatly? There are many reasons, but here are three.

First, some fishermen, although they see the natural hundreds of times, think a change in color here or a change there might produce a more effective imitation. Evolution, especially in fly patterns, is not always more useful or more successful.

It's a revelation to journey up and downstream on Penn's Creek just before a hatch of Green Drakes to observe which artificial each fly fisherman is using. Each fisherman has his own pet pattern which is a real "killer." Invariably, each fisherman relives accounts of success his Drake pattern has engendered. On these walks, before the hatch begins and while all other anglers are at streamside waiting for the emergence, I've seen a host of weird imitations. These patterns vary in hook size from 6 to 16, and in body color from green to bright yellow. Remember, all these diverse imitations represent one species which varies little from individual to individual.

A second reason for pattern variation might be that color in the same species does vary from location to location. Leonard and Leonard in *Mayflies of Michigan Trout Streams* suggest that *Stenacron canadense* (the Light Cahill) varies from cream to dark brown depending on the locale. Many other species, too, deviate in color from stream to stream.

Our early dependence on English imitations is a third explanation for the divergence in patterns. Along with the name "mayfly," the English gave us such patterns as the March Brown, the Green Drake, and the Iron Blue Dun. These patterns, intended for use on English streams, only vaguely represent the mayfly for which they're intended here.

There are other reasons for this evident diversity of patterns. Two fly tiers might use different materials for the wings or the body, for example. They do this often because one material might be more accessible than others.

The imitations listed in the following pages represent both the male and female dun of a species. If the two sexes vary in coloration, then we've included both duns.

Only occasionally do male imagos take on importance as trout food. Therefore, we've included only one male-spinner pattern, *Tricorythodes stygiatus*. This male spinner is short-lived (usually three hours or less), and sometimes dies in numbers over the water. Another male spinner, the Jenny Spinner, which represents many species (especially in the Family Leptophlebiidae), does find its way to the surface, on occasion.

MATERIALS

You'll note some changes in materials used for the imitations. For spent wings of the spinner, I like white or very pale gray polypropylene tied perpendicular and flat. This relatively new material is exceptionally buoyant, durable, and versatile, and comes in almost any color.

In the patterns I repeatedly recommend spun fur and hackle stems as appropriate body materials, and mallard-quill sections for wings. Spun furs are easy to find, easy to work with, and available in many colors (as is polypropylene). Hackle stems (peacock also), when stripped, effectively duplicate the ribbed appearance of many mayflies.

Most fly tiers loathe using mallard-quill sections for wings. The main disadvantage when using these is that they split easily after a few casts. You can overcome this problem by applying a drop of Pliobond adhesive to each wing. You can use hackle tips also for wings – but when you want a dark-slate wing you can't beat mallard sections. The dark-slate color of the mallard quill is very similar to the wing coloration of many mayflies, such as the Slate Drake, Blue-Winged Olive Dun, Blue Quill, and many others.

CAUTIONS IN IMITATING THE HATCHES

A word of caution in the following descriptions. What one person interprets as yellowish cream might be yellow or cream to someone else. Also, don't forget that body color can vary radically for the same species on different streams. Not only does color vary with the same insect from stream to stream, but also it can vary for the same species on the same stream. Furthermore, a day or two after emergence, the coloration of the dun can become much darker, and the spinner too often becomes darker the longer it lives. Some *Baetis* species exemplify this color change. Immediately after changing from dun to spinner, many *Baetis* species have tannish brown abdomens. Two days after the change, the body has evolved into a very dark brown color.

With all the aforementioned cautions in mind, and probably many not mentioned, we can look at the natural and suggested imitation for the various species. We've recorded some of the more important species to imitate in the following section. We describe the dun and spinner on the left and suggest a pattern on the right. Immediately following the description of each species, we have listed possible commercial patterns that you can purchase, which may prove as effective, or nearly so, as the recommended imitation.

We have placed duns in approximate chronological order – those emerging early in the season appear first on the list.

You'll probably note changes in some of the common names. If a species has no common name, I have used a common name that usually describes its general coloration.

NATURALS AND IMITATIONS (*Eastern*)

Order Ephemeroptera – Mayflies

Baetis vagans	Imitation – Little Blue Dun
Dun – 5–7 mm	Hook size – 18 or 20
Wing – Medium slate gray	Gray mallard quill
Body – Dark slate, ribbed lighter, and with a decided olive cast	Gray muskrat dyed olive and dubbed
Legs – Tannish gray with pale gray tips	Pale dun hackle
Tail – Gray	Dark dun hackle fibers
Spinner	Rusty Spinner
Wing – Glassy clear	Pale gray hackle tips
Body – Dark rusty brown, ribbed with tan	Dark brown hackle stem stripped
Legs – Dark grayish brown	Dark brown hackle
Tail – Dark grayish brown	Dark brown hackle fibers

Commercial pattern, dun: Blue Dun
Commercial pattern, spinner: Rusty Spinner or Red Quill

I have seen this species on central Pennsylvania waters as early as March 5, so it's important to include patterns copying *Baetis vagans* at the beginning of the season.

To get the proper color for the body of the dun, place a piece of dark gray muskrat fur in a hot (but not boiling) bath of Rit Olive Dye. Leave the fur in the dye for only a minute or two, then rinse the fur with cold water to set the dye.

The dark brown body of the female spinner is ribbed with a lighter tan. To obtain this ribbed effect, strip a dark brown hackle stem of its fibers and wind. As with the Red Quill body, place a drop of lacquer on the completed body to prevent it from splitting. Don't forget, *Baetis vagans* has overlapping broods and can be found on many streams two or three times a year.

Paraleptophlebia adoptiva, P. mollis,	
P. guttata, and similar species	Imitation – Dark Blue Quill
Dun – 6–9 mm	Hook size – 18
Wing – Dark slate gray	Dark gray mallard quill
Body – Dark brownish gray	Peacock quill (not from the eye)
Legs – Grayish tan with darker markings	Light to medium blue dun hackle
Tail – Grayish brown	Dark blue dun hackle fibers
Spinner	Dark Brown Spinner
Wing – Glassy clear	Pale gray polypropylene tied spent
Body – Dark brown	Dark brown polypropylene
Legs – Dark brown	Dark brown hackle
Tail – Dark brown	Dark brown hackle fibers
Commercial pattern, dun: Dark Blue Quill	
Commercial pattern, spinner: Early Brown Spinner	

The legs of many *Paraleptophlebia* species appear lighter than others. When tying the lighter species, you can use a lighter dun hackle. Female spinners of most species have dark brown bodies, legs, and tails. Few commercial imitations have this dark brown combination. However, artificials of the imago are extremely effective, especially early in the season. Make certain you carry copies.

Many male spinners have amber or white bodies with only the last couple segments dark brown. These male imagos are the familiar Jenny Spinners.

Epeorus pleuralis	Imitation – Quill Gordon
Dun – 9–12 mm	Hook size – 12
Wing – Slate gray	Dark gray mallard quill
Body – Dark gray, ribbed faintly with lighter gray	Eyed peacock quill, stripped
Legs – Tannish gray with darker markings	Blue dun variant hackle
Tail – Dark gray	Dark blue dun hackle fibers
Spinner	Red Quill Spinner
Wing – Glassy clear	White polypropylene, tied spent
Body – Reddish to tannish brown, ribbed finely with tannish cream	Dark reddish brown hackle stem, stripped
Legs – Grayish tan with reddish brown markings	Medium blue dun hackle
Tail – Dark brown	Dark brown hackle fibers
Commercial pattern, dun: Quill Gordon	
Commercial pattern, spinner: Red Quill	

Immediately you'll note a difference in the suggested pattern over what you're accustomed to seeing: The imitation I suggest has a wing of gray mallard and not barred wood duck. The wings of the natural are actually dark slate, so why use wood duck? I posed this question to Fred Ramage of Pittston, who theorizes that the configuration (barred effect) imitates a mayfly with fluttering wings. I guess that's as good an explanation as any. If you feel your artificial is not complete without the wood duck, include it.

Mallard quill is easy to use as wing material if you follow the advice given to me by John Perhach. Cut out two equal sections (the width will depend on the hook size), one from a right wing and one from a left wing of a mallard. Place the sections together so they appear concave (shiny sides together). Put the wings (sections) between the thumb and index finger and place both over the shank of the hook with the tips headed toward the eye. Take one loose turn with the thread, then a tight turn to secure the wings. Pull the wings upright by the tips and make five or six complete winds of thread in front. Now take a loose piece of thread about 3 to 4 inches long, and make a loop with it, under the hook and in front of the wings. The loose thread should look like the letter U. Bring the two ends (or the open ends of the U) up and through the wings, pulling gently. This tension will divide the wings and pull them toward the rear slightly. Tie down the loose ends of the thread with the thread attached to the bobbin. Don't forget to apply a drop of Pliobond cement to the completed wings for protection.

Ephemerella subvaria	Imitation – Hendrickson (female); Red Quill (male)
Dun – 9–12 mm	Hook size – 12 (female); 14 (male)
Wing – Slate gray	Gray mallard quill
Body – Female: creamish to dark tan, ribbed lighter (sometimes with pinkish cast)	Female: Tan fox belly fur
Male: Pinkish tan with lighter ribbing	Male: Brown hackle stem
Legs – Creamish yellow marked with tannish gray	Tannish gray hackle with a turn or two of dirty cream hackle
Tail – Dark tannish gray	Dark bronze dun hackle fibers
Spinner	Red Quill Spinner
Wing – Glassy clear	White polypropylene tied spent
Body – Dark tannish brown ribbed finely with tan	Reddish brown hackle stem
Legs – Tannish gray with reddish brown markings	Bronze dun hackle
Tail – Tannish gray with dark brown markings	Bronze dun hackle fibers

Commercial pattern, dun: Hendrickson (female); Red Quill (male)
Commercial pattern, spinner: Red Quill

Again we suggest a dark mallard wing for the dun rather than the usual barred wood duck. Wood duck, however, does work well for the spinner.

The body of the Red Quill is formed from a reddish brown hackle, stripped of its barbules. To tie the body, strip the stem, and place it in water for a few minutes to make it more pliable. Tie the tip of the stripped stem on the hook at the bend and wind toward the eye. Using the tip of the stem first makes the rear segments appear smaller than the front ones, much the same as in the natural.

The female spinner imitation is usually called the Female Beaverkill or the Female Hendrickson. The pattern most suggested has a body of cream, ribbed with yellow. However, the spinners I've observed possess a tannish-brown body ribbed with tan. Therefore, I am recommending that you use a brown hackle stem as the basis for the body rather than the "cream-with-yellow-ribbing." Granted, the coloration of this species varies from location to location, but I still think the Red Quill might be more appropriate. If you want, you can add a turn or two of yellow polypropylene at the tip to imitate the egg sac of the female spinner.

Caution: Individuals of this species vary considerably in body color from stream to stream.

Leptophlebia cupida
Dun – 9–12 mm   Imitation – Black Quill
                                            Hook size – 12

Leptophlebia cupida	Imitation – Black Quill
Dun – 9–12 mm	Hook size – 12
Wing – Medium to dark slate gray	Dark gray mallard quill
Body – Dark slate gray (with brown cast), and ribbed lighter	Eyed peacock herl, stripped
Legs – Front are dark brown (almost black), and rear two pair are dark tan	Dark brown hackle with a turn or two of tan hackle in the rear
Tail – Grayish banded with brown	Dark bronze dun hackle fibers
Spinner	Early Brown Spinner
Wing – Glassy clear with some brown in stigmatic (front) area of wing	Pale tan polypropylene
Body – Dark reddish brown banded with pale yellow	Dark reddish brown polypropylene, ribbed with pale yellow thread
Legs – Front are dark (almost black), and rear two pair are dark tannish brown	Dark brown hackle
Tail – Dark grayish brown (almost black)	Dark brown hackle fibers

Commercial pattern, dun: Black Quill
Commercial pattern, spinner: Early Brown Spinner or Black Quill

This species, although not as common as many others discussed in this chapter, can be important in late April and early May. The Black Quill is common on lakes and ponds and on slow stretches of streams. All duns I have ever observed escape rapidly from the surface, and this phase of the insect is of questionable value to imitate. The spinner is active all afternoon and the female does fall spent on the surface. The latter is probably the more important phase to imitate.

Ephemerella rotunda   Imitation – Pale Evening Dun
Dun – 7–9 mm   Hook size – 14 or 16
  Wing – Pale gray   Pale gray mallard quill
  Body – Creamish yellow with distinct   Creamish yellow polypropylene dyed pale
      olive cast   olive
  Legs – Pale creamish yellow   Cream hackle
  Tail – Pale creamish yellow   Cream hackle fibers

Spinner   Pale Evening Spinner
  Wing – Glassy clear   White polypropylene tied spent
  Body – Tan   Red fox belly fur
  Legs – Tan   Pale ginger hackle
  Tail – Tan with darker ribbing   Pale ginger hackle fibers
Commercial pattern, dun: Pale Evening Dun
Commercial pattern, spinner: Pale Evening Spinner

The body of the dun of this species has a distinct olive cast. I have never seen a commercially tied pattern which combines the correct color pattern.

I have on rare occasions noted a male of this species. Needham *et al.*[1] suggests possible intermittent parthenogenesis (fertilization of eggs without males) in this species.

Ephemerella septentrionalis
Dun – 7–9 mm
  Wing – White
  Body – Creamish yellow with orangish
        cast
  Legs – Creamish yellow
  Tail – Creamish yellow

Spinner
  Wing – Glassy clear
  Body – Creamish yellow
  Legs – Creamish yellow
  Tail – Creamish yellow
Commercial pattern, dun and spinner: Pale Evening Dun

I list this species because I have never seen it described in any fishing text, and because I have noted this species and similar-looking ones (*Ephemerella dorothea*) on many streams from late May to mid-July.

Duns tend to emerge near the edge of streams around 8:00 p.m. The Pale Evening Dun is effective during the hatch – therefore no other imitation is necessary. You might, however, make a few imitations with white wings rather than the pale gray, if you feel the small variation is important.

[1] James G. Needham, Jay R. Traver, and Yin-chi Hsu, *The Biology of Mayflies* (Hampton, England: E. W. Classey Ltd., 1972), p. 105.

Heptagenia aphrodite and *Heptagenia hebe*
Dun — 6–8 mm (*H. aphrodite*) and 5–7 mm (*H. hebe*)
  Wing – Pale gray and barred
  Body – Creamish yellow with olive cast
        (*H. hebe* has no olive cast)
  Legs – Yellowish cream
  Tail – Creamish yellow

Spinner
  Wing – Glassy clear
  Body – Pale yellow
  Legs – Pale yellow
  Tail – Cream

Imitation – Pale Evening Dun

Hook size – 14 or 16

Commercial pattern, dun and spinner: Pale Evening Dun

Again, I don't suggest a pattern for these species, since the Pale Evening Dun, in the correct sizes, should suffice.

Since most *Heptagenia* species alight from the surface rapidly, you might need an imitation of one very infrequently. These and similar-looking species can be found on many streams from late May until late September. Most duns have yellowish cream bodies (sometimes with an olive cast), cream legs with darker markings, cream tails, and medium gray wings.

Heptagenia aphrodite, since it appears in mid-May, when temperatures in the evening cool quickly, does often rest before takeoff. Species emerging in July and August escape much more rapidly.

Stenonema fuscum
Dun – 9–12 mm
  Wing – Pale yellow, barred, and with a grayish cast
  Body – Pale creamish yellow to tan with fine, lighter ribbing
  Legs – Creamish yellow with darker markings
  Tail – Amber with dark brown markings

Spinner
  Wing – Glassy clear with dark brown barring, and darker area in stigmatic (front tip) section
  Body – Grayish tan, ribbed with pale tan
  Legs – Grayish tan with dark brown markings
  Tail – Tan with dark brown markings

Imitation – Gray Fox
Hook size – 12
Pale yellow mallard flank

Creamish yellow angora, dubbed

Cream variant hackle

Ginger hackle fibers

Ginger Quill Spinner
Pale amber mallard quill

Tan peacock eye, stripped

Cream ginger hackle

Ginger hackle fibers

Commercial pattern, dun: Gray Fox or Light Cahill
Commercial pattern, spinner: Ginger Quill

This species has typical *Stenonema* leg coloration – pale creamish yellow legs with brown markings. To obtain the desired coloration with the dark markings, use a badger or natural cream variant neck. The badger neck is cream with a dark center, while the cream variant is cream with ginger or light brown horizontal markings. Both colors do an effective job, but I lean toward the cream variant. The Light Cahill sometimes substitutes effectively during an emergence of *Stenonema fuscum* subimagos.

Caution: Coloration of this species varies from stream to stream.

Stenonema vicarium — Imitation – American March Brown

Dun – 10–16 mm — Hook size – 10–12

Wing – Tannish yellow, usually heavily barred with profuse black markings — Teal or mallard flank dyed pale tannish yellow

Body – Creamish tan to dark tan, ribbed faintly with reddish brown — Creamish tan polypropylene or fox belly fur, ribbed with brown thread

Legs – Cream with dark brown markings — Cream variant or creamish yellow hackle, with grizzly dark brown hackle fibers

Tail – Dark brown barred — Dark brown hackle fibers

Spinner — Great Red Spinner

Wing – Glassy clear, with brown markings, and a brown area in the stigmatic region — Creamish tan mallard flank

Body – Tan, ribbed with dark brown — Fox belly fur, dubbed, and ribbed with dark brown thread

Legs – Amber, with dark brown markings — Cream ginger and dark brown hackle mixed

Tail – Dark brown, mottled — Dark brown hackle fibers

Commercial pattern, dun: American March Brown
Commercial pattern, spinner: Great Red Spinner

Most members of this species would be more correctly imitated with a size 10 hook. However, this larger hook is more difficult to float for any distance, and I recommend a size 12.

Teal flank feathers contain much heavier barring than mallard flank. The former, therefore, better duplicates the wings of the American March Brown.

Caution: Color and size of individuals of this species vary considerably.

Stenacron canadense — Imitation – Light Cahill

Dun – 9–12 mm — Hook size – 12 or 14

Wing – Pale yellow, barred slightly — Pale yellow mallard flank feather

Body – Creamish yellow (female has orange cast) — Creamish yellow polypropylene (with orange cast to imitate female)

Legs – Creamish yellow, marked with dark brown — Cream variant hackle or creamish yellow with a turn of brown hackle

Tail – Creamish yellow — Creamish yellow hackle fibers

Spinner

    Wing – Glassy clear with faint yellow
            cast

    Body – Pale yellow (the female, with
            eggs, has a creamish-orange
            cast)

    Legs – Creamish yellow, marked with
            dark brown

    Tail – Creamish

Salmon Spinner
Very pale yellow mallard flank feather

Pale cream polypropylene

Same as dun

Cream hackle fibers

Commercial pattern, dun: Light Cahill
Commercial pattern, spinner: Little Salmon Spinner or Light Cahill

The Light Cahill effectively copies both the dun and the spinner of this species. However, as with many *Stenonema* and *Stenacron* species, male and female duns differ greatly in body coloration. The male dun is correctly imitated with the Light Cahill, while the female is not. The artificial for the female dun should contain a distinct orange cast to the body. Several other similar species have orange or pink bodies; it's important to have on hand dry flies copying these body colors.

Note: Until recently this and several other species were placed in the genus *Stenonema*.

Caution: Coloration of this species varies from stream to stream.

Litobrancha recurvata

Dun – 20–28 mm

    Wing – Black, heavily barred, with
            dark green reflections

    Body – Dark slate, ribbed finely with
            yellow

    Legs – Front – Dark brown
           Rear – Tannish brown

    Tail – Black

Imitation – Dark Green Drake
Hook size – 8 or 10
Green teal flank feather

Peacock (not from the eye), stripped and
   ribbed with yellow thread
Dark brown hackle

Black hackle fibers

Spinner

    Wing – Glassy, heavily barred with
            dark brown

    Body – Reddish brown, ribbed with
            yellow

    Legs – Dark brown

    Tail – Black

Brown Drake
Brown teal flank

Dark brown polypropylene, ribbed with
   fine yellow thread
Dark brown hackle
Black hackle fibers

Commercial pattern, dun: Dark Green Drake
Commercial pattern, spinner: Brown Drake

As with the Black Quill, this species does not often produce a fishable hatch. These mayflies tend to emerge around the end of May in cold streams containing some slow water. Duns appear as early as 1:00 p.m., but seldom rest long enough to allow trout to feed on them. However, female spinners, after their mating ritual, ride the water spent for great distances. Note the change from the genus *Hexagenia* to *Litobrancha*.

Ephemera simulans	Imitation – Brown Drake
Dun – 11–15 mm	Hook size – 10 or 12
Wing – Grayish with dark brown markings	Mallard flank feathers
Body – Grayish yellow with dark brown markings	Yellow polypropylene (dyed gray)
Legs – Tan	Tan or ginger hackle
Tail – Tan	Tan or ginger hackle fibers
Spinner	Brown Drake Spinner
Wing – Glassy clear, heavily barred	Mallard flank feather
Body – Tannish yellow, with dark brown markings	Tannish yellow polypropylene
Legs – Tannish with some dark brown markings	Two tan and one brown hackle
Tail – Tan	Tan or ginger hackle fibers

Commercial pattern, dun and spinner: Brown Drake or Ginger Quill

Don't be without imitations of this species if you plan to fish large streams in late May or early June. On June 3, 1975, I met a spinner fall of this species that would match any I have ever seen. I was without any appropriate imitation. Tons of trout rose around me as I fruitlessly cast a Black Quill over them. A Ginger Quill would have been a better pattern. The spinner has brown markings on both sides of its belly. To make these markings, I use a brown felt waterproof marking pen.

Isonychia bicolor, I. sadleri, and *I. harperi*	Imitation – Slate Drake
Dun – 12–16 mm	Hook size – 12
Wing – Dark slate gray	Dark gray mallard quill
Body – Dark slate gray	Peacock (not from eye) stripped
Legs – Front are dark brown and rear pair are cream	One cream and one dark brown hackle
Tail – Medium gray	Medium blue dun fibers
Spinner	White-Gloved Howdy
Wing – Glassy clear	White polypropylene or hackle tips tied spent
Body – Dark reddish mahogany	Dark reddish mahogany raffia
Legs – Same as dun	One cream and one dark brown hackle
Tail – Medium gray	Medium blue dun fibers

Commercial pattern, dun: Leadwing Coachman
Commercial pattern, spinner: White-Gloved Howdy

On several imitations listed, I've recommended peacock fibers stripped. With the Slate Drake and others the fiber should be taken from the lower part of the tail feather. Fibers from this area don't contain the light and dark sides that the eyed peacock ones have, but rather have a uniform dark slate color.

Fast-water versions of the Slate Drake are very effective. Use impala dyed a dark gray for the wings and the same material but dyed pale gray for the tail.

Ephemera guttulata

Dun – 16–22 mm
    Wing – Yellowish green heavily barred with dark brown or black
    Body – Pale cream
    Legs – Front are dark brown and rear are cream
    Tail – Dark brownish black

Spinner
    Wing – Glassy, but heavily barred, and with a yellow cast
    Body – Chalky white

    Legs – Front are dark brown and rear are cream
    Tail – Tannish mottled with dark brown

Commercial pattern, dun: Green Drake
Commercial pattern, spinner: Coffin Fly or White Wulff

Imitation – Green Drake
Hook size – 8 or 10
Yellowish green mallard flank

Cream polypropylene or cream raffia
Two cream hackles in rear and one dark brown hackle in front
Dark brown moose or dark brown hackle stems

Coffin Fly
Pale yellow mallard flank

White polypropylene or 10 long white bucktail hairs
Same as dun

Ginger hackle stems, stripped of barbules

For the female spinner I suggest white polypropylene or white bucktail. John Perhach first showed me an effective method of using the bucktail. Take about ten white hairs from a tail, and tie in by their tips at the bend of the hook. Wind over the extended body and forward toward the wing. Not only is the bucktail more buoyant, but also the chalky white color of the material is very similar to the natural.

I suggest pale cream polypropylene to imitate the body of the dun. If you plan to tie the Drake with an extended body, you can use the polypropylene or cream raffia. If you prefer the raffia, soak it for a few minutes in water to make it more pliable.

You can extend the body by adding a 3-inch piece of 20- or 30-pound monofilament line. To make the monofilament easier to secure to the hook, flatten the end to be tied with pliers. After you secure the line, take three very dark moose mane hairs or hackle stems. If you use the stems, strip them of their barbules. Tie in the hairs or the stems by their butts. Now tie in the cream polypropylene or raffia midway on the shank. Wind the body material back over the extended body (monofilament) for an inch or two (depending on the size of the fly), and wind forward to the wings. Cut off the monofilament where the body ends, and shape the tail, if necessary.

Caution: Size of this species varies from stream to stream.

Epeorus vitreus

Dun – 7–9 mm
    Wing – Pale grayish with yellow cast – not barred

Imitation – Light Cahill (male); Pink Cahill (female)
Hook size – 16
Pale yellow mallard flank

Body – Male: pale yellow; Female: pinkish cream – top has dark reddish brown markings	Pale yellow or pinkish cream polypropylene, depending on sex
Legs – Creamish yellow marked with brown	Creamish yellow hackle
Tail – Dark grayish brown	Dark blue dun hackle fibers

Spinner	Salmon Spinner
Wing – Glassy clear	Pale gray polypropylene
Body – Pinkish red	Coral polypropylene
Legs – Creamish tan, barred	Cream ginger hackle
Tail – Creamish tan	Cream ginger hackle fibers

Commercial pattern, dun: Light Cahill
Commercial pattern, spinner: Salmon Spinner

I have encountered this species only on Six Mile Run in north-central Pennsylvania. Male and female body colors vary considerably.

Ephemerella invaria	Imitation – Pale Evening Dun
Dun – 6–9 mm	Hook size – 16
Wing – Pale to medium gray	Gray mallard quills
Body – Creamish yellow with heavy orange cast	Creamish yellow polypropylene with orange cast
Legs – Creamish yellow	Creamish yellow hackle
Tail – Creamish yellow	Creamish yellow hackle fibers

Spinner	Pale Evening Spinner
Wing – Glassy clear	White polypropylene, tied spent
Body – Orangish tan	Tan polypropylene
Legs – Tan	Ginger hackle
Tail – Pale cream	Cream hackle fibers

Commercial pattern, dun: Pale Evening Dun
Commercial pattern, spinner: Pale Evening Spinner

The body of this dun has a distinct orange cast to it. To copy the body color, soak white polypropylene in Rit Yellow Dye for five to ten minutes. This dye has a hint of orange, and when the material is saturated it will produce a body almost indistinguishable from the natural.

Male duns are much darker than the females. Males of this species appear to be much less common than females.

Wings for this imitation should be very pale gray, so select sections from the base of two mallard quills.

Ephemerella dorothea	Imitation – Pale Evening Dun
Dun – 5–7 mm	Hook size – 16 or 18
Wing – Pale gray	Pale gray mallard quill
Body – Creamish yellow	Pale yellow polypropylene
Legs – Pale yellowish cream	Yellowish cream hackle
Tail – Yellowish cream	Yellowish cream hackle fibers

Spinner | Pale Evening Spinner
  Wing – Glassy clear | White polypropylene
  Body – Creamish yellow | Creamish yellow polypropylene
  Legs – Creamish yellow | Creamish yellow hackle
  Tail – Cream | Cream hackle fibers

Commercial pattern, dun and spinner: Pale Evening Dun

This species is often compared with *Ephemerella rotunda* and *Ephemerella invaria*. *Ephemerella dorothea*, however, is usually pale yellow with no olive or orange cast, and usually emerges later in the season than the other two.

You'll note that the spinner of this and several similar-looking species are called ''Pale Evening Duns'' in the Insect Emergence Chart. This is deliberate on my part, since the Pale Evening Dun and not the Pale Evening Spinner more nearly resembles the imago.

Ephemerella attenuata | Imitation – Blue-Winged Olive Dun
Dun – 7–10 mm | Hook size – 14
  Wing – Dark bluish gray | Dark gray mallard quill
  Body – Medium olive faintly ribbed and with a gray cast | Medium olive hackle stem or muskrat, dyed olive
  Legs – Medium olive | Medium olive hackle
  Tail – Grayish | Blue dun hackle fibers

Spinner | Dark Olive Quill
  Wing – Glassy clear | Pale gray hackle tips
  Body – Rusty brown with an olive cast | Dark brown fur with an olive cast
  Legs – Tannish gray | Blue dun hackle
  Tail – Tannish gray | Blue dun hackle fibers

Commercial pattern, dun: Blue-Winged Olive Dun
Commercial pattern, spinner: Dark Olive Quill

I have seen this species on two occasions, both on the Beaverkill in early June. This species appears to have an olive body with a distinct gray cast. You might want to use the same muskrat placed in the olive dye as suggested for some of the *Baetis* species.

Ephemerella needhami | Imitation – Chocolate Dun
Dun – 6–9 mm | Hook size – 16
  Wing – Dark slate | Dark mallard quill
  Body – Chocolate brown, ribbed finely with tan | Dark brown polypropylene, ribbed with fine gold wire
  Legs – Creamish tan | Cream ginger hackle
  Tail – Medium gray | Medium dun hackle fibers

Spinner | Chocolate Spinner
  Wing – Glassy clear | Pale gray hackle tips
  Body – Dark rusty brown | Dark brown polypropylene
  Legs – Cream | Cream hackle
  Tail – Tannish gray | Bronze dun hackle fibers

Commercial pattern, dun and spinner: Little Marryat

I have observed both dun and spinner of this species on small streams in late May and early June shortly after noon. Artificials imitating the dun have proved very productive during hatches of this species.

Stenonema species, *pulchellum*-group	Imitation – Cream Cahill
Dun – 9–13 mm	Hook size – 12
Wing – Pale cream and very slightly barred	Very pale cream mallard flank feather
Body – Very pale cream, almost white	White or pale cream polypropylene
Legs – Pale cream with darker markings	Cream hackle
Tail – Pale tan	Tan hackle fibers
Spinner	Cream Cahill Spinner
Wing – Glassy clear with brown shading in stigmatic (front) region	Use dun imitation
Body – White (female with eggs has pale cream body)	
Legs – Pale cream with darker markings	
Tail – Pale tan mottled	

Commercial pattern, dun and spinner: White Wulff

Since dun and spinner of this species are similar except for wings, one imitation will suffice for both. Duns emerge sporadically during the day with the heaviest appearances from 10 a.m. to 2 p.m. The spinner can be an important source of food for trout. Spinners usually appear about 8:00 p.m., lay their eggs, and move back toward shore. While laying eggs the female does alight and rest briefly on the surface. Emergence begins about mid-June and continues through August in sparser numbers. The spinner of the species appears in the evening shortly before the Yellow Drake.

Although we presently know only the group and not the species to which this mayfly belongs, it is still important to imitate it.

Stenonema luteum	Imitation – Light Cahill
Dun – 9–13 mm	Hook size – 12
Wing – Yellow, slightly barred	Yellow mallard flank
Body – Yellowish cream	Yellowish cream polypropylene
Legs – Yellow with grayish tan markings	One cream and one blue dun hackle
Tail – Dark brown	Dark brown hackle fibers
Spinner	Olive Cahill Spinner
Wing – Glassy clear with some dark brown in stigmatic (front) region	Pale gray hackle tips
Body – Grayish cream	Fox belly fur dubbed

Legs – Front – Dark grayish brown	Front dark brown and rear cream hackle
Rear – Yellowish cream with	
darker markings	
Tail – Dark grayish brown	Dark brown hackle fibers

Commercial pattern, dun: Light Cahill
Commercial pattern, spinner: Light Hendrickson

The dun of this species is almost identical to that of *Stenacron canadense*, and the imitation of the latter will prove effective for this species. The spinner, however, is probably the more important phase to copy. Although emergence of the dun is very sparse from its beginning in mid-June to its end in September, there are enough spinners over fast water to make it common, and an imitation is required. Female imagos are active about 8:00 p.m. and hover a few inches above rapids laying eggs. Since the adult is so near the water's surface, it is often difficult or downright impossible to detect its presence. On several occasions I've observed trout jump completely out of the water to seize the naturals. I've tied the spinner imitation with a very long hackle to attempt to duplicate the hovering spinner. Sometimes dragging the artificial upstream during this egglaying flight can be effective.

Ephemerella cornuta	Imitation – Blue-Winged Olive Dun
Dun – 7–10 mm	Hook size – 14
Wing – Dark slate	Dark mallard quill
Body – Medium olive (may have	Fox belly fur dyed olive
grayish cast)	
Legs – Amber with olive cast	Ginger cream hackle
Tail – Pale grayish olive	Pale blue dun hackle fibers
Spinner	Dark Olive Spinner
Wing – Glassy clear	Pale gray hackle tips
Body – Dark olive (male has brown-	Muskrat fur, dyed olive
olive body)	
Legs – Dark olive brown	Dark brown hackle
Tail – Dark gray	Dark blue dun hackle fibers

Commercial pattern, dun: Blue-Winged Olive Dun
Commercial pattern, spinner: Dark Olive Spinner

This species too is seldom mentioned in fly-fishing literature, but is highly important to imitate in the dun and spinner stages. When it emerges in July and August it escapes quite rapidly, but still some remain long enough to encourage surface feeding. Meeting and fishing the dun most often occurs in the morning, while the spinner is most active just at dusk.

Baetis species	Imitation – Little Blue Dun
Dun – 4–6 mm	Hook size – 20
Wing – Medium gray	Mallard quill
Body – Medium olive	Muskrat, dyed olive
Legs – Creamish tan	Cream ginger hackle
Tail – Medium gray	Medium blue dun hackle fibers

Spinner
  Wing – Glassy clear
  Body – Medium brown
  Legs – Tannish
  Tail – Tannish
Commercial pattern, dun: Blue Dun or Blue-Winged Olive Dun
Commercial pattern, spinner: Rusty Spinner

Rusty Spinner
Pale gray hackle tips
Medium to dark brown polypropylene
Dark ginger hackle
Dark ginger hackle fibers

Although I have not yet had this species identified, it is an extremely important mayfly to imitate. The species appears on many streams in July during the afternoon and evening. Furthermore, the dun of the species rests a long time before taking flight.

This species has a deeper olive color to its body than does *Baetis vagans*. To duplicate the body color, place the gray muskrat fur in Rit Olive Dye for several minutes.

The male spinner resembles the Jenny Spinners of the genus *Paraleptophlebia*.

Tricorythodes stygiatus
Dun – 3–4 mm
  Wing – Pale gray
  Body – Pale creamish olive
  Legs – Pale cream
  Tail – Cream

Imitation – Pale Olive Dun
Hook size – 24–26
Pale gray hackle tips
Creamish olive fur
Cream hackle
Cream hackle fibers

Spinner

  Wing – Glassy clear

Body, female – rear half of abdomen is pale cream and front half is dark brown
Body, male – dark brown faintly ribbed
Legs, female – pale cream
Legs, male – front are dark brown and rear are cream
Commercial pattern, dun: Pale Sulphur Dun

Dark Brown Spinner (male); Reverse Jenny Spinner (female)
White or pale gray polypropylene tied spent
Rear half pale cream polypropylene, front half dark brown polypropylene

Dark brown polypropylene

Female, pale dun;
  male, pale dun with a turn of dark brown in front

Many fly tiers have asked how to tie wings on a size 24 hook. I always say, "Very carefully." For the dun imitation I use two hackle tips from a hen's neck, trim them to size, and tie them on.

Wing placement on spinner imitations is an easier task. Tie in the polypropylene perpendicular to and on the same plane as the shank of the hook. Wind over and around each wing to secure.

When tying the body of the female spinner imitation, take a piece of white or pale cream polypropylene and tie it in at the bend of the hook. After making two or three complete turns with the pale cream, next take the dark brown, tie in, and wind up the shank to the spent wings.

Hexagenia atrocaudata
Dun – 16–26 mm
  Wing – Dark slate
  Body – Dark slate (may be finely
         ribbed)
  Legs – Dark brown
  Tail – Dark grayish brown

Spinner
  Wing – Glassy clear with rear of front
         and rear wing ringed with dark
         brown
  Body – Tannish yellow ribbed finely
         with dark brown
  Legs – Front are dark brown and rear
         are tannish yellow
  Tail – Dark brown
Commercial pattern, dun: Dark Cahill
Commercial pattern, spinner: American March Brown

Imitation – Big Slate Drake
Hook size – 6 or 8
Dark gray calf tail
Peacock, stripped (take from bottom of
  herl)
Dark brown hackle
Dark gray hackle fibers

Dark Rusty Spinner
Brown mallard flank feathers

Tannish yellow polypropylene ribbed with
  dark brown thread
One dark brown hackle in front and a
  tannish yellow in the rear
Dark brown hackle fibers

How do you tie a size 6 or 8 dry-fly hook to make it float consistently? That's difficult to do, but if you make the body of trimmed deer hair it will probably work. I prefer, however, to tie the imitation on a size 10 or 12 hook. I've always thought that an imitation smaller than the natural emerging is much more successful than one larger than the actual mayfly.

Ephoron leukon
Dun – 9–12 mm
  Wing – Very pale gray
  Body – female – pale cream
  Body – male – white with rear two
         segments pale brown
  Legs – Front: very dark brown
         Rear: white
  Tail – Pale gray

Spinner (male only)
  Wing – Clear
  Body – White (rear two brown)
  Legs – Front: dark brown
         Rear: white
  Tail – Pale gray
Commercial pattern, dun and spinner: White Wulff

Imitation – White Mayfly
Hook size – 12–14
Pale gray hackle tips
Pale cream or white polypropylene
Same

White hackle with a turn of dark brown in
  front
Pale blue dun hackle fibers

Again one imitation should suffice for both dun and spinner. *Ephoron leukon* can be a locally important species in August and September. The species is not as common as many of the others discussed in this chapter. However, when you discover a stream that contains these nymphs you're probably in for some excellent late-season fly fishing.

The female never sheds its subimago skin and therefore mates and lays its eggs as a dun. The male dun, however, does change to the spinner stage almost immediately after emerging. Many times the male spinner carries the partially shed subimago skin while in flight. The male is noticeably smaller and more streamlined than is the female.

Caution: Size of this species varies from stream to stream.

Order Tricoptera – Caddis Flies

Rhyacophila lobifera
Adult – 8–12 mm
Wing – Medium brown, heavily flecked
Body – Medium green
Legs – Tan

Imitation – Green Caddis
Hook size – 14–16*
Brown deer body hair
Green polypropylene
Tan hackle (optional with deer hair)

Brachycentrus fuliginosus
Adult – 10–12 mm
Wing – Dark brown, heavily flecked
Body – Dark brownish black
Legs – Dark brown

Imitation – Grannom
Hook size – 12–14
Dark turkey tail
Black fur dubbed
Dark brown hackle

Hydropsyche slossanae
Adult – 7–10 mm
Wing – Tan, flecked
Body – Tan
Legs – Amber

Imitation – Spotted Sedge
Hook size – 14 or 16
Light turkey
Fox fur
Ginger cream hackle

Psilotreta frontalis
Adult – 10–12 mm
Wing – Dark bluish gray
Body – Dark slate gray
Legs – Dark brownish black

Imitation – Dark Blue Sedge
Hook size – 12
Dark bluish gray hackle tips
Peacock herl (not eyed)
Dark brown hackle

Chimarrha atterima
Adult – 6–10 mm
Wing – Medium gray
Body – Black
Legs – Dark brown

Imitation – Little Black Caddis
Hook size – 16
Medium gray mallard quill
Black fur dubbed
Dark brown hackle

* Mustad 94840 recommended for imitations unless another hook is specifically mentioned.

For the Green Caddis, and for that matter for any of the caddis imitations, you can utilize a method Barry Beck first showed me. After tying on the body material, take a bunch of deer hair and tie it in at the head of the fly. The deer hair imitates the wings, legs, and tail, and also does an effective job of floating the fly.

If you prefer, you can substitute turkey-wing sections for the deer hair. If you choose this latter material, tie in the tail and body first. Then take two quills from matching turkey feathers (tail feathers for dark wings and secondary wing feathers for light wings). Place the wings down over the body and secure with a few turns of thread and a drop of lacquer. Now take two stiff hackles and tie them on in front of the wing. Make certain you don't place the wing too far forward, because you need plenty of space for the hackle.

Order Plecoptera – Stoneflies

Taeniopteryx faciata
    Adult – 8–10 mm
    Wing – Dark brown barred
    Body – Dark brownish gray
    Legs – Dark brown
    Tail – Dark brown

Imitation – Early Brown Stonefly
Hook size – 14
Mallard flank feather dyed brown
Peacock (not eyed) stripped
Dark brown hackle
Dark brown hackle fibers

Isoperla signata
    Adult – 10–14 mm
    Wing – Pale yellow barred

    Body – Pale yellow ribbed with tannish
        brown
    Legs – Cream ginger
    Tail – Cream ginger

Imitation – Light Stonefly
Hook size – 12–14
Mallard flank feather dyed pale tannish
    yellow
Pale yellow floss ribbed with tannish
    brown thread
Cream ginger hackle
Cream ginger hackle fibers

Wings of stoneflies are tied like caddis-fly imitations. Again, you can use deer hair to imitate the wings, legs, and tail by tying one small bunch of hair in just back from the eye.

Terrestrial Imitations

Cricket Imitation
    Hook size – 10 Mustad 9672
    Wing – Black goose quill section tied downwing
    Body – Black floss or black angora
    Legs – Black deer hair spun around the hook, just behind the eye

The deer hair is buoyant and floats this large artificial rather well. The deer hair is spun around and clipped to form the head.

Grasshopper
    Hook size – 10–18 Mustad 9672
    Wing – Medium turkey wing tied downwing
    Body – Tan, yellow, or cream fur
    Legs – Brown deer hair tied similar to the cricket

Beetle
    Hook size – 14–18 Mustad 94840

Take a bunch of black deer body hair and tie on at the bend of the hook by the butt. After tying in the butt, wind the thread toward the eye of the hook. Now pull the tips of the deer hair up over the top of the shank. Tie in the tips just behind the eye and finish off, and clip off the end of the hair. If you want to imitate more closely the body coloration of the Japanese Beetle, you can use peacock for the body.

Ant
   Hook size – 16–22 Mustad 94840

Take a piece of black, brown, or for that matter any color polypropylene and tie it in at the bend of the hook. Make a few turns on the rear half of the shank of the hook to give it a humped effect. Now take a black hackle, tie it in at the middle of the shank, and make a few turns. Next take the black polypropylene and make another hump on the front part of the shank. To imitate one of the many winged species of ants, add two pale dun hackle tips at the head of the hook and place downwing over the body.

You can use black deer hair also to tie the ant imitation. Tie the deer hair in at the bend of the hook similar to the beetle. Halfway up the shank tie in the deer hair, leaving some of the smaller, loose hairs as legs. Continue the deer hair to the eye and tie in at the eye. Clip and cement, and you have a realistic, buoyant imitation.

PATTERN SELECTION (*Eastern and Midwestern*)

In the following chart we suggest specific patterns that might be best during certain times of the season. We base these selections on the hatches that are prevalent at different times and days of the fishing months. This chart should narrow the number of imitations you carry with you.

Morning	*Afternoon*	*Evening*
APRIL		
Blue Quill – 18	Blue Quill – 18	Dark Brown Spinner – 18
Blue Dun – 18 or 20	Quill Gordon – 12	Red Quill – 12
	Red Quill – 14	
	Hendrickson – 12	
	Black Quill – 12	
	Little Black Caddis – 16	
MAY		
Blue Quill – 18	Hendrickson – 12	Red Quill – 12
Blue Dun – 18 or 20	Red Quill – 14	Gray Fox – 12
Blue-Winged Olive	Green Caddis – 14	Grannom – 12
Dun – 14	Grannom – 12	Pale Evening Dun – 16
	Pale Evening Dun – 16	Spotted Sedge – 16
	Spotted Sedge – 16	March Brown – 12
	March Brown – 12	Slate Drake – 12
	Gray Fox – 12	Light Cahill – 12
		Green Drake – 10
		Brown Drake – 12
		Ginger Quill – 12

Blue-Winged Olive	March Brown – 12	Ginger Quill – 12
Dun – 14	Gray Fox – 12	Green Drake – 10
Blue Quill – 18	Blue Quill – 18	Coffin Fly – 10
	Blue-Winged Olive	Dark Olive Spinner – 14
	Dun – 14	Dark Blue Sedge – 12
	Chocolate Dun – 16	Brown Drake – 12
		Pale Evening Dun – 16
		Light Cahill – 12
		Yellow Drake – 12
		Golden Drake – 12

JULY

Blue-Winged Olive	Blue Dun – 20	Slate Drake – 12
Dun – 14	Blue-Winged Olive	Light Cahill – 12
Blue Quill – 18	Dun – 14	Pale Evening Dun – 16
Dark Brown Spinner – 24		Yellow Drake – 12
Reverse Jenny Dark		Dark Olive Spinner – 14
Brown Spinner – 24		

AUGUST

Blue Quill – 18	Blue Dun – 20	White Wulff – 12
Reverse Jenny	Blue-Winged Olive	Slate Drake – 12
Spinner – 24	Dun – 14	Pale Evening Dun – 16
Dark Brown Spinner – 24		Light Cahill – 12

NATURALS AND IMITATIONS (*Western*)

Although I've suggested using mallard-quill sections for wings on many of the following Western patterns, I feel that calf's tail or impala is much better. This latter material should withstand much more abuse on the faster Western waters. Calf's tail is easily dyed. Place the tail in charcoal gray dye for five or ten minutes to achieve the same color as the mallard quill.

For the tail I also recommend the stiffest material available. Dark brown moose mane imitates the tail of the Western Green Drake (*Ephemerella grandis*) rather closely, plus many other species. Use this tail material whenever a pattern calls for a dark brown tail.

I also strongly urge you to use the stiffest hackle for the legs of your dry-fly imitations. In fact, on many Western patterns, I use three rather than two hackles. Remember, most Western waters are higher and faster than their Eastern and Midwestern counterparts until late July.

Many of the species listed in the following pages have no common patterns to match them effectively. Furthermore, many of the species vary considerably in color from stream to stream. In most cases where color varies I have attempted to indicate this. In some instances, because of color variation, the pattern suggested might be inappropriate for your particular stream.

Baetis tricaudatus and *B. intermedius*
Dun – 5–7 mm
  Wing – Medium gray
  Body – Light brown (*tricaudatus*) to
         tannish gray with an olive cast
         (*intermedius*)
  Legs – Tannish cream
  Tail – Pale gray

Spinner
  Wing – Glassy clear
  Body – Light tan (*intermedius*) to dark
         rusty brown (*tricaudatus*)
  Legs – Tan
  Tail – Pale gray
Commercial pattern, dun: Blue Dun
Commercial pattern, spinner: Rusty Spinner

I have not suggested one pattern, but rather suggest that you carry several patterns with grayish tan, tan, and olive gray bodies in hook sizes from 18 to 22.

These mayflies can be important all season. The duns seem to be most important in the afternoon and the spinners in the evening.

Ephemera simulans – see previous section on Eastern patterns

Cinygmula ramaleyi	Imitation – Dark Red Quill
Dun – 7–9 mm	Hook size – 16 or 18
Wing – Dark slate	Dark mallard quill or dark gray calf tail
Body – Reddish brown, ringed lighter	Dark reddish brown hackle stem, stripped
Legs – Brownish gray	Bronze dun hackle
Tail – Medium gray	Medium dun hackle fibers
Spinner	Red Quill Spinner
Wing – Glassy clear with tan cast	Very pale tan polypropylene tied spent
Body – Reddish brown	Reddish brown hackle stem
Legs – Reddish brown	Brown hackle
Tail – Pale gray	Pale dun hackle fibers

Commercial pattern, dun and spinner: Red Quill

Here is one of the many Western species so ably duplicated by the Red Quill.

Most *Cinygmula* species are found on small and medium-sized streams with characteristically colder water temperatures.

Ephemerella inermis
Dun – 6–8 mm
  Wing – Pale gray
  Body – Creamish yellow with an olive
         cast
  Legs – Creamish yellow with an olive
         cast
  Tail – Creamish yellow

Spinner
    Wing – Glassy clear
    Body – Yellowish olive
    Legs – Dark tan
    Tail – Dark tan
Commercial pattern, dun: Pale Morning Dun
Commercial pattern, spinner: Pale Morning Spinner

This is one of the most common, yet diverse species found on Western streams. *Ephemerella inermis* is found on streams as far north as Alaska.

The color pattern listed here was taken from a hatch on Henry's Fork in Idaho. The color varies so much, even on the same stream, that it's important to carry imitations with bodies of tan, reddish brown, olive, and the most common color, pale yellow with an olive cast. Since the color is so variable, I have not suggested one specific pattern.

I have seen this species emerging in the morning, afternoon, and evening – so it's important to have imitations available all day.

Caution: Color of this species varies more than any other mayfly of which I am aware.

Paraleptophlebia bicornuta, P. heteronea, P. memorialis, P. vaciva, and *P. debilis* — Imitation – Dark Blue Quill

Dun – 6–10 mm — Hook size – 16–20
    Wing – Dark slate — Dark mallard quill
    Body – Dark slate to dark reddish brown — Dark brown polypropylene, ribbed with lighter thread; or peacock herl
    Legs – Tannish cream — Ginger cream hackle
    Tail – Medium gray — Medium dun hackle fibers

Spinner — Dark Brown Spinner
    Wing – Glassy clear — Pale gray polypropylene
    Body – Dark brown to dark reddish brown — Same as dun
    Legs – Creamish gray with dark brown — Pale dun hackle with a turn of dark brown
    Tail – Pale gray — Pale dun
Commercial pattern, dun: Blue Quill or Dark Blue Quill
Commercial pattern, spinner: Dark Brown Spinner

I have witnessed *Paraleptophlebia debilis* duns on Henry's Fork, *P. memorialis* on the Bitterroot River, and *P. bicornuta* on the Colorado River, so it's extremely important to carry imitations with you always.

If you plan to fish any North American stream in the morning or afternoon, the Blue Quill is an important pattern.

Epeorus longimanus — Imitation – Quill Gordon or Blue Dun
Dun – 10–12 mm — Hook size – 12 or 14
    Wing – Dark slate — Dark mallard quill or dark gray calf tail

Body – Pale gray; tergites (back) are darker	Pale to medium gray polypropylene or muskrat fur dubbed
Legs – Tannish gray with darker markings	Pale tannish gray hackle
Tail – Grayish	Medium dun hackle

Spinner	Red Quill Spinner
Wing – Glassy clear with an amber cast	Pale tan polypropylene
Body – Pale yellowish brown	Pale yellowish brown polypropylene
Legs – Pale yellowish brown with darker markings	Ginger hackle with a turn of brown
Tail – Dark brown	Moose mane

Commercial pattern, dun: Quill Gordon or Blue Dun
Commercial pattern, spinner: Brown Drake

Many *Epeorus*, *Rhithrogena*, and *Cinygmula* species exhibit the general coloration of this species, so it's important to have these gray or gray-brown imitations on hand.

Ephemerella tibialis	Imitation – Red Quill
Dun – 7–9 mm	Hook size – 16 or 18
Wing – Pale gray	
Body – Dark reddish brown	
Legs – Creamish yellow	
Tail – Pale gray	

Spinner	White-Gloved Howdy
Wing – Cloudy	
Body – Dark purplish brown	
Legs – Pale yellow	
Tail – Gray	

Commercial pattern, dun: Red Quill
Commercial pattern, spinner: White-Gloved Howdy

This is another species imitated by the Red Quill; therefore, I have not suggested a pattern.

Baetis parvus	Imitation – Dark Brown Dun
Dun – 4–5 mm	Hook size – 20
Wing – Dark gray	Gray mallard quill
Body – Dark brown	Dark brown polypropylene
Legs – Tannish cream	Ginger cream hackle
Tail – Tannish cream	Ginger cream hackle fibers

Spinner	Dark Brown Spinner
Wing – Glassy clear	Pale gray polypropylene
Body – Dark brown	Dark brown polypropylene
Legs – Tannish cream	Ginger cream hackle
Tail – Pale gray	Pale dun hackle fibers

Commercial pattern, dun and spinner: Dark Brown Dun

Don't ever be without this pattern when fishing Western waters. As with *Baetis bicaudatus*, *B. parvus* does not have the typical *Baetis* body coloration. I tried the Little Blue Dun two times during hatches of *Baetis parvus* and had very little success until I switched to the Dark Brown Dun.

Hexagenia limbata
Dun – 17–26 mm
    Wing – Smoky gray with a distinct olive cast
    Body – Yellowish brown, with dark brown markings on top (coloration of this species varies from tannish yellow to brown)
    Legs – Tannish yellow with darker markings
    Tail – Brown

Spinner
    Wing – Glassy clear with dark purple markings in the costal area (front area)
    Body – Varies from yellow to yellowish brown
    Legs – Front legs are dark brown and rear two pair are yellow
    Tail – Tannish yellow
Commercial pattern, dun: Michigan Caddis
Commercial pattern, spinner: Michigan Spinner

Imitation – Michigan Caddis
Hook size – 6X
Teal flank feather, dyed smoky gray and with an olive cast
Yellowish brown polypropylene

Cream ginger hackle with a couple turns of brown
Brown hackle fibers

Michigan Spinner
Mallard flank feather

Brownish yellow polypropylene

One dark brown and two cream ginger hackles
Cream ginger hackle fibers

Although this species is mainly Midwestern it is locally important on Eastern and Western streams and lakes. An example of this is the impressive hatch on Flathead Lake in Montana. I have also had reports of this species on south-central Pennsylvania streams.

Caution: Coloration of species varies considerably from location to location.

Heptagenia elegantula
Dun – 9–10 mm
    Wing – Gray, slightly barred
    Body – Creamish yellow
    Legs – Cream
    Tail – Cream

Spinner
    Wing – Glassy clear
    Body – Cream
    Legs – Pale cream
    Tail – Tannish
Commercial pattern, dun: Pale Evening Dun
Commercial pattern, spinner: Pale Evening Spinner

Imitation – Pale Evening Dun
Hook size – 14
Pale gray calf tail
Creamish yellow polypropylene
Cream hackle
Cream hackle fibers

Pale Evening Spinner

I have seen *Heptagenia elegantula* spinners on the Colorado River in large enough numbers to consider it important to imitate much of the summer. A size 14 Light Cahill will substitute for the dun and spinner of this species. Since the imitation suggested for the dun works well for the spinner fall, I have not recommended a pattern for the latter.

Callibaetis coloradensis	Imitation – Speckle-Winged Dun
Dun – 6–9 mm	Hook size – 16
Wing – Dark gray with white venation	Dark gray mallard flank
Body – Grayish tan	Grayish tan polypropylene
Legs – Pale grayish tan with darker tips	Pale bronze dun hackle
Tail – Pale tan	Cream ginger hackle fibers
Spinner	Speckle-Winged Spinner
Wing – Glassy clear with heavy gray flecks in the front part of the fore wing (male doesn't have as much)	Mallard flank feather
Body – Pale gray	Pale gray polypropylene
Legs – Tannish gray	Pale bronze dun hackle
Tail – Pale tan	Cream ginger hackle fibers

Commercial pattern, dun and spinner: Dark Cahill

The commercial pattern I've listed, the Dark Cahill, does not copy the natural very closely; therefore, several copies of the above pattern should be tied.

I have seen *Callibaetis* species on Western waters as late as September, and on streams with some slow water, like the Blue River in Colorado. Always carry imitations of this and other closely related species with you if you plan to fish slow water in the morning.

Ephemerella flavilinea	Imitation – Blue-Winged Olive Dun
Dun – 7–10 mm	Hook size – 14 or 16
Wing – Dark gray	Dark gray mallard quill
Body – Olive green	Olive green polypropylene
Legs – Dark olive brown with creamish tan tips	Dark olive brown hackle
Tail – Dark olive brown	Dark brown moose mane
Spinner	Dark Olive Spinner
Wing – Glassy clear	Pale gray polypropylene
Body – Dark olive brown	Dark olive brown polypropylene
Legs – Dark olive	Dark olive hackle
Tail – Dark olive	Dark olive hackle fibers

Commercial pattern, dun: Blue-Winged Olive Dun
Commercial pattern, spinner: Dark Olive Spinner

Although the Blue-Winged Olive Dun is an effective pattern, I prefer to mix some green polypropylene with olive to get the desired body color for the pattern.

Ephemerella grandis
Dun – 14–16 mm
   Wing – Dark grayish black
   Body – Dark grayish black with pale
         yellow ribbing and greenish
         olive reflections
   Legs – Grayish black with pale yellow
         tarsi (tips)
   Tail – Base is dark brown, and tip is
         pale gray

Spinner
   Wing – Glassy clear with veining
   Body – Black ringed with pale yellow
         (faint olive cast)
   Legs – Dark brownish black
   Tail – Dark brown

Imitation – Western Green Drake
Hook size – 10 or 12
Impala, dyed dark gray
Olive black polypropylene, ribbed with
   pale yellow thread

Grayish black hackle

Moose mane

Great Red Spinner
White polypropylene, tied spent
Same as dun

Brownish black hackle
Moose mane

Commercial pattern, dun: Western Green Drake
Commercial pattern, spinner: Great Red Spinner

Evidently the color of this species too varies tremendously from stream to stream. The coloration described above is taken from hatches on the Bitterroot River in Montana. The same species observed on other waters has a much brighter green body.

However, the pattern I have suggested works well. It works well also when the common *Ephemerella doddsi* emerges.

Caution: Color of duns varies considerably from stream to stream.

Baetis bicaudatus
Dun – 4–5 mm
   Wing – Pale gray
   Body – Pale olive
   Legs – Pale olive
   Tail – Pale olive

Spinner
   Wing – Glassy clear
   Body – Tan with olive cast
   Legs – Tannish
   Tail – Tan

Imitation – Pale Olive Dun
Hook size – 20
Pale gray hackle tips
Pale olive polypropylene
Pale olive hackle
Pale olive hackle fibers

Light Rusty Spinner
Pale gray polypropylene
Tan polypropylene
Ginger hackle
Ginger hackle fibers

Commercial pattern, dun: Pale Olive Dun
Commercial pattern, spinner: Rusty Spinner

Charlie Brooks says he has seen *Baetis* species on Western streams from mid-January to late October. Although *Baetis* species are small, imitations of them are a must for any fly fisherman fishing Western waters.

We spotlight *Baetis bicaudatus* first because its coloration is atypical for *Baetis* species. Many *Baetis* species have bodies of olive gray or olive tan – not so with the pale-olive-bodied *Baetis bicaudatus*. Second, this mayfly is extremely common on many Western streams.

I have witnessed heavy afternoon hatches in mid-July on Henry's Fork in Idaho, and have seen many trout surface-feeding on them.

Cinygma dimicki	Imitation – Light Cahill
Dun – 9–11 mm	Hook size – 12
Wing – Tannish cream, barred	Wood duck or imitation flank feather
Body – Pale creamish yellow	Pale creamish yellow polypropylene
Legs – Creamish, with darker markings	Ginger cream hackle
Tail – Tannish	Ginger hackle fibers
Spinner	Light Cahill
Wing – Glassy clear	Pale gray polypropylene
Body – Yellowish cream	Yellowish cream polypropylene
Legs – Yellowish cream, with darker markings	Yellowish cream hackle
Tail – Tan	Ginger hackle fibers

Commercial pattern, dun and spinner: Light Cahill

I list this species first because it's fairly common, and second, because the dun and spinner concentrate their activity into a two-hour period in the evening. *Cinygma dimicki* appears on Western waters for more than a month. The imitation, the Light Cahill, is an important one when evening fishing.

Both male and female spinners are available as food for trout. Imagos of this species characteristically mate just a few inches above the water, similar to *Stenonema luteum* in the East.

Cinygmula reticulata	Imitation – Pale Brown Dun
Dun – 8–10 mm	Hook size – 12 or 14
Wing – Yellow	Yellow mallard flank
Body – Tannish brown	Pale brown polypropylene
Legs – Tannish cream	Ginger cream hackle
Tail – Tannish cream	Ginger cream hackle fibers
Spinner	Dark Rusty Spinner
Wing – Yellow tan	Pale yellow polypropylene
Body – Dark rusty brown	Dark brown polypropylene
Legs – Dark rusty brown	Dark brown hackle
Tail – Dark brown	Dark brown hackle fibers

Commercial pattern, dun and spinner: Dark Cahill

Spinners of this species concentrate their activity around early morning. The commercial pattern listed is a poor one, so a few copies of the one I suggest might be in order.

Like *Cinygmula ramaleyi*, this species is often found on small and moderate-sized streams with plenty of cold water. I first met *Cinygmula reticulata* on the upper section of the Gallatin River in Yellowstone Park. During that first meeting I recorded a water temperature of 45 degrees – and that was in the middle of July.

Epeorus albertae
Dun – 9–11 mm
  Wing – Medium gray
  Body – Grayish cream; female has a
      pinkish cast
  Legs – Cream with darker markings
  Tail – Creamish tan

Spinner
  Wing – Glassy clear
  Body – Cream gray (female has a pink
      body)
  Legs – Cream gray with darker
      markings
  Tail – Olive brown

Imitation – Light Cahill or Pink Lady
Hook size – 12
Gray mallard quills
Grayish cream polypropylene

Cream or badger hackle
Cream ginger hackle fibers

Salmon Spinner
Pale gray polypropylene
Female – pinkish red polypropylene
Male – cream gray polypropylene
Pale blue dun hackle

Dark brown moose mane

Commercial pattern, dun: Light Cahill or Pink Lady
Commercial pattern, spinner: Salmon Spinner

This is an extremely common species on many Western rivers on summer evenings. I have seen spinners mating on Henry's Fork in the Box Canyon area, on the Buffalo River in Idaho, and on the Madison River in Yellowstone Park.

Siphlonurus occidentalis
Dun – 11–15 mm
  Wing – Brownish gray with distinct
      veining
  Body – Brownish black, ribbed lighter

  Legs – Pale grayish tan
  Tail – Gray

Spinner
  Wing – Glassy clear
  Body – Dark reddish brown with lighter
      ribbing
  Legs – Dark brown
  Tail – Dark brown

Imitation – Gray Drake
Hook size – 12
Dark gray mallard flank

Brownish black polypropylene with tan
    thread for ribbing
Pale bronze dun hackle
Medium dun hackle fibers

Brown Quill Spinner
Pale gray polypropylene
Dark reddish brown polypropylene ribbed
    with tan thread
Dark brown hackle
Dark brown moose mane

Commercial pattern, dun: Gray Drake
Commercial pattern, spinner: Brown Quill Spinner

I have seen enough duns of this species appear on afternoons even in mid-July to know the importance of carrying imitations to copy the emerging dun.

   Caution: Size of this species seems to vary from stream to stream.

Heptagenia solitaria
Dun – 10–12 mm
  Wing – Pale gray with yellow cast
  Body – Yellowish tan (top is tan)
  Legs – Tannish gray with darker
      markings
  Tail – Tannish gray

Imitation – Gray Fox
Pale gray mallard quill

Yellowish tan polypropylene
Bronze dun hackle

Bronze dun hackle fibers

Spinner   Ginger Quill Spinner
   Wing – Glassy clear   Pale gray polypropylene
   Body – Tan ribbed with yellow   Eyed peacock herl, dyed tan and stripped
   Legs – Tan with darker markings   Ginger hackle
   Tail   – Grayish tan   Ginger hackle fibers
Commercial pattern, dun: Gray Fox
Commercial pattern, spinner: Ginger Quill

If you plan to fish Western streams after mid-July and especially in early September, don't fish without imitations of this dun and spinner. This species is one of the most important of the season.

The Ginger Quill is very effective during a spinner fall.

Ephemerella infrequens   Imitation – Pale Morning Dun
Dun – 7–9 mm   Hook size – 16 or 18
   Wing – Pale gray with yellow cast   Pale gray mallard
   Body – Creamish yellow with faint   Creamish yellow polypropylene, soaked in
         olive cast; can vary to tan   olive dye
   Legs – Creamish yellow   Creamish yellow hackle
   Tail   – Creamish yellow   Creamish yellow hackle fibers

Spinner   Rusty Spinner
   Wing – Glassy clear   Pale gray polypropylene, tied spent
   Body – Creamish tan   Cream ginger hackle
   Legs – Yellow, marked with tan   Cream ginger hackle fibers
   Tail   – Pale tan   Tan hackle fibers
Commercial pattern, dun: Pale Morning Dun
Commercial pattern, spinner: Rusty Spinner

As we have indicated, coloration of this species too varies considerably from stream to stream – in fact, color varies from time to time on the same stream.

The specimen I have described above exhibits probably the most common color for the species. This species resembles the Eastern *Ephemerella* species, like *E. invaria*.

Caution: Color varies considerably.

Rhithrogena hageni   Imitation – Pale Brown Dun
Dun – 9–11 mm   Hook size – 12
   Wing – Medium gray   Gray mallard quill
   Body – Tannish olive   Tannish olive polypropylene
   Legs – Creamish tan   Cream ginger hackle
   Tail   – Cream   Cream hackle fibers

Spinner   Dark Tan Spinner
   Wing – Glassy clear   Pale gray polypropylene
   Body – Pale olive tan   Pale olive tan polypropylene
   Legs – Dark tannish olive with cream   Cream, mixed with dark tan hackle
         tarsi (tips)
   Tail   – Gray   Gray hackle fibers
Commercial pattern, dun and spinner: none.

I have seen thousands of these duns emerge on the Madison River above Ennis, Montana. Duns escape rapidly from the surface, but, since emergence is fairly concentrated, it's important to have imitations. Imitations of the nymph should work well when this species emerges.

Ameletus cooki — Imitation – Dark Brown Dun

Dun – 8–10 mm	Hook size – 12 or 14
Wing – Dark gray, barred	Teal flank feather
Body – Dark brown	Dark brown polypropylene
Legs – Dark brown	Dark brown hackle
Tail – Dark brown	Dark brown hackle fibers
Spinner	Dark Brown Spinner
Wing – Glassy clear with black and yellow markings	Teal flank feather, dyed yellow
Body – Dark brown	Dark brown polypropylene
Legs – Dark brown	Dark brown hackle
Tail – Dark brown	Dark brown hackle fibers

Commercial pattern, dun and spinner: Dark Brown Dun

Duns of this species emerge sporadically during the day, and spinners fall in the afternoon. The species can be important to imitate.

Rhithrogena futilis — Imitation – Quill Gordon

Dun – 9–11 mm	Hook size – 12
Wing – Pale to medium gray	Gray mallard quill
Body – Pale tannish gray with olive cast (top of abdomen is much darker)	Tannish gray polypropylene
Legs – Tannish gray	Rusty dun hackle
Tail – Tannish gray	Rusty dun hackle fibers
Spinner	Quill Gordon Spinner
Wing – Glassy clear	Pale gray polypropylene
Body – Black, ribbed lighter	Peacock herl, eyed, stripped
Legs – Dark gray	Dark dun hackle
Tail – Dark gray	Dark dun hackle fibers

Commercial pattern, dun and spinner: Quill Gordon

This species can be an important one to imitate. On several occasions while fishing in the evening I've encountered the spinner mating and laying eggs, and have had success with the Quill Gordon Spinner imitation.

Rhithrogena undulata — Imitation – Dark Red Quill

Dun – 8–11 mm	Hook size – 12 or 14
Wing – Dark gray	Gray mallard quills
Body – Dark reddish brown	Dark brown hackle stem
Legs – Brown	Dark brown hackle
Tail – Gray	Dark blue dun hackle fibers

Spinner
  Wing – Glassy clear
  Body – Light to dark reddish brown
  Legs – Light to dark brown
  Tail – Light to dark brown

Red Quill or Dark Red Quill
White or pale gray hackle tips
Red to dark brown hackle stems
Ginger to dark brown hackle
Ginger to dark brown hackle fibers

Commercial pattern, dun and spinner: Red Quill and Dark Red Quill

This species is important on many Western waters like the Blackfoot in Montana. Either color patterns of this species vary considerably from stream to stream or I have confused the lighter variation with another species. I think it's probably the former explanation. However, both patterns are important on Western waters.

Caution: Coloration of species varies considerably from stream to stream.

Ephemerella hecuba
Dun – 14–16 mm
  Wing – Dark gray
  Body – Reddish, ribbed lighter
  Legs – Dark brownish black with
    cream tarsi (tips)
  Tail – Dark brownish black

Imitation – Great Red Quill
Hook size – 10 or 12
Dark gray impala
Large reddish brown hackle stem, stripped
Dark brown hackle

Moose mane

Spinner
  Wing – Glassy clear
  Body – Dark reddish brown, ribbed
    lighter
  Legs – Dark blackish brown
  Tail – Dark blackish brown

Great Red Spinner
Pale gray hackle tips
Dark brown hackle stems, stripped

Dark brown hackle
Moose mane

Commercial pattern, dun: Red Quill
Commercial pattern, spinner: Great Red Spinner

I have observed this species in limited numbers on only one occasion in late July. The few I noted emerging did so in the evening. Other writers suggest this species appears around midday. Nevertheless, carry some large Red Quill dry flies with you on trips in July, August, or September.

I have indicated above that the dun has a bright-red body – this body color, as with most other species, does vary considerably from stream to stream.

Tricorythodes minutus
Dun – 3 mm
  Wing – Pale gray

Body – Medium to dark olive
Legs – Pale cream with dark brown on
    front legs
  Tail – Pale gray

Imitation – Pale Olive Dun
Hook size – 24 or 26
Pale gray polypropylene, upright and not
  divided
Medium olive polypropylene
Pale cream hackle

Pale gray hackle fibers

Spinner

  Wing – Glassy clear with dark brown on
    front edge

Brown Spinner (male); Dark Reverse
  Jenny Spinner (female)
Pale gray polypropylene, tied spent

Body, male – Dark blackish with faint lighter ribbing	Dark brownish black polypropylene
Body, female – Cream with faint olive cast	Cream polypropylene
Legs – Cream with gray markings	Cream hackle
Tail, male – Pale gray	Pale gray hackle fibers
Tail, female – Cream	Same

Commercial pattern, dun and spinner: none.

I have seen this hatch on many slower silted rivers in the West in late July, August, and September. The Colorado River near Kremmling, Colorado, has a heavy *Tricorythodes* hatch and spinner fall.

On several occasions I have noted a larger *Tricorythodes* dun emerging also in the morning. This latter species, in its spinner stage, has a reddish brown body in both sexes. This species is also somewhat larger than the 3 mm suggested for *Tricorythodes minutus*. This latter species might well be a subspecies (T. *minutus fallax*).

Ephemerella coloradensis	Imitation – Dark Olive Dun
Dun – 12–13 mm	Hook size – 12
Wing – Dark gray	Gray mallard quill
Body – Dark olive brownish	Dark olive brown polypropylene
Legs – Tan	Ginger hackle
Tail – Gray	Gray hackle fibers
Spinner	Dark Brown Spinner
Wing – Glassy clear with heavy brown veining	Pale tan polypropylene
Body – Dark brown	Dark brown polypropylene
Legs – Dark brown	Dark brown hackle
Tail – Dark brown	Dark brown moose mane

Commercial pattern, dun and spinner: none

I have noted members of this species emerging on high-altitude streams well past midday. Since the pattern is not a common one, it's important to have a few imitations with you if you plan to fish Western streams in August.

Ephoron album	
Dun – 11–13 mm	Hook size – 12
Wing – Pale gray	
Body – White with grayish cast	
Legs – Front are dark with rear ones white	
Tail – Pale gray	
Spinner (male only)	
Wing – Clear	
Body – White (rear may be darker)	
Legs – Same as dun	
Tail – Pale gray	

Commercial pattern, dun and spinner: White Wulff

The White Wulff in appropriate sizes will effectively copy the dun and spinner of this species, so we have not listed any recommended pattern. This species can be important on lower stretches of warmer streams in August.

Western Stoneflies

Pteronarcys californica
  35–45 mm
    Wing – Creamish tan with heavy black
      veins
    Body – Burnt orange; underside of
      thorax and head is bright orange

    Legs – Brownish black with small
      orange markings
    Tail – Short and dark brown
Commercial pattern: Troth Salmon Fly

Salmon Fly
Hook size – 4 or 6, 8XL, Mustad 94720
Creamish tan dyed mallard flank tied
  downwing
Abdomen, burnt orange polypropylene;
  thorax and head, bright orange poly-
  propylene
Brownish black hackle

Dark moose mane

This pattern is extremely difficult to tie, and unless you plan to tie many of them I suggest purchasing the commercial pattern recommended. These large dry flies are really effective during the egglaying phase of this stonefly – don't be on Western streams in June or July without several of these imitations.

Acroneuria pacifica
  25–35 mm
    Wing – Creamish, barred heavily
    Body – Creamish brown
    Legs – Brown
    Tail – Brown
Commercial pattern: Willow Fly

Willow Stonefly
Hook size – 6, 8XL, Mustad 94720
Creamish mallard flank
Creamish brown polypropylene
Brown hackle
Short brown hackle fibers

This large stonefly is important on many Western streams in June and July. Again, carry several imitations if you plan to fish water like the Yellowstone River.

PATTERN SELECTION (*Western*)

Again, to assist you in narrowing the quantity of patterns, we recommend some of the important imitations. These patterns are listed by month and time of day. Remember, these are only a few of the more important imitations; many more mayflies appear, and patterns for many of these have not been included.

The imitations suggested for each month successfully copy many of the mayfly species found on Western waters. We have included one imitation, the Cream Spinner, in July, August, and September. Although this is an *Ephemerella* species, I have never encountered a male of the species, and therefore have been unable to have the species correctly identified. Females of this species lay their eggs around 7:00 p.m. on the shore next to the water. Many of the female spinners then fall into the water and become available as food for trout.

Morning

MAY
Blue Dun – 18
Dark Red Quill – 16
Light Rusty Spinner – 18
Dark Rusty Spinner – 18

JUNE
Quill Gordon – 12
W. Green Drake – 12
Speckle-Winged Dun and
  Spinner – 14 or 16
Blue-Winged Olive
  Dun – 14
Pale Morning Dun – 16
  or 18
Salmon Fly – 6
Blue Dun – 18
Dark Brown Dun – 20
Dark Brown Spinner – 20
Dark Blue Quill – 16 or 18
Dark Brown Spinner – 16
  or 18
Pale Olive Dun – 20
Pale Morning Spinner – 16
  or 18
Dark Red Quill – 16

JULY
Pale Morning Dun – 16
  or 18
Quill Gordon – 12
W. Green Drake – 12
Gray Drake – 12
Speckle-Winged Dun and
  Spinner – 14 or 16
Blue Dun – 18
Dark Brown Dun – 20
Dark Brown Spinner – 20
Dark Blue Quill – 18
Dark Brown Spinner – 18
Pale Olive Dun – 20 and
  24
Dark Brown Spinner – 24
Reverse Jenny Spinner –
  24
Salmon Spinner – 12
Pale Brown Dun – 12
Dark Brown Dun – 14

Afternoon

Blue Dun – 18
Salmon Fly – 6
Dark Red Quill – 16

Quill Gordon – 12
W. Green Drake – 12
Speckle-Winged Dun and
  Spinner – 14 or 16
Pale Morning Dun – 16
  or 18
Salmon Fly – 6
Blue Dun – 18
Dark Brown Dun – 20
Dark Brown Spinner – 20
Dark Blue Quill – 16 or 18
Dark Brown Spinner – 16
  or 18
Pale Olive Dun – 20
Dark Red Quill – 16

Pale Morning Dun – 16
  or 18
Salmon Fly – 6
Speckle-Winged Dun and
  Spinner – 14 or 16
W. Green Drake – 12
Quill Gordon – 12
Red Quill – 14, 16, & 18
Dark Red Quill – 14
Dark Blue Quill – 18
Dark Brown Spinner – 18

Evening

Brown Drake – 12
Salmon Fly – 6
Light Rusty Spinner – 18
Dark Rusty Spinner – 18

Brown Drake – 12
Salmon Fly – 6
Light Rusty Spinner – 18
  or 20
Dark Rusty Spinner – 18
Great Red Spinner – 12
Pale Morning Dun and
  Spinner – 16 or 18

Pale Morning Dun – 16
  or 18
Salmon Fly – 6
Ginger Quill – 12
Light Cahill – 12
Pink Lady – 12
Salmon Spinner – 12
Red Quill – 16
Dark Red Quill – 14
Red Quill – 16
Cream Spinner – 16
Cream Spinner – 16
Blue-Winged Olive
  Dun – 14

AUGUST

Dark Blue Quill – 18
Dark Brown Spinner – 18
Gray Drake – 12
Pale Olive Dun – 20 and 24
Reverse Jenny Spinner – 24
Dark Brown Spinner – 24
Pale Morning Dun – 16 or 18
Ginger Quill – 14
Red Quill – 14 or 16

Dark Blue Quill – 18
Dark Brown Spinner – 18
Gray Drake – 12
Blue Dun – 18 or 20
Red Quill – 14 and 16
Pale Morning Dun – 16 or 18
Gray Fox – 14

Pale Evening Dun – 14
Gray Fox – 14
Pale Evening Spinner – 14
Ginger Quill – 14
Brown Quill Spinner – 12
Cream Spinner – 16
Gray Fox – 14

SEPTEMBER

Dark Blue Quill – 18
Dark Brown Spinner – 18 and 24
Blue Dun – 18 and 20
Pale Olive Dun – 24
Reverse Jenny Spinner – 24
Speckle-Winged Dun and Spinner – 14 or 16
Ginger Quill – 14

Gray Fox – 14
Pale Evening Dun – 14
Dark Blue Quill – 18
Blue Dun – 18 and 20
Dark Brown Spinner – 18
Speckle-Winged Dun and Spinner – 14 and 16

Gray Fox – 14
Ginger Quill – 14
Brown Quill Spinner – 12
Dark Rusty Spinner – 20
Pale Evening Spinner – 14
Cream Spinner – 16

Tying a caddis imitation is fairly simple whether it's intended for Eastern, Midwestern, or Western streams. The pictures demonstrate the process.

Dub a small amount of poly material onto the waxed tying thread.

Wrap the dubbing toward the eye of the hook, then backwards toward the bend, and finally forward toward the eye. Tying the dubbing in this manner produces a well-tapered body. If you plan to include hackle, leave plenty of space at the eye.

Tie a small bunch of deer hair (light or dark depending on the wing color of the natural) near the eye after removing all short hair. The length of the deer hair wings should be slightly longer than the length of the body.

Trim the base and tie in firmly.

If you prefer more buoyancy, add hackle to the imitation. Tie one or two hackles in front of the deer hair and wind.

Finished caddis or stonefly imitation with hackle.

For many of the spinner imitations I suggest polypropylene, tied spent, to duplicate the wings. An imitation of a female *Tricorythodes* is typical. To aid in detailing the sequence, I have used a size 14 hook.

Tie in a strand of polypropylene material near the eye of the hook. Remember, leave plenty of room for the hackle.

Clip and shape polypropylene. Tie in several pale dun hackle fibers at the bend of the hook for the tail. Dub a small amount of cream poly material for the rear half of the abdomen.

Finish body by dubbing dark brown poly material for the front half of the body.

Body, wings, and tail complete.

Tie in one or two pale dun hackles and wind.

Finish with a whip finish, and lacquer.

Chapter VI

Fishing the Morning Hatches
(*Eastern and Midwestern*)

In the list below, (A) indicates that hatches or spinner falls also often occur in the afternoon, (E) that they often occur in the evening. Dates listed are, of course, very approximate.

Duns

Baetis vagans[1] (A) – Little Blue Dun; 10:00 a.m.–6:00 p.m.; April 1[2]

Paraleptophlebia adoptiva (A) – Dark Blue Quill; 11:00 a.m.–4:00 p.m.; April 15

Stenonema fuscum (A & E) – Gray Fox; 4:00–8:30 p.m. (some days hatches may occur earlier); May 15

Stenonema vicarium (A & E) – American March Brown; 10:00 a.m.–7:00 p.m.; May 20

Ephemerella bicolor (A) – Chocolate Dun; late morning and early afternoon; May 25

Ephemerella species (A & E) – Blue-Winged Olive Dun; morning and afternoon with a peak sometimes around 11:30 a.m.; May 26

Ephemerella needhami (A) – Chocolate Dun; late morning and early afternoon; May 30

Paraleptophlebia mollis (A & E) – Dark Blue Quill; 10:00 a.m.–4:00 p.m. (sometimes hatches occur into the evening); June 3

Ephemerella attenuata (A) – Blue-Winged Olive Dun; sporadic during the day; June 5

Paraleptophlebia strigula (A) – Blue Quill; 9:00 a.m.–4:00 p.m.; June 5[2]

Leptophlebia johnsoni (A) – Iron Blue Dun; 11:00 a.m.; June 9

Stenonema species, Pulchellum Group (A) – Cream Cahill; sporadic around midday; June 15[2]

Ephemerella deficiens (A) – Dark Blue Quill; 11:00 a.m.; June 18

Paraleptophlebia guttata (A) – Dark Blue Quill; sporadic during day; June 25[2]

Ephemerella lata (A) – Blue-Winged Olive Dun; sporadic during day; June 25

Ephemerella cornuta (A) – Blue-Winged Olive Dun; sporadic in morning, but mainly around 11:00 a.m.; June 25[2]

Tricorythodes stygiatus – Pale Olive Dun; 7:00–9:00 a.m.; July 23[2]

Tricorythodes attratus – Pale Olive Dun; 7:00–9:00 a.m.; July 23[2]

Spinners

Baetis vagans (A & E) – Rusty Spinner; 10:00 a.m.–6:00 p.m. (and later); April 3[2]

[1] Species may produce several broods per season.
[2] Hatches appear for many days.

Epeorus pleuralis (A) – Red Quill Spinner; 11:30 a.m.–2:00 p.m. (sometimes later); April 20

Ephemerella bicolor – Chocolate Spinner; afternoon; May 26

Paraleptophlebia mollis (A & E) – Dark Brown Spinner; morning and afternoon (and sometimes evening); June 4

Paraleptophlebia strigula (A & E) – Dark Brown Spinner; morning and afternoon (and sometimes evening); June 6

Paraleptophlebia guttata (A & E) – Dark Brown Spinner; morning and afternoon (and sometimes evening); June 26

Tricorythodes stygiatus – Reverse Jenny Spinner (female), Dark Brown Spinner (male) – 8:00–11:00 a.m.; July 23

Tricorythodes attratus – Reverse Jenny Spinner (female), Dark Brown Spinner (male) – 8:00–11:00 a.m., July 23

A good morning imitation is the Dark Blue Quill, which copies many *Paraleptophlebia* species.

The Blue-Winged Olive Dun imitates many of the morning-emerging *Ephe-merellas*.

The Reverse Jenny Spinner duplicates *Tricorythodes* species appearing in the morning in the East, Midwest, and West.

A stretch of Spring Creek in central Pennsylvania, which contains good hatches of *Tricorythodes* and *Ephemerella cornuta*, both morning emerges.

We take a rather uncommon approach to fishing the hatches and spinner falls. Most writers have categorized aquatic insects according to the time of season they emerge – that is, early, middle, or late. This method is useful and follows one of the four rules set forth for meeting and fishing the hatches – emergence dates. But no matter how good you are at predicting the season an insect emerges, you'll likely miss the hatch if you aren't on the stream at the proper time. Therefore, I prefer to utilize another one of the four rules to group aquatic insects – time of day. Using this latter approach, we have divided the hatches into those that normally appear in the morning, afternoon, or evening. There is nothing sacred about this type of grouping, however, since many insects that are listed in one category may emerge in fishable numbers during another time of the day. For example, the Green Drake, normally an evening hatch, sometimes appears in heavy numbers in the afternoon. Another evening emerger, the Slate Drake, often appears in the morning or afternoon on cloudy days in June or July. Many other mayflies fall into this exception-to-the-rule category. Furthermore, many mayflies and caddis flies that appear in the afternoon in May emerge later, usually in the evening, in June or July. In addition, many *Paraleptophlebia* species that begin appearing in the morning continue through the afternoon, and on into the evening.

I enjoy fly fishing in the morning probably more than at any other time of day. In direct contrast to the problems associated with late-evening fishing, you don't have to worry about changing imitations in almost total darkness, and locating rising trout from distant sounds. No reflex casting needed here; just pinpoint casting to clearly visible rises.

Morning is not without its disadvantages, however. As the fly fisherman sees better during the day, so too does the trout, making new demands on the angler. It requires a more refined approach to the stream, a better presentation of the artificial, and a finer leader, among other things, to achieve success.

When I think of morning fly fishing I think of Blue Quills, which effectively copy most *Paraleptophlebia* species; Blue-Winged Olive Duns, which imitate some important *Ephemerella* species; and the Pale Olive Dun (and of course the spinners of this species), which imitate several of the *Tricorythodes* species.

THE TIME TO USE THE
BLUE QUILL IS NOW

I had just tied a dozen size 18 Blue Quills and presented them to a friend. After he thanked me for the dry flies, he asked the all-important question: "When should I use these artificials?"

"If you plan to be on the stream any morning or afternoon, the time to use the Blue Quill is now," I urged.

"What do you mean?"

"Well, the Blue Quill effectively copies many *Paraleptophlebia* species, and members of this genus can be found on most waters from early morning until late afternoon almost every day from mid-April until late October."

Yes, the Blue Quill and Dark Blue Quill imitate rather closely species like *P. adoptiva*, *P. mollis*, *P. strigula*, and *P. guttata* in the East and Midwest, and *P. debilis* and *P. packii* in the West, and many, many other members of this common genus. Most of these subimagos have dark slate gray wings, dark grayish brown bodies, dark gray tails, and pale tan to pale gray legs.

Not only are the duns similar in appearance, but so are most spinners (especially females). Females, because of their body coloration, are sometimes called Dark Brown Spinners. This is a very appropriate common name for this genus; and although there are few commercial imitations that adequately copy the natural, the one suggested in Chapter III does extremely well during a spinner fall.

In addition to similarity in size and general coloration, most species emerge at corresponding times – mainly mornings (but remember, they may continue into the evening). Even in April, when mornings can be extremely cold, some brave *Paraleptophlebia adoptiva* duns appear by 11:00 a.m., but the largest number of this species usually appears around 2:00 p.m.

Probably the most important subimago is *Paraleptophlebia mollis*, with *P. adoptiva* a close second. Both duns are often sluggish and drift on the surface quite some distance before taking flight.

But there are two other *Paraleptophlebia* species – *P. strigula* and *P. guttata*. Both have proved to be important to meet and fish during June, July, and August on many Eastern streams. Although neither has been mentioned very often in fly-fishing literature, both species produce rising trout while emerging.

I first met *Paraleptophlebia strigula* on Big Fishing Creek in mid-June several years ago. I arrived at a stretch above Lamar called the Narrows at 9:00 a.m. This stream contains fantastically fertile limestone water with a good steady flow throughout the season. The water temperature seldom rises above 60 degrees even on the warmest summer days on this section of the stream.

When I arrived at the stream I was greeted by a heavy morning fog, typical on this stream because of the difference in air and water temperatures. A few Blue Quills (*P. strigula*) already had appeared on the surface and several trout rose, but not enough to motivate me to cast to them. I spent the first two hours collecting duns and taking photographs.

It was now 11:00 a.m. and hundreds of the motionless duns rode the surface of the pool in front of me. Most had emerged in the fast water at the head of the pool and traveled possibly 300 feet without taking flight. The legs of this species are extremely pale, so I searched in my Blue Quill compartment until I found an imitation containing very pale dun hackle. I tied the artificial onto the 6X tippet and waded into the pool just below a half-dozen rising trout. I disturbed the first two fish, and now moved toward a third fish which was still feeding. More trout now joined the half-dozen surface-feeding, and all actively gulped in the small slate-colored duns passing near them. A major hatch was underway and the trout seemed to sense it.

The first cast barely landed on the surface in front of a heavy trout and the dry fly immediately disappeared with a huge swirl. The rainbow showed his annoyance with the strike by leaping out of the water and then heading upstream past two boulders. My leader caught on one of the rocks but I successfully mended it. After a few minutes of following the rainbow up through the pool, I turned it and it headed toward me. I scooped my net under the trout and proudly lifted the 3-pounder out of the water. It had probably gained some of that weight today feeding on the thousands of mayflies available to it.

Duns emerged and trout rose until 2:00 p.m., when the hatch finally subsided. Coincidentally, while subimagos appeared, thousands of imagos from yesterday's hatch undulated in their mating flight so characteristic for most *Paraleptophlebia* species.

Another important species in the dun stage is *Paraleptophlebia adoptiva*. Even though it most often appears in greatest numbers in the afternoon rather than the morning, we'll discuss it here.

Jim Heltzel and I arrived at Cedar Run in north-central Pennsylvania just before 11:00 a.m. A brisk breeze chilled the late-April morning. It had rained, drizzled, and flurried for the past three days, but at last the leaden gray color had given way to a bright blue sky.

My thermometer registered a 55-degree air temperature and a 45-degree water temperature – both poor indicators of the tremendous mayfly hatches which were to follow shortly. We had stopped at a long, deep, eroded pool on Cedar Run which was probably created by water unendingly pounding a huge rock ledge for years. A small stream cascaded in as a miniature waterfall on the far side of Cedar Run. The pool was 50 to 60 feet long and 10 feet deep at its deepest spot.

Only a few gray midges dotted the surface when we arrived, and no trout rose, so I tied on a Lady Ghost streamer. The water seemed void of trout – for two hours I methodically cast that streamer without success.

Around 1:30 p.m. several Blue Quills braved the cold water and air temperatures and appeared on the surface. However, they were too dazed to fly, and after several abortive attempts, floated aimlessly around and around in an eddy near the far shore. Now more Blue Quills emerged – two dozen or more immobile duns rested in the small eddy. Occasionally a small native brook trout rose to capture one of the motionless duns.

By 2:00 p.m. hundreds of Blue Quill duns had appeared and now ten to fifteen trout actively fed on the surface. I tied on a size 18 Blue Quill and cast toward what appeared to be a large trout now feeding in the fast water at the head of the pool. The first cast adequately covered the feeding fish and it gulped in the imitation almost immediately. I struck – too late! Don't forget it had been six long months since I had last had a strike on a dry fly. I was more successful with the next four trout, all taken in the fast water at the head of this picturesque pool.

About 2:30 p.m. another species, the Quill Gordon, began emerging in large numbers, and about 3:00 p.m. enough Hendricksons appeared to encourage trout to switch a third time. With each imitation I caught more than ten trout.

Who would believe that all this activity, all this dry-fly fishing, occurred on a cold blustery April late morning and afternoon? I had been conditioned not to expect a sizable mayfly hatch until the water temperature neared 50 degrees.

The Dark Blue Quill imitation also effectively duplicates other species that also appear in the morning. For several years I met and fished a small mayfly that habitually emerged at 11:00 a.m. I was confident it was a *Paraleptophlebia* species. However, after I examined it under a microscope I was surprised to find out it was *Ephemerella deficiens*. This species appears on Elk Creek in Central Pennsylvania for weeks – always at 11:00 a.m. A Dark Blue Quill tied on a size 20 hook effectively copies this species. I have had other reports that this species is important to duplicate.

When should you use the Blue Quill? If you're fly fishing any morning of the season from mid-April to October – the time to use the Blue Quill is now.

WHEN BLUE-WINGED OLIVES EMERGE

"I've never seen an Olive Dun emerge," a fishing friend once said to me. "Evidently they're not common to our streams." I had to agree with the angler; for many years I too hadn't seen the emergence of any of the *Ephemerella* species, usually tagged with the appropriate common name of Blue-Winged Olive Dun.

Then one evening in June, around the 8th, I met the Dark Olive Quill, the spinner of the Blue-Winged Olive Dun, on Bowman's Creek. I got a late start that evening, and it was 7:00 p.m. when I finally arrived at the stream. The long deep pool where I parked my car was silent – not one fish rose in a 100-yard section. Only a couple Slate Drakes (*Isonychia bicolor*) emerged along the shores at the fast stretch at the head of the pool. As I often do when no trout are working, and as I suggested you do earlier, I moved upstream to the fast stretch above the pool to look for any spinner activity. There, at the upper end of the fast water, directly out from a tall hemlock, were thousands of clear-winged adults performing their final act. I captured a few of the imagos, noted the brownish olive body and the three dark tails, and surmised that this might be the spinner of one of the Blue-Winged Olive Duns.

I had only one poorly tied imitation, and it only vaguely copied the mating spinner. I had very limited success that evening – but I had finally seen what I thought was a spinner of one of the elusive species of Blue-Winged Olive Duns.

The duns of these species usually emerge sporadically during the morning and afternoon. Now I realized why I hadn't seen the duns appear before; from June to the end of the season I had been fly fishing only evenings. Sure, evening fishing is the best time to tempt lunkers to the surface, but it's not the time to meet and fish while a hatch of Blue-Winged Olives appears.

The next morning I set out again for the same stretch on Bowman's Creek. I had tied a few Olive Duns the night before. I alternately fished and waited from 9:00 to 11:00 a.m., by the Barn Pool. At about 11:00 a few sizable duns emerged on the slow water directly in front of me. Soon the four duns became eight, and eight duns sixteen, and a sporadic hatch was on. I waded out to the nearest dun, captured it, and held it toward the light. The dun had a medium olive body and dark slate wings – it was a Blue-Winged Olive Dun.

Now was my chance – trout rose throughout the pool. I walked down the path along the stream until I was 20 feet below a free-ranging trout seizing every dun nearby. The dry fly hit the water and disappeared. The heavy fish immediately headed toward his protective home under a ledge. I pulled as hard as I dared to discourage him, but only a short minute or two later the imitation flew out of the water and the lunker moved to the safety of the ledge. More than a dozen trout took the artificial that morning.

White Deer Creek also has a good population of this or a closely related species. This hatch too occurs in late May and early June. Several years ago, in early June, I traveled to that fertile stream to search for that species.

When I arrived at the stream I immediately noticed that the water was about 2 feet higher than normal – patches of grass near the far shore were now submerged. Fast water and pockets were impossible to fish with a dry fly.

As I approached the stream I noted several Blue-Winged Olive Duns rise rapidly from the fast water. No trout, however, rose, and I was ready to retrace my steps back to the car. I cast two times in a deep pool – the only area nearby that contained any relatively slow water. On the second cast a heavy stream-bred brown hit the artificial. Three more browns succumbed to the Blue-Winged Olive Dun imitation in that pool. Now upstream to the next fairly slow stretch. Four browns in this stretch took the dry fly.

In all, in two hours of morning fishing, I caught twenty-two trout on the Blue-Winged Olive Dun. All this action occurred on a hot early-June morning with air temperatures hovering around 90 degrees – and on a stream almost in flood stage. Furthermore, none of the trout had been rising to the naturals.

The same species appears on Bald Eagle Creek and on Cedar Run around the end of May. We have listed it in the Insect Emergence Chart as *Ephemerella* species. An entomologist listed it as *Ephemerella sp. nov.* (near *cornuta* and *lata*), possibly a new species. Whatever it is, it is important on many streams in Pennsylvania (and probably other Eastern states) in late May and early June.

Another Blue-Winged Olive, *Ephemerella cornuta*, has been overlooked as an important species until recently. Sporadic hatches occur almost daily on many Eastern and Midwestern waters from late June into September. Although *E. cornuta* seems to escape more rapidly than the former species, it is on the water many more days.

The Dark Olive Quill effectively imitates both previously mentioned species. These spinners usually fall near dusk, although I have seen rare occasions where *Ephemerella* spinner falls have occurred in the morning. The spinner fall is explosive and concentrated, and can be extremely important.

Have you ever witnessed a hatch of Blue-Winged Olive Duns? If not, try fly fishing on mornings in late May, June, July, or August.

THE HATCH FEW PEOPLE SEE

Who'd ever think that a mayfly 3 mm long could cause a lot of excitement and create fantastic rises on almost any summer morning? *Tricorythodes* can and does! I certainly didn't realize the importance of these mayflies until Vince Marinaro and others thoroughly discussed *Caenis* and *Tricorythodes* species in several articles in the mid-1960s. These stories related the fantastic hatches on Falling Springs, the Letort, and to a lesser extent on the Yellow Breeches – all fertile south-central Pennsylvania limestone waters.

At that time (during the mid-1960s) I lived in northeastern Pennsylvania, heart of freestone fishing, and didn't expect the *Tricorythodes* species to be found anywhere but on limestone waters. A fishing event was to change my thinking on this genus completely.

A male *Tricorythodes* spinner.

Joe McMullen holds a rainbow caught during a *Tricorythodes* hatch on Spruce Creek.

Bowman's Creek is a freestone in northeastern Pennsylvania. Several years ago, in late July, Lloyd Williams and I were night-fishing for lunker brown trout. Lloyd had located two such brown trout by a picnic area. He had caught a 24-inch brown in that stretch of water the night before on a Giant Stonefly imitation.

We fished that evening (really it was early morning) until 3:00 a.m. and returned home without any trout to show for our five hours of fishing. When I arrived home that morning I noticed a small unfamiliar mayfly clinging to my fishing vest. It was now a spinner, but its shiny wings were still attached to the subimagal skin. I placed the mayfly under a stereomicroscope, and after a careful inspection of the wing venation, felt sure it was a member of the genus *Tricorythodes*.

I had some question about the identification – for I still doubted that this species emerged on Bowman's Creek. Besides, I visited the stream almost daily and I knew at least fifteen other fly fishermen who did too. Wouldn't I, or one of the other anglers, have experienced this hatch? If not experienced, then at least have seen the mating formation?

I still had serious doubts about a *Tricorythodes* hatch on Bowman's, but concluded that there was only one way to clarify the ambiguity – visit the stream at 8:00 a.m. the next day.

I arrived the next morning at the fly-fishing area of Bowman's, just a few hundred yards above the picnic area. As I approached the fast water above the barn, I was greeted with the exhilarating sight of thousands of glistening wings. As I looked down toward the surface of the water, I saw hundreds of spent spinners and more than ten actively feeding trout.

This was the proof I needed. I hurried home and tied a dozen artificials to imitate both male and female spinners. The next morning, Sunday, I arrived at the stream at 7:30. An all-night rain had just stopped, and the water was slightly discolored. Duns were emerging from the slow water by the hundreds – I'd wait until the first spinners fell spent before I started fishing. By 8:30 females that had moved upstream and mated now fell spent into the fast water. Soon ten or more trout started feeding. The rises to the spent spinners were not typical rises, but rather almost imperceptible swirls. Trout seemed to capture three or four spinners on each rise.

I tied on a size 24 Reverse Jenny Spinner, which effectively copies the female imago. Five casts, ten casts – finally the trout sucked in the dry fly and I gently set the fine wire hook. The rainbow jumped, shook, slapped, then swam upstream. A few minutes later I netted and released the 15-inch fighter. Now upstream a few feet to cast to the next rising trout. Again, several casts, and finally a strike. This was a 14-inch brown trout which was again netted and released.

About 9:30 I noticed a darker spinner on the water, so I switched to the male imitation, the Dark Brown Spinner. Five trout hit that dry fly before the spinner fall waned.

The Beaverkill too has a sizable *Tricorythodes* hatch, especially in late July and early August. The hatches I've experienced have appeared from Hendrickson's Pool upstream to Junction Pool.

I first met the hatch on the fast water above Barnhart's Pool, several years ago in late July. The intensity of the hatch seems to vary considerably from day to day. However, as I arrived at Barnhart's that morning, I saw thousands of spinners mating above the fast water, and I was confident that a sizable spinner fall would occur.

Soon twenty to thirty trout started feeding on spent spinners. Most of the trout seemed to be concentrated a short distance out from a large boulder, and 20 feet below the last fast water. I quickly grabbed for an imitation so I could enjoy the rewards of meeting and fishing the hatches. Guess what – I had left all the *Tricorythodes* imitations in my car, which was parked a half-mile away. I found a Dark Brown Spinner in my fly compartment, hook size 20, and reluctantly tied it onto the leader. During the spinner fall, even with a size 20 imitation, I managed to hook ten trout. As with some other notable hatches, not one other fly fisherman was on hand to meet and fish the hatch.

I have included a suggested imitation for the dun in Chapter V, since this phase too can be important. On several occasions, when I've arrived before 7:30 a.m., I've seen many trout feed on the duns.

On a couple spinner imitations (female) you might want to add the olive egg sac. I have never tied an imitation with the sac, but feel it might be effective.

Next time you're fly-fishing any morning in late July or August look carefully for the hatch few people see. The hatch might occur every day on your favorite stream and you might not be aware of it. If you find this species on a productive stream, you're in for some great midsummer morning fly fishing.

Chapter VII

Fishing the Afternoon Hatches
(*Eastern and Midwestern*)

In the list below, (M) indicates that hatches or spinner falls also often occur in the morning, (E) that they often occur in the evening. Dates listed are very approximate.

Duns

Baetis vagans[1] (M) – Little Blue Dun; 10:00 a.m.–6:00 p.m. (sometimes with heavy emergence around 1:00 p.m.); April 1

Paraleptophlebia adoptiva (M) – Dark Blue Quill; 11:00 a.m.–4:00 p.m. (heavy emergence often from 2:00–4:00 p.m.); April 15

Epeorus pleuralis – Quill Gordon; 1:00–3:00 p.m.; April 18

Ephemerella subvaria – Hendrickson (female), Red Quill (male); 2:00–4:00 p.m.; April 26

Leptophlebia cupida – Black Quill; 2:00–4:00 p.m.; April 27

Ephemerella rotunda (E) – Pale Evening Dun; 2:00–8:00 p.m.; May 8

Stenonema fuscum (M & E) – Gray Fox; 4:00–8:30 p.m. (many days hatches occur earlier); May 15

Pseudocloeon species[1,2] (E) – Little Blue Dun; afternoon and evening; May 10

Ephemerella invaria (E) – Pale Evening Dun; 3:00–8:00 p.m.; May 20[3]

Ephemerella septentrionalis (E) – Pale Evening Dun; appears mainly in the evening but does emerge sporadically in the afternoon; May 18

Stenonema vicarium (M & E) – American March Brown; 10:00 a.m.–7:00 p.m.; May 20

Stenacron canadense (E) – Light Cahill; sporadic during afternoon with a concentration at dusk in June; May 25[3]

Litobrancha recurvata (E) – Dark Green Drake; 1:00–8:00 p.m.; May 25

Ephemera simulans (E) – Brown Drake; sporadic in afternoon; May 25

Ephemera guttulata (E) – Green Drake; mainly evening, but many smaller streams have heavy hatches in the afternoon; May 25

Ephemerella bicolor (M) – Chocolate Dun; late morning and early afternoon; May 25

Ephemerella species (M) – Blue-Winged Olive Dun; morning and afternoon; May 26

Ephemerella needhami (M) – Chocolate Dun[4]; late morning and early afternoon; May 30

Ephemerella minimella (M & E) – Chocolate Dun; afternoon; June 1

[1] Species may produce several broods per year.
[2] Species are not listed in the Insect Emergence Chart, but can be important on occasion.
[3] Hatches appear for many days.
[4] Color may vary.
[5] Dates are approximate and emergence may begin earlier in the season.

Paraleptophlebia mollis (M & E) – Dark Blue Quill; 10:00 a.m.–4:00 p.m. (often continues into early evening); June 3
Ephemerella attenuata (M) – Blue-Winged Olive Dun; morning and afternoon; June 5
Leptophlebia johnsoni (M) – Iron Blue Dun; 11:00 a.m. (sporadic in the afternoon); June 9
Stenonema species, *pulchellum* group (M) – Cream Cahill; sporadic around midday; June 15[3]
Paraleptophlebia guttata (M) – Dark Blue Quill; sporadic during day; June 25[3]
Ephemerella cornuta (M) – Blue-Winged Olive Dun; sporadic during morning and afternoon (often around 11:00 a.m.); June 25[3]
Baetis species (E) – Little Blue Dun; afternoon and evening; July 5[3]

Spinners

Baetis vagans[1] (M) – Rusty Spinner; 10:00 a.m.–6:00 p.m. (and later); April 3[3]
Paraleptophlebia adoptiva (E) – Dark Brown Spinner; 4:00–7:00 p.m.; April 17
Epeorus pleuralis (M) – Red Quill Spinner; 11:30 a.m.–2:00 p.m.; April 20
Ephemerella subvaria (E) – Red Quill Spinner; 3:00–8:00 p.m.; April 28
Leptophlebia cupida (E) – Early Brown Spinner; 1:00–6:00 p.m.; April 28
Ephemerella bicolor (E) – Chocolate Spinner; afternoon and evening; May 27
Ephemerella needhami (E) – Chocolate Spinner; afternoon and evening, May 30
Paraleptophlebia mollis (M) – Dark Brown Spinner; morning and afternoon; June 4
Paraleptophlebia guttata (M) – Dark Brown Spinner; morning and afternoon; June 25

Caddis Flies

Chimarrha atterima (M & E) – Little Black Caddis; 11:00 a.m.–6:00 p.m.; April 26
Brachycentrus fuliginosus (M & E) – Grannom; 3:00–7:00 p.m. (sometimes in morning); May 10[5]
Rhyacophila lobifera (M & E) – Green Caddis; 4:00–9:00 p.m.; May 10[5]
Hydropsyche slossanae (M & E) – Spotted Sedge; 1:00–6:00 p.m.; May 23

Stoneflies

Taeniopteryx faciata (M) – Early Brown Stonefly; afternoon; April 10
Isoperla signata (E) – Light Stonefly; afternoon; May 8[5]

Many anglers believe that afternoon is a lousy time to be on the stream. Fly fishermen plan to be on their favorite water while a comforting morning fog still covers waters, cooled by the darkness before. Even more anglers schedule their trips to meet sunset and the well-known hatches and spinner falls this period produces. But how many credible anglers fish trout waters in midafternoon – especially in mid- and late season?

Anglers might qualify their degradation of afternoon fishing by saying: "Sure, this is the time when the Quill Gordon, Hendrickson, Black Quill, American March Brown, and some Gray Foxes emerge – but these hatches occur only the first month and a half of the season. After June, however, it's useless to cast over waters heated by a hot afternoon sun. Certainly, you wouldn't waste an afternoon in July or August in uncomfortable, sweaty waders with temperatures hovering around 90 degrees. Besides, no hatches appear on these midsummer afternoons."

To these comments I say try this time slot before you condemn it to oblivion. Sure, fishing in the afternoon can be hot and uncomfortable. Yes, afternoon is a notoriously poor time to try for lunker trout, because they characteristically don't feed during daylight hours. But, as you'll see, or as you already know, this is not a time necessarily void of emerging insects, or for that matter, rising trout.

A visit to your favorite stream in June, July, or August might surprise you. There can be sporadic hatches of several *Ephemerella* species, many of which are effectively duplicated by the Blue-Winged Olive Dun. Many *Baetis* species also choose hot, humid summer afternoons to appear. These, of course, are imitated by the Little Blue Dun.

But, in addition, there are other little-known, but significant, *Ephemerella* species that appear on many afternoons in late May and June. A lot of these afternoon-emergers are effectively matched with the Chocolate Dun. On any given June afternoon enough of these lethargic duns can appear to encourage trout to feed.

Most of these species are members of the Bicolor Group (subgenus *Eurylophella*) of the genus *Ephemerella*. One of these, *Ephemerella bicolor*, begins emerging around noon and continues throughout the afternoon. Another species, *Ephemerella minimella*, appears on Pine Creek in early June from late morning until early evening.

Both species, plus others like *Ephemerella needhami* (not a member of the bicolor group), are all effectively copied by a size 16 Chocolate Dun. *Always* include several Chocolate Duns in your selection of artificials for use in afternoon fly fishing.

Not only does afternoon have its own insect hatches, but it also harbors holdovers from the morning and premature appearances from the evening. This is only natural, since this time span is a connecting link between the other two time periods. Holdovers and premature hatches and spinner falls most often occur in April, May, or June, but some (*Paraleptophlebia*, *Baetis*, and *Ephemerella* species) spill over into July and August.

Holdovers from the morning are aquatic insects that initially appear in the earlier time slot, but many times continue, in profuse or limited numbers, into the afternoon. Many of the Blue Quills (*Paraleptophlebia* species) often appear heaviest in the morning, but often continue emerging in more limited numbers through mid-afternoon. I've noted *Paraleptophlebia mollis* duns emerging on Cedar Run in late May as late as 6:00 p.m. – in large enough numbers to produce many rising trout. At least one *Paraleptophlebia* species, *P. adoptiva*, appears in heaviest numbers in the afternoon, rather than the morning.

The other large group of holdovers comes from the genus *Ephemerella* (subgenus *Drunella*). These Blue-Winged Olive Duns begin their emergence in the morning, sometimes with a concentration between 11:00 a.m. and noon. Many continue well into the afternoon, often in sparser numbers. Still, enough can appear on some days to encourage trout to feed on escaping duns.

Premature hatches of species that usually emerge in the evening occur in late

May and early June. The Pale Evening Dun (both *Ephemerella rotunda* and *invaria*) and Light Cahill (*Stenacron canadense*) commonly appear in the afternoon during May and June, and they sometimes appear in heavy enough numbers to encourage trout to feed.

What about July? No decent mayfly would emerge during the afternoon in this month? Wrong again! Hatches aren't as frequent, but several species of *Baetis* appear almost daily on these hot July afternoons. One *Baetis* species, as yet unidentified, appears almost daily on central-Pennsylvania streams in July. Other *Baetis* species appear in August and September in the afternoon.

Caddis flies, too, appear in the afternoon. One of the most important I have met and fished is the Green Caddis. In early May it emerges in the afternoon, as well as the evening.

Afternoon fishing is lousy? Bunk! Sure, it's not the most productive time, but it's still a good time to meet and fish some of the hatches, and often a good time to fly-fish over feeding trout.

DRY FLIES IN APRIL

What a time to be alive! A beautiful warm spring afternoon in late April or early May. After months of snow, just plain cold weather, and patient waiting, I thrive on outside activities at this time – fly fishing over rising trout is just an added bonus. Some of the best-known and heaviest hatches appear on these cool (and sometimes downright cold) afternoons. Who hasn't heard of the Quill Gordon or the Hendrickson? Both species, *Epeorus pleuralis* and *Ephemerella subvaria*, emerge on many Eastern and Midwestern streams in late April. Some afternoons during this early season, air temperatures barely rise above 40 degrees and water temperatures barely above 45 degrees. On many of these days, however, these two species brave the elements and announce the coming of a new fly-fishing season.

Since the Hendrickson usually follows the Quill Gordon by less than a week, and since both hatches appear about the same time, it's logical to discuss them concurrently. On some fertile streams I've noted Quill Gordon duns emerging around 1:30 p.m., shadowed by a Blue Quill (*Paraleptophlebia adoptiva*) peak at 2:00 p.m., and Hendricksons at 3:00 p.m. However, the peak emergence of the Quill Gordon is usually a week ahead of the Hendrickson, and the two hatches never seem to appear in equal numbers on the same day. Between April 18 and 25, in north-central Pennsylvania, the Quill Gordon is often the heavier hatch, with only a few precursory Hendricksons emerging. From April 26 until the second week in May the Hendrickson seems to dominate. On many streams you'll witness one of the two hatches, but less often both, and of course on many of our marginal waters neither of the hatches.

Earlier I suggested that emergence dates can vary from year to year by as much as several weeks. Recently we experienced an extremely warm April. All early hatches, including the Quill Gordon and Hendrickson, emerged well before the season began in Pennsylvania – all artificials tied to meet and fish these hatches had to be placed aside for another year.

For four years, as if part of an enforced ritual, Jack Conyngham, Guthrie Conyngham, Dick Mills, and I planned annual trips to coincide with either the Quill Gordon or Hendrickson. We planned these treks to the productive Loyalsock Creek, because this stream has heavy hatches of both species. We schedule these trips to be on this north-central Pennsylvania water any weekend that falls between April 20 and April 27. On these trips, we usually meet either or both of the hatches. Sure, we agree after four years of meeting these hatches, that it's extremely risky to expect many rising trout on some of the cold blustery days often encountered then; but we're anxious to be on the stream to meet and fish while the first species appear.

Of all these planned trips, the third was by far the most memorable to date. We arrived in separate cars and met at a section of the stream near Barbours at 1:00 p.m. Predictably, at this time of year, a cold north wind blew downstream. Our only asset for meeting and fishing the hatch that afternoon was the semi-pleasant 55-degree air temperature.

Only two or three mayflies appeared in the first half-hour, so I backed out of the snow-chilled water to survey the entire stretch for any signs of a major hatch. While patiently waiting (I never wait patiently), I checked the water temperature and recorded the 46-degree reading in my notebook. Still no hatch. But the elements improved – the north wind slowed to a breeze, the air temperature rose several degrees, and the water temperature neared 50 degrees.

By 1:20 p.m. several duns abruptly appeared in front of me on the high spring waters. I followed their path on the water's surface for more than 100 feet, through the entire length of a pool, but none was seized. Within a half-hour, more than a hundred newly emerged duns appeared on the fast stretch several feet upstream. As the dazed, motionless duns entered the pool below, eight to ten trout took up feeding positions and occasionally fed on the laggards.

All four of us, witnessing the emerging Quill Gordons and concomitant feeding, scattered out quickly in the large pool to fish over rising trout. I selected an area where four trout occasionally rose to the dark duns. I tied on a fresh Quill Gordon imitation with dark slate wings, and cast toward two trout closest to me. After a half-dozen or so casts, the first catch of the year. The trout was barely 6 inches long, but I get excited every new season when I experience success with dry flies in April. Several other trout also seized the artificial before the hatch began to wane.

The Quill Gordon subsided as quickly as it had begun a half-hour before. Quite a few half-drowned subimagos still floated past, but these had probably emerged earlier on stretches several pools upstream.

That afternoon the four of us had a half-mile section of the productive Loyalsock to ourselves – not one other fisherman had planned to meet and fish the hatch in this area of the stream. We decided to go to our cabin for the evening, and on the way we anxiously entered into a discussion of the next day's tactics to meet and fish the hatch.

There's no need to arise early on these spring days, since little emergence activity occurs before 10:00 or 11:00 a.m. However, when we awoke in midmorning we were greeted by a freak 2-inch snowstorm – totally unexpected and unpredicted. By noon most of the snow had melted, but the temperature had only risen to 40 degrees, and scattered snow flurries still spewed from the leaden gray skies. Even with the tremendous uncertainty of the weather, we decided to travel to the stream to see if another hatch might appear. We arrived on the stream just in time to be greeted by snow squalls, and we immediately built a fire to warm ourselves from the chilling winter wind. One o'clock passed, now it was two o'clock – and only a couple dazed, bewildered, frozen duns had appeared. No hatch appeared, and no trout showed.

I state this latter unsuccessful experience because weather often affects your chances of meeting and fishing the hatches in April and early May. These changeable spring weather conditions often affect the quantity of mayflies appearing and the quality of fly fishing.

The Red Quill Spinner, or the imago of *Epeorus pleuralis*, has been of little consequence in my experience. I have noted several mating flights around noon or later, but have seen little or no feeding on the spinners. The same Red Quill used to imitate the male dun of *Ephemerella subvaria* can be effective should the need ever arise to imitate the *Epeorus pleuralis* spinner.

The Hendrickson is one of the most common and fishable mayflies. I have recorded this species on large streams like the Beaverkill and Loyalsock; on small streams like Cedar Run and White Deer Creek; on medium-sized streams like Bowman's Creek; and on slightly acid streams like the Lehigh River.

Since emergence for this species is usually concentrated into a two-week period on most streams, and since duns most often appear from 2:00 to 4:00 p.m., dense hatches are the rule (except on smaller streams). Furthermore, the late-afternoon-early-evening spinner fall, unlike that of the Red Quill Spinner (*Epeorus pleuralis*), sometimes produces rising trout.

Coloration of male and female duns of *Ephemerella subvaria* varies substantially, so a separate imitation for each sex is in order. From above (dorsal) both appear similar; but a ventral view portrays the difference: the female has a dark pinkish tan abdomen, whereas the male has a reddish body that is slightly ringed. Some writers have indicated that males and females emerge from different stretches of water. On many occasions, during an emergence, rather than fish, I have checked the male-and-female ratio on a particular stretch. From my observations, the sexes emerge together. This suggests that trout might do one of two things – they may be selective and take only male or female, or they may take male and female indiscriminately.

I have had more success with the Hendrickson imitation than with the Red Quill. Since the female is slightly larger than the male, it might be that trout are selective in taking the more substantial piece of food, the female dun. Nevertheless, make certain you have Red Quill artificials with you, since it effectively copies the female spinner (the female spinner imitation should have spent wings).

The spinner fall for *Ephemerella subvaria* usually occurs late in the afternoon or early in the evening. The imago can be an important source of food on these otherwise-void early-season trips. The spinner is fairly easy to identify on wing, because of the orange egg sac which it carries under its curved abdomen.

For many years I reserved my dry-fly fishing for June, July, and August. Not now! Now I prepare myself so I can fish dry flies in April.

CADDIS IMITATIONS CAN BE EFFECTIVE

The Little Juniata River, in central Pennsylvania, is now a fantastic stretch of trout water. Large brown trout abound in every pool. Annually, fly fishermen take many 3- and 4-pounders. The river is 80 to 90 feet wide, and it is almost impossible to wade from one shore to another. Until a few years ago the stream was heavily polluted from an upstream paper mill, and from raw, untreated sewage. Now, all that's changed. Before the cleanup, the dark brown water had a pungent, nauseous odor. Now, there is no such odor near the chalky green water.

Since its comeback (and possibly before), the river has some profuse mayfly hatches. But probably more common than the mayflies is the almost-daily emergence of several caddis-fly species. From early May until the end of July, on many afternoons and evenings, there are enough Green Caddis (*Rhyacophila* species) on or near the water to encourage the large browns to feed on the surface.

Several years ago on these same productive waters of the Little Juniata, I learned the value of meeting and fishing the hatch when caddis flies appeared. I traveled with Larry Wilson to the Barn Pool at the lower end of the Espy Farm on a chilly mid-May afternoon. As we approached the deep pool, I noted hundreds of mothlike insects moving upstream in unison 2 or 3 feet above the surface. I quickly waded into the cold water and positioned myself below three surfacing trout. For a minute or two I searched for insects resting on the surface. I scooped at several riding past me, caught one of them, examined the abdomen, and concluded it was a Green Caddis. Soon, more caddis floated past me, and dozens of trout began surfacing for some of the partially emerged caddis. A major hatch was underway. I had prepared for just this circumstance by tying a half dozen downwing artificials of the Green Caddis a few days before. With the first cast I caught an overhanging bush on the far shore. But that wasn't the only problem – there were several current speeds between me and the feeding fish, and the caddis imitation floated only a foot or two before severe drag set in. Finally, a good cast, a mend upstream, and the Caddis drifted drag-free directly over a trout that had been casually sipping in naturals. The brown sucked in the artificial and I struck. The trout swam toward the center of the stream, leaped into the air, and headed upstream. A gentle nudge on the fly rod moved the fish back downstream toward me. In ten minutes I landed the 3-pound trout that had gorged itself on the easily accessible food.

Earlier, in the Preface, I mentioned rather assertively that I prefer dry-fly fishing and most often choose not to use wet flies. On many occasions, however, during a hatch of stoneflies, and to a greater extent caddis flies, trout seem to refuse surface imitations. On one of these instances on the Little Juniata, I noted caddis fly after caddis fly float directly over what I thought were rising trout. Not one of these naturals was seized, however. Trout seemingly surfaced throughout the pool that day but few actually took naturals on the surface.

During this frustrating experience my caddis dry fly sank and became a wet fly drifting a few inches beneath the surface. On the very first drift I noted a huge swirl at the "wet fly" as it made the turn at the end of the natural drift. I roll-cast in the same direction again, letting the imitation sink a few inches. This time a brown rose to the fly and I hooked it. Trout after trout that afternoon took the imitation only when it was fished a few inches beneath the surface.

Again, during an emergence of the Light Stonefly in early May, I tried the same tactic. During this hatch too, trout easily succumbed to a dry-fly imitation stonefly fished just under the surface.

Why does an imitation of either of these two orders prove so effective when fished in this manner? Several fishermen I know theorize that stoneflies and caddis flies usually escape rapidly from the surface, and were trout to seize these surface naturals they would expend more energy on them then they would gain from the food value. Furthermore, the easiest time to capture the caddis is when it is escaping to the surface to emerge.

The Spotted Sedge is a common caddis fly on many streams the third or fourth week in May. Several years ago John Hagan, Dick Mills, and I arrived at Bowman's Creek four hours after it had been stocked. Close to a hundred newly introduced trout formed a tight school in front of me. Spotted Sedges soon appeared directly over the school, and the fish seized them with little apprehension. Ten or more sedges now skittered above the trout. I tied on an imitation and made the same movement the natural did. Cast after cast with that imitation produced trout after trout. John Hagan used a size 16 Light Cahill, which is almost identical to the natural except for the upright wings. For every trout John caught, I caught and released five. After a frustrating hour of saying, "These trout shouldn't notice the difference," John switched to a downwing Spotted Sedge imitation. His rate of success immediately increased. Were the upright wings the problem with these relatively unsophisticated trout?

I have used downwing patterns for caddis flies and stoneflies for about ten years, and although I've been scoffed at by some upright purists, I feel they're important to include in any dry-fly assortment (in fact, in any assortment). Why? First and foremost, these downwing imitations more accurately copy the natural. When the caddis fly rests on the surface, its wings are folded tentlike back over the body, and the downwing imitation copies this pose correctly.

Second, I feel that caddis flies and caddis-fly patterns, which have been overlooked for years, are important as a source of food for trout and are therefore important to imitate. I once met a real expert fly fisherman on the same Little Juniata River. This man took more trout and larger trout than any other fisherman on the stream. On several occasions when he was fishing I sat back and watched. He was not one to come over and converse, but he mechanically went on with his expert skill of casting, catching, and releasing trout. Finally, on about the third or fourth meeting, I asked him what pattern he used. "Caddis – nothing but caddis. Day in, day out they catch more fish for me," he said as he showed me his Green Caddis imitation.

If you learn nothing more from this book than the fact that caddis imitations on Eastern, Midwestern, and Western streams have been neglected but are extremely important, you'll probably be a more successful fly fisherman.

We discussed in Chapter V methods of tying the caddis fly and stonefly. I prefer the first of the two recommended methods – with a body of polypropylene and deer-hair wings. (I strongly recommend an imitation with two hackles for all Western patterns.) It's important, however, to select the color of deer hair which best matches the wings of the insect. Light deer hair, for example, effectively copies the wings of the Light Stonefly and Spotted Sedge, whereas darker deer hair is used for the Grannom. These suggested patterns don't ride as high on the surface as do regular dry flies, but apparently are much more effective during a hatch of the naturals.

Although we've discussed only a couple caddis-fly species, many others are important to match. Tie caddis imitations with cream, yellow, tan, brown, dark brown, gray, green, olive, and black in sizes 12–20. This range of colors and hook sizes should prepare you adequately to meet and fish most caddis-fly and also most stonefly hatches.

You haven't tried a downwing caddis imitation yet? Try one; it might make a potentially uneventful trip into a successful one.

THE CREAM DUNS ARE COMING

The Pale Evening Duns (*Ephemerella invaria*, *E. rotunda*, and *E. dorothea*), the American March Brown (*Stenonema vicarium*), the Gray Fox (*Stenonema fuscum*), and the Light Cahill (*Stenacron canadense*) have many things in common as mayfly hatches. All begin appearing in mid-May – some earlier and some a little later – and all are moderate-sized. But more important, all species have cream, creamish yellow, yellowish cream, or tannish cream bodies (some have an orange or olive cast also).

Rather than discuss all together, however, we'll look at the Pale Evening Dun, then the Gray Fox, then the American March Brown, and finally the Light Cahill. Remember, although we're discussing these as afternoon hatches, most tend to appear in heaviest numbers in the evening, and could be examined under that heading. Most, however, initially appear in the afternoon (and morning for the

An Eastern *Heptagenia* species well represented by the Pale Evening Dun.
This species most often appears near dusk.

A good cream dun imitation is the Light Cahill shown here.

The Pale Evening Dun is another effective cream dun imitation.

The American March Brown, a cream dun imitation.

The Gray Fox, which imitates a cream dun. Although the Gray Fox pictured here is tied with badger hackle, I recommend cream variant.

Gray Fox and American Brown), and as warm weather arrives and June approaches, most species appear in larger numbers in the evening.

On May 8 several years ago I visited the Barn Pool on the Little Juniata River to look for a hatch of Green Caddis. Caddis flies were already in the air and on the water when I arrived. By 4:00 p.m. a few Pale Evening Duns (*Ephemerella invaria*) rested on the surface with the Green Caddis. I thought this was only a premature emergence and didn't expect the hatch to last very long. But by 5:00 p.m. the hatch became heavier – now, hundreds of duns rode the surface. Trout now switched their surface feeding from the Green Caddis to the more plentiful Pale

A section of the Little Juniata River where many of the cream duns appear.

Evening Dun. Thirty feet from me, at the head of the pool, a huge trout now devoured every dun in his path. From its characteristic "slurp" I knew it was a lunker. On the third cast I successfully covered the rise – the monster took the fly and I set the hook. The brown immediately leaped out of the water, displayed its golden brown belly, and broke free. This was the biggest trout I had ever seen take a dry fly, especially this early (5:00 p.m.) in the day. I conservatively estimated the trout I had just lost to be about 26 inches long.

I rested for a while after the episode – I still trembled fifteen minutes later. While resting on the bank and trying to regain my composure, I surveyed the pool once again, hoping against hope that that monster would feed again on some of the hundreds of duns still floating downstream. He did not; I had put him down, wiser and more difficult for the next angler to catch. But there were several smaller trout working. I waded back into the pool again, but not with the same enthusiasm I had earlier – losing that large trout still haunted me.

A week later I visited the same stretch of the Little Juniata with Jim Heltzel. I had described to him the previous week's hatch and the huge trout I had lost, and he was anxious to meet and fish while a hatch progressed.

For the middle of May the day was absolutely chilling, with a wind blowing out of the north at about 15–20 miles per hour. The temperature hovered around 45 degrees all afternoon. A few duns already greeted us as we arrived at the Long Pool at 3:00 p.m.

No trout rose to the few *Ephemerella invaria* duns on the Long Pool, so I moved downstream several hundred yards to see if there was any surface feeding in the pools below. Hundreds of dazed subimagos now floated on these pools, but still few trout showed. On my return trip to the Long Pool, Jim Heltzel motioned for me to hurry to the middle section. When I arrived I knew why he wanted me – ten or more trout now methodically took these pale duns, seemingly too cold to take flight. Four fish rose 15 feet from where we stood. I entered the water, false-cast the Pale Evening Dun several times, and landed the artificial 2 feet in front of the closest trout. A heavy rainbow hit and broke loose after a couple leaps. Another cast above a rising trout and another rise to the artificial. More casts, more trout – in all, six large trout struck the imitation within ten minutes.

The Pale Evening Dun appeared on the Little Juniata River that year until the middle of June. As the season progressed, the duns emerged later and later, until early June when the species appeared at dusk.

A few days after the Pale Evening Dun first appears, the Gray Fox (*Stenonema fuscum*) emerges. Although the Gray Fox is apt to appear morning, afternoon, or evening, hatches most often occur between 4:00 and 8:00 p.m. Earlier I suggested that the Gray Fox might not emerge in the numbers that the Pale Evening Dun does. However, on one stream, and I'm sure there are others, the Gray Fox emerges in unbelievable numbers. When it appears in the quantity it does on Bald Eagle in central Pennsylvania, it can be the most impressive hatch of the season.

Stenonema fuscum first arrives about May 15 (remember, earlier or later depending on location and weather conditions), but the most profuse hatches occur from May 20 to June 5. On some streams, especially headwaters, the species continues in limited numbers into July.

Several years before, someone had reported to me that a brown-and-cream mayfly emerged the last two weeks in May on the Bald Eagle Creek. Now, on May 20, I arrived at the stream, curious to see if the species would appear, and which species it was. I arrived at the stream at 3:00 p.m. and decided to take an exploratory trip. I followed a well-traveled path upstream a couple hundred yards to a clearing. Flycatchers perched at vantage points on many of the elms and willows near the stream. Barn swallows, too, made their characteristic low, swerving flight just above the middle of the stream. Occasionally a flycatcher took off, headed for the stream, hovered, then returned to its perch. Several times two flycatchers from opposite sides of the stream met in the center and fought over an insect. I observed the surface carefully now, and saw that the birds were feeding on *Stenonema fuscum* subimagos. I stared at the same stretch and noted possibly thirty duns emerge in a twenty-minute period, but saw only one make it to the safety of a nearby tree. I wondered how mayflies have any chance to multiply when they are taken freely as nymphs by fish, captured on the surface by trout and birds, and taken in flight by many winged predators.

Some of the duns floated 10 to 20 feet on the surface before their fateful escape. Not once did I observe a trout rise for these lethargic mayflies. Since there was no action, I returned to my car for photographic equipment and sat by a pool at the bridge, capturing duns and taking pictures of them.

An old fisherman wandered by about 5:30 p.m. and watched carefully as I took photos of the mayflies. He complained at the apparent lack of trout in the stream. I shook my head in agreement as I looked through my single-lens reflex and snapped one final shot. I had to agree with the old man, since I had been on the stream more than two hours, experienced a fairly sizable hatch, and not observed one feeding trout.

The old man left in a few minutes, certain that the fishing would not improve later. I decided to stay until dusk. About 8:15 or 8:30 p.m. every Gray Fox dun in that section of the stream must have decided to emerge. Hundreds and hundreds of brown-and-cream subimagos appeared in the air, and still more rested on the water, after breaking free from their nymphal cases. These duns appeared only minutes after the last flycatcher and barn swallow left the area for the day. The mayflies seemed to realize they were now free from attack from above. In a short fast stretch at the head of the pool, fifteen trout – no exaggeration – now actively gulped resting duns. This action occurred in an area which, for the past several hours, had seemed to contain no trout at all.

Earlier, I had tied a Gray Fox onto the leader in case any hatch appeared, but not really expecting anything like this. Almost every cast produced a rise to the artificial. Trout after trout hooked, then released. The hatch continued through the half-light and on into darkness – the trout continued feeding in unison with the hatch. Finally, I quit because I no longer had any idea whether trout were rising to the imitation or the natural.

Here, in a pool that I had sworn earlier had no trout, in a stream that was heavily fished, I met and fished a spectacular Gray Fox hatch. While all this action occurred, not one other fly fisherman was in sight; not one other fisherman enjoyed the rewards of meeting and fishing the hatch.

A day or two after the dun emerges, it changes into a completely different-looking imago – the Ginger Quill. The spinner fall also provides memorable fly fishing. Females fall spent to the surface around 8:30 p.m.

For years and years I had not experienced a sizable, fishable hatch of American March Brown (*Stenonema vicarium*) duns or spinners. After all these observations, I was convinced this species was truly a sporadic emerger, and was not an important species to meet and fish.

Then, two years ago, on June 1, I traveled to the diminutive, but fertile, Big Fill Run in central Pennsylvania. On this 10-foot-wide mountain stream, I saw hundreds of American March Brown duns appear. Sure, they emerged sporadically, but duns were continuously on the water from noon until after 4:00 p.m. Furthermore, these duns rode the surface for great distances before struggling free of the surface film. Hundreds of March Browns rested on rocks by the stream, presumably too tired to reach safety in nearby trees.

But, more important than experiencing a sizable hatch, I observed trout rising to the duns all afternoon. Upstream and downstream in fast water, pockets, and pools, trout fed eagerly on the large duns. All afternoon I fished over trout rising to the naturals, and all afternoon I caught trout. Don't let anybody tell you that sporadic hatches can't be important!

A year later I encountered a good hatch of March Browns on the Beaverkill. It was June 8 and several of us traveled to this hallowed stream to meet and fish while the Green Drake appeared. We arrived at Mountain Pool at 6:00 p.m. and were greeted by an early-evening hatch of March Browns. It was a sparse hatch, but several trout rose to take the duns. Since we still had an hour and a half before any Green Drakes might appear, I tied on an imitation of the March Brown. I selected what I thought was the largest trout rising to the naturals, and waded toward the center of the stream. Several casts and the trout took the artificial. I landed the 16-inch brown in a few minutes. Three more heavy trout took the artificial that night before the Green Drake appeared.

The imago, the Great Red Spinner, might be important on evenings in late May and early June. I say "might be" because although I have seen heavy flights, I have rarely seen the spent spinners on the water. The spinner appears over fast water around 8:00 p.m.

The final cream dun performer is the Light Cahill (*Stenacron canadense*). This large stream species appears before May has ended and continues well into July. As with other cream duns, the Cahill appears sporadically in the afternoon in late May, when it often emerges with the Pale Evening Dun (*Ephemerella invaria*). In late June and until the species has ended its annual appearance in mid-July, the Light Cahill emerges at dusk in an explosive hatch. During the latter half of this species' emergence, the Cahill often co-emerges at dusk with the Yellow Drake (*Ephemera varia*). Trout, during this latter period, will often indiscriminately take either species. Therefore, it's imperative to use imitations which correctly copy the yellowish cream body of both species (this color copies only the male *Stenacron canadense*).

I place *Stenacron canadense* as one of the best hatches of the season for several reasons. First, it has an extremely lengthy appearance. I have encountered fishable hatches as early as May 25 and as late as July 15. Furthermore, when the Cahill appears, it often does in numbers large enough to produce rising trout. Finally, because the species often appears sporadically, duns on any given day might emerge for four to five hours, providing plenty of time for rising trout to gorge themselves.

The *Stenacron canadense* (Light Cahill) is a cream dun that commonly appears on many Eastern and Midwestern streams.

Another common Eastern and Midwestern cream dun is the *Stenacron interpunctatum* (Light Cahill).

The *Ephemerella septentrionalis* (Pale Evening Dun) is a cream dun frequently seen by Eastern and Midwestern anglers.

Hatches of the cream dun *Ephemerella invaria* (Pale Evening Dun) are common on many Eastern and Midwestern streams.

The *Ephemerella rotunda* (Pale Evening Dun) is a cream dun of the East and Midwest.

Spring Creek in central Pennsylvania was rated in 1954 as one of the top one hundred trout streams in the nation. Shortly after this rating, the stream experienced some bad times. First, excessive organic material was pumped into an upper branch, as a result of an overload on a municipal sewage system. This material lowered the oxygen content of the stream and killed much of the aquatic life. Additionally, in the last ten years, the stream has suffered from chemical spills, gasoline spills, and any other catastrophe that you can think of. All of this had a detrimental effect on the benthos of the stream. Huge hatches of Green Drakes were common prior to 1957 – now there are none. Only recently has the stream made a gallant attempt to return to its original fertile condition. Along with this recent revitalization some mayfly species have reappeared. Presently, heavy hatches of *Ephemerella invaria*, *Stenacron canadense*, and some *Baetis* species have returned.

I recently heard a Bellefonte angler say that mayfly hatches had returned to the lower end of Spring Creek. He said that in late May and early June the stream had a large hatch of large pale yellow mayflies. I traveled to a section below Fisherman's Paradise on a chilly late May evening. By the time I arrived, several yellow duns were already emerging. I captured a dun still riding the surface, and assumed from its coloration, size, and two tails that it might be the Light Cahill (*Stenacron canadense*).

I rested on a bank by a large pool, waiting for trout to surface to the sparse hatch. A trout at the lower end of the pool casually took the cream duns, but to reach that fish I might disturb the entire pool. More duns appeared on the fast stretch at the head of the pool, and trout surfaced for them. I noticed one large swirl to the duns and cast above what I thought was a large trout. The trout seized the imitation immediately and swam downstream toward the center of the pool. As I guided the heavy brown toward my net, I heard two boys, who had been watching this whole episode from behind, say, "Boy, is that a big trout!"

"Would I like to catch a trout like that!" one of them said.

"Do you really want the fish?" I asked.

"Yeah," the smaller boy said as his mouth opened wide.

I waded to the shore and handed the 18-inch brown to the older boy with outstretched arms. He quickly grabbed the fish and ran up a steep hill through shoulder-high briars to his parents' house, screaming words of excitement. I dislike keeping trout, and I detest even more keeping trout for friends – but here were two youngsters who might take more interest in fishing if they experienced success. Besides, their parents owned the farmland through which this stream flowed, and one should be courteous to the landowner.

This *Stenacron* imago produces heavy, concentrated spinner falls in June and July. Mating activity usually occurs after 8:00 p.m. On many evenings I've seen thousands of spinners available to trout.

Female duns have a decided orange cast to their creamish yellow bodies. I've tied artificials with this orange cast to the body and they have proved extremely effective.

There are four other cream duns which, on occasion, can be important to meet and fish. All again are placed under the heading of Pale Evening Duns for the fisherman, since they too have pale yellow or orangish yellow bodies. *Ephemerella dorothea* and *Ephemerella rotunda* we discussed briefly – to these two we can add *Heptagenia aphrodite* and *Ephemerella septentrionalis*.

To the Light Cahill list we can also add *Stenacron areion*, *Stenacron interpunctatum interpunctatum*, *Stenacron interpunctatum heterotarsale*, *Stenonema luteum*, *Stenonema pulchellum*, and others which appear mainly during the late season. These species too can be extremely important on those late-season days when few hatches or falls occur. We list here subspecies of *Stenacron interpunc-*

tatum. The Light Cahill (*Stenacron canadense*) is also considered a subspecies of *S. interpunctatum* and should properly be listed as *Stenacron interpunctatum canadense*.

For the first month or so we witness the emergence of several dark species. But when mid-May arrives in the East and Midwest, we can be assured that the cream duns are coming.

Chapter VIII

Fishing the Evening Hatches

(*Eastern and Midwestern*)

In the list below, (M) indicates that hatches or spinner falls also often occur in the morning, (A) that they often occur in the afternoon. Dates listed are very approximate.

Duns

Ephemerella rotunda (A) – Pale Evening Dun; 3:00–8:00 p.m.; May 8
Stenonema fuscum (A) – Gray Fox; 4:00–8:30 p.m.; May 15
Heptagenia aphrodite (A) – Pale Evening Dun; 8:00 p.m.; May 18
Ephemerella septentrionalis – Pale Evening Dun; 8:00 p.m.; May 18
Ephemerella invaria (A) – Pale Evening Dun; 3:00–8:00 p.m.; May 20[1]
Stenonema vicarium (A) – American March Brown; 10:00 a.m.–7:00 p.m.; May 20
Stenacron canadense (A) – Light Cahill; 6:00–8:30 p.m.; May 25[1,2]
Litobrancha recurvata (A) – Dark Green Drake; 1:00–8:00 p.m.; May 25[3]
Ephemera simulans – Brown Drake; 8:00 p.m.; May 25
Ephemera guttulata – Green Drake; 8:00 p.m.; May 25
Epeorus vitreus – Light Cahill (male), Pink Cahill (female); 8:00 p.m.; May 25[1]
Isonychia sadleri – Slate Drake; Evening; May 25
Stenonema ithaca – Light Cahill; Evening; May 25[1]
Stenacron interpunctatum – Light Cahill; Evening; May 25
Isonychia bicolor – Slate Drake; 7:00 p.m.; May 30[1]
Ephemerella dorothea – Pale Evening Dun; 8:00 p.m.; June 1[1]
Stenacron areion – Light Cahill; 7:00 p.m.; June 10[2]
Stenonema luteum – Light Cahill; 8:00 p.m.; June 15[1]
Stenacron heterotarsale – Light Cahill; Evening; June 15
Heptagenia hebe – Pale Evening Dun; 8:00 p.m.; June 22[1]
Ephemera varia – Yellow Drake; 8:00–9:15 p.m.; June 22[1]
Potamanthus distinctus – Golden Drake; 9:00 p.m.; June 28
Isonychia harperi (M & A) – Slate Drake; 7:00 p.m.; July 20[1]
Ephoron leukon – White Mayfly; 7:00 p.m.; August 15
Hexagenia atrocaudata – Big Slate Drake; 8:00 p.m.; August 18

[1] Hatches usually appear for many days.
[2] Formerly *Stenonema*.
[3] Most appropriate imitation.

Spinners

Paraleptophlebia adoptiva (A) – Dark Brown Spinner; 4:00–7:00 p.m.; April 17
Ephemerella subvaria (A) – Red Quill; 3:00–8:00 p.m.; April 28
Leptophlebia cupida (A) – Early Brown Spinner; 1:00–6:00 p.m.; April 28
Ephemerella rotunda (A) – Pale Evening Spinner; 6:00–8:00 p.m.; May 10
Stenonema fuscum – Ginger Quill Spinner; 7:00–9:00 p.m.; May 18[1]
Heptagenia aphrodite – Pale Evening Dun[3]; 8:00 p.m.; May 20
Ephemerella septentrionalis – Pale Evening Dun[3]; 8:00 p.m.; May 20
Ephemerella invaria – Pale Evening Spinner; 7:00–8:30 p.m.; May 22[1]
Stenonema vicarium – Great Red Spinner; 8:00 p.m.; May 22
Stenacron canadense – Light Cahill[3]; 7:00–9:00 p.m.; May 27[2]
Litobrancha recurvata – Brown Drake; 7:00–9:00 p.m.; May 27
Ephemera simulans – Brown Drake; 8:00 p.m.; May 27
Ephemera guttulata – Coffin Fly; 8:00 p.m.; May 27
Epeorus vitreus – Salmon Spinner – Evening; May 26[1]
Isonychia sadleri – White-Gloved Howdy – Evening; May 26[1]
Stenonema ithaca – Light Cahill – Evening; May 26
Stenacron interpunctatum – Light Cahill – Evening; May 26
Ephemerella species – Dark Olive Spinner; 7:00–9:00 p.m.; May 27
Isonychia bicolor – White-Gloved Howdy; 8:00 p.m.; May 31[1]
Stenacron areion – Light Cahill[3]; 8:00 p.m.; June 11
Leptophlebia johnsoni – Blue Quill Spinner; 6:00–8:00 p.m.; June 11
Stenonema luteum – Olive Cahill Spinner; 8:00 p.m.; June 16[1]
Stenacron heterotarsale – Light Cahill, Evening; May 26
Stenonema species, *pulchellum* group – Cream Cahill Spinner; 8:00 p.m.; June 16
Heptagenia hebe – Pale Evening Dun[3]; 8:00 p.m.; June 23[1]
Ephemera varia – Yellow Drake; 8:00 p.m.; June 23[1]
Potamanthus distinctus – Golden Spinner; 9:00 p.m.; June 28
Ephemerella cornuta – Dark Olive Spinner; 7:00–9:00 p.m.; July 3[1]
Isonychia harperi – White-Gloved Howdy; 8:00 p.m.; July 21[1]
Ephoron leukon – White Mayfly; 7:00–8:00 p.m.; August 15
Hexagenia atrocaudata – Dark Rusty Spinner; 6:00–7:00 p.m.; August 19

Caddis Flies

Chimarra atterima (A) – Little Black Caddis; 11:00–6:00 p.m.; April 26
Brachycentrus fuliginosus (A) – Grannom; 3:00–7:00 p.m.; May 10
Rhyacophila lobifera (A) – Green Caddis; 3:00–9:00 p.m.; May 10[1]
Hydropsyche slossanae (A) – Spotted Sedge; 1:00–6:00 p.m.; May 23
Psilotreta frontalis – Dark Blue Sedge; 8:00 p.m.; June 8

Evening . . . that time of huge drake hatches and resultant, ranging trout. Evening is that period of daylight, sunset, half-light, and darkness – all vying for recognition and only the last one prevailing. Evening fly fishing can be more rewarding or more frustrating than any other part of the day. It can be more rewarding because this is the time to match the Green Drake, Light Cahill, Yellow Drake, and many, many other productive hatches. It can be satisfying too during one of the hundreds of spinner falls that seem to occur almost every summer night over fertile fast-water stretches. It can be more fruitful also because this is typically the time of day that the lunker trout lose their timidity and range freely in their search for food.

However, fly fishing in the evening can be profoundly frustrating. The fly fisherman has to fight darkness, praying for a few more minutes of enough light to view his imitation float flawlessly over a methodically feeding trout. Evening fishing is especially trying when the angler hurriedly attempts to test one more pattern over one more feeding trout. In the process he has extreme difficulty holding the rod, dry fly, and line overhead toward the last hint of daylight, and trying to place the leader through the eye of the hook.

Evening fly fishing is not consistently productive during all months of the season. Few duns emerge and spinners fall until after mid-May. Most mayflies in April and early May appear during the warmest part of the day – from noon until 4:00 p.m. But midway through May a noticeable shift occurs – duns and spinners now appear more often in the evening hours.

Late May, June, July, and August harbor the bulk of the evening hatches and attendant spinner falls. The emergence of the Gray Fox and the subsequent Ginger Quill Spinner herald the advent of premier evening fly fishing. This select angling begins around May 18 (a few days earlier, or a few days later), and continues through June with the emergence of Brown Drakes (*Ephemera simulans*), Green Drakes (*E. guttulata*), and Yellow Drakes (*E. varia*). This outstanding time to meet and fish while the hatches appear wanes in August after the appearance of the White Mayfly (*Ephoron leukon*), the Big Slate Drake (*Hexagenia atrocaudata*), and some late Light Cahills (*Stenonema* species).

Although evening fishing can be productive throughout the summer, the greater part of the hatches appear near the beginning of June. Within a couple weeks we see the likes of the Green Drake, Gray Fox, Slate Drake, Light Cahill, Brown Drake, and others.

Caddis flies during this early part of June can produce exciting action on selected streams during the evening hours. Species like those imitated by the Green Caddis and the Dark Blue Sedge engender prolific hatches during early June.

In June, with many mayflies and caddis flies emerging concurrently, it's important to determine what food item (insect) trout are selecting. On these multi-hatch nights it's imperative to "fish the hatches and not the hatch." Make certain you have with you imitations of all species which might emerge. Predicting which hatch will be the major one can be difficult, and forecasting which species trout will prefer can be downright frustrating.

Spinners too are productive at dusk. Imagos associated with the aforementioned duns, plus many others where the subimago appears sporadically during the day, can create productive spinner falls. We indicated earlier that spinners of many species meet, mate, lay eggs, and fall spent on the water, just at dusk.

If you're not certain which spinner will fall spent onto the water on a given night, try this strategy. Most females mating at dusk do so over fast water. This might ensure that the fertilized eggs, when deposited on a fast stretch, will be well distributed. Just before dark, if emerging duns are absent, move upstream to a moderate or fast stretch where mating imagos are likely to be present. Try to identify what species is present in the largest formation (try to catch a female spinner), and match it with an imitation you have with you. It's of value to know what method of egglaying the spinner uses – for if the species never touches the surface in its ritual, the fall might be unimportant. Furthermore, if the female drops the eggs from a foot or two above the surface, or if the female dies away from the water after egglaying, the fall will be unproductive. Return downstream to the head of the pool and wait for the spent spinners to appear on the water.

This advice has made fishing spinner falls more meaningful and much less frustrating for me. These falls can be baffling, because by the time you decide on the proper imitation, the fall and the feeding have subsided. Many times I have wasted fifteen or twenty minutes during an explosive fall on the Beaverkill trying, unsuccessfully, to match the actual spinner with the correct imitation in almost complete darkness. With the method I'm suggesting, you'll be prepared well ahead of the spinner fall.

On many of our better streams like the Beaverkill, Big Fishing Creek, and Penn's in central Pennsylvania, and the Willowemoc, spinner falls occur almost every evening. Many duns which appear sporadically throughout the day produce fantastic, concentrated falls. Often the imagos appear on the water in great quantities for a very short period in the evening. Several species of the genus *Ephemerella*, commonly imitated by the Blue-Winged Olive Dun, emerge in a less than explosive manner as a subimago. Their emergence is usually diffused throughout the day, with a possible peak around 11:00 a.m. Most imagos of these species appear over the water in the evening to mate and fall in huge numbers at a time when lunker trout are more readily apt to feed.

In this chapter we'll look at three of the evening hatches and their spinner falls – the Green Drake, Yellow Drake, and Slate Drake. All three are important, but other species listed at the beginning of this chapter can also be productive.

FISHING THE GREEN DRAKE HATCH
ON PENN'S CREEK

Were the reports we had heard true? Did the annual appearance of the Green Drake really excite the big trout on Penn's Creek as much as we had been told? Or was it another exaggerated tale of an overzealous fisherman? It had been ten years since I last saw the hatch. Was it as prolific as ever? We would soon find out!

Three of us arrived at Penn's Creek at 6:00 a.m. Why so early, when the Green Drake usually doesn't appear until the evening? First, we didn't want to take any chance of missing the hatch, and second, we wanted to put in a "full day" on this productive limestone stream. During the first five or six hours we caught and released thirty trout. Few of them, however, were large. We caught most of these trout on Light Cahill dry flies fished wet with a fast retrieve.

We only halfheartedly fished that morning in anticipation of the Drake hatch

The Green Drake imitates the *Ephemera guttulata* dun.

The Coffin Fly copies the *Ephemera guttulata* spinner.

later in the day. Shortly after noon we moved downstream, several miles below the village of Coburn. This area is apparently ideal for the *Ephemera guttulata* nymph, since the stream contains large stretches of slow to moderate water and a bottom of mud and silt.

At 3:00 p.m. we arrived at an old railroad tunnel. During the next four hours we experienced little success, and we were about ready to call it a day. Only one thing kept us at the stream – the largest hatch of duns usually occurs after 8:00 p.m. We did see a few duns emerging during the day, but very sporadically.

It was now 7:00 p.m. and fishermen started arriving in droves. They hurriedly assembled their gear and took their positions on the stream. It was reminiscent of the scene on opening day of trout season. Dick Mills, Tom Taylor, and I kept on fishing, while twenty to thirty other fishermen in our immediate area just sat there and watched. When I asked one of the natives why he wasn't fishing, I received the same reply I had several years ago when I first saw this unforgettable hatch: "You gotta wait until the fish start working."

It was now 7:45 p.m. and no trout were rising, and all fishermen were still waiting. One of the natives across the stream collected naturals (duns) from some of the low-lying trees and placed them in a paper bag. He'd use these duns later when the hatch began. I couldn't wait for the hatch to begin and continued to fish. Since we had had so much success during the day using a Light Cahill dry fly fished wet, I decided to tie on an extended-bodied Green Drake and fish it wet also. After several casts and quick retrieves I noted a huge swirl. The line tightened, and I knew I had on a heavy trout. The fish stayed deep and started swimming downstream away from the fast water toward a large deep pool. Twenty hectic minutes later and 100 yards downstream, I netted one of the finest orange-bellied brown trout I had ever caught.

Now it grew darker. The sun moved behind some tall oak trees to the west of the stream, and the lengthening shadows brought a slight chill to the air. Large white mayfly spinners met over the water and formed a cloudlike cover. These white spinners were dull-colored Green Drake duns a couple days before, but had cast away their subimago skins in preparation for their final most important act of the life cycle – mating.

Up to this point only a few dark green duns rested on the chalky water before they took flight. However, the deepening shadows of evening seemed to remind the large grayish brown nymphs that it was time for them to emerge . . . and the famous Green Drake hatch at Penn's Creek began. Upstream and downstream fishermen started casting, while they bellowed in nervous anticipation, "They're working, they're working," as hundreds of duns appeared on the water. As I looked upstream at a stretch of about 100 yards, I saw at least twenty large trout now methodically, brazenly feeding on the newly emerged duns. Nearer to me, five large fish, oblivious to all the fishermen near them, devoured dun after dun. On my first cast, I hooked a heavy fish. It went to the bottom, shook several times, and left me with the artificial hanging in a nearby bush. Quickly I retrieved the fly and cast just above a second rising trout. It immediately struck, and in a few minutes I netted a 14-inch rainbow. Now almost complete darkness had come to the stream. To the west a faint glow lingered in the sky, and as I looked upstream toward that faint glow, I saw ten to twenty duns float past me. I quickly cast for a third trout which I heard gulping in subimagos directly in front of me, and only a few feet out from the bank. The fish struck the imitation, turned upstream, plunged deep toward the center of the pool, and broke my 4-pound leader.

The hatch continued until well after dark, and when we decided to quit at 10:00 p.m., fishermen still fished, duns still emerged, and trout still rose. We hated to leave the stream, but our casting arms were numb from the almost steady sixteen-hour ordeal.

The emergence of the dun at any given spot on the stream lasts for a few evenings and constantly moves upstream nightly. You can stretch your meeting and fishing of this particular hatch by being on the stream for the indescribable spinner falls. Spinner falls occur simultaneously with the dun emergence in the evening, and last a couple days after the dun has dissipated. Although the dun lasts only a few days in the same area, on any given evening it is capable of emerging for three or four hours.

The Beaverkill in New York's Catskills has a memorable *Ephemera guttulata* hatch. On this fertile stream, the Green Drake appears several days later than on Penn's Creek. Although the mayfly numbers are not as prominent as on Penn's Creek, the trout seem to be more numerous and the fishermen are more successful on the Beaverkill.

If you enjoy catching lunker trout or get a thrill hearing them splash, don't miss the unforgettable experience of the Green Drake hatch.

THE SLATE DRAKE – A FLY FOR ALL SUMMER

The American March Brown emerges about the third week in May and is present on most fast waters for the next couple weeks. Similarly, the Gray Fox appears about the same time, and duns of this species continue to emerge well into June. Imitations of either of these mayflies are especially effective during emergence time. Most mayfly species, as we have seen throughout this book, follow this pattern – annually emerging for a few weeks out of the year.

However, there are three mayflies, all imitated by the Slate Drake, that begin appearing in late May and continue to appear until late September. *Isonychia bicolor* is the first of the trio to emerge, usually in late May, followed closely by *I. sadleri*. Finally, in mid-July and until September, *I. harperi* appears. These three homogeneous species, all effectively imitated by the Slate Drake, appear for four months of the fishing season. Therefore, if artificials imitating the American March Brown and Gray Fox are effective in late May and June, an artificial imitating the three *Isonychia* species (as the Slate Drake imitation does) should be "a fly for all summer."

Present imitations of the three species are few, and those existing don't do an adequate job. The pattern most fly fishermen use when a hatch of "bicolors" appears is the Leadwing Coachman or the Dun Variant. Let's look at the Coachman versus the natural:

The Slate Drake imitation effectively copies many of the *Isonychia* species.

Leadwing Coachman
Tail – None
Body – Peacock
Wings – Gray quill
Hackle – Brown

Isonychia species
Tail – Medium gray
Body – Dark slate gray
Wings – Dark slate gray
Legs – Front, dark brown
      Rear, cream

    Schwiebert, in his classic *Matching the Hatch,* has suggested that the Leadwing Coachman does not duplicate closely enough the hatch when it appears. Perplexed by the need for a closer imitation, but frustrated by the lack of a more realistic pattern, I designed an artificial and dubbed it the Slate Drake after the nomenclature from Donald DuBois' comprehensive book *The Fisherman's Handbook of Trout Flies*. I attempted to make the artificial as lifelike as possible by using medium gray hackle fibers for the tail, stripped peacock quill for the body, dark gray mallard quill for the wings, and one cream hackle in the rear and one dark brown hackle in front for the legs.

How effective is the Slate Drake as an artificial? I tied about a dozen of the new imitations and put them in my "frustration box" – a box containing a hundred or so seldom-used patterns. Early in July that year several of us traveled to the Loyalsock Creek in north-central Pennsylvania. We hit the "Sock" on one of those evenings when no artificial, large or small, seemed to work.

Evening had arrived and the pool I waded into was now in complete shadow. The pool was a deep one about a quarter-mile long with plenty of fast water at its head. Large dark gray mayflies began emerging profusely along the edges. I captured an emerging dun and recognized it as a Slate Drake. Now I had my chance to go to my frustration box and select a realistic pattern to fish the hatch. On the second cast a large rainbow sucked in the dry fly almost imperceptibly in the fastest water in the pool. When I netted the 15-inch trout I was smiling, elated with the initial feeling of success a new pattern always produces. Meanwhile, Dick Mills had a large hook-jawed rainbow rise to the same artificial 2 feet away from him, but when he lifted his rod to cast again he lost the large fish. That evening we caught three additional trout – none larger than a foot – but this was the beginning of success with the pattern.

In early August of that same year I fished the fabled Willowemoc in New York. It was the middle of the afternoon, and I had fished for two hours without even one strike. Finally, I tied on a fast-water version of the Slate Drake which contained pale gray calf for the tail and dark grayish brown calf for the wings. In less than an hour I had five nice brown trout – all caught on the Slate Drake, and all this action in the middle of an extremely hot afternoon in August when most trout are supposedly inactive.

The imitation is productive in September too. On White Deer Creek, a small but productive trout stream in central Pennsylvania, I saw hundreds of "bicolor" duns appear one early September afternoon. Shortly after noon I entered the stream and began casting the Slate Drake. I casually made one or two casts in a small pool and was ready to move upstream when I saw a flash beneath the artificial. A few casts later to the same area – a strike, and I netted a 15-inch brown trout. Twenty feet upstream I saw another trout working, and on the first cast it hit and I promptly lost it. For most of the day I had similar success, hole after hole, riffle after riffle, pocket after pocket, with the Slate Drake.

In my position with Penn State University I travel quite a bit, registering adults in continuing-education classes. Recently, in September, I had an hour before a scheduled registration in Tunkhannock in northeastern Pennsylvania. On my way to the registration, I stopped off at Bowman's Creek, an excellent but heavily fished stream. I had only a short time to fish, so I left my car with my rod, net, and a box of Slate Drake imitations. I had no time to change clothes, but arrived at the stream with a bright orange shirt, tie, and new shoes. As I approached the stream, I realized how I was dressed, and how I must have appeared to any passerby. On about the tenth cast I hooked a rainbow about 13 inches long, released it, and proceeded to the next pool – one with a large hole under a root. After five fruitless casts I was ready to quit, but like most fly fishermen, I had to make one more cast. The fly landed an inch from the root and immediately disappeared. When it disappeared I heard a noise that sounded as if somebody had thrown a large log in the creek. Nervously, I set the hook and played what I now realized was a large fish. After fifteen minutes and two wet shoes, I landed the 18-inch brown trout which too had succumbed to the Slate Drake.

Since the method of emergence of the *Isonychia* species is unusual, a brief look at the life cycle is important. The nymph is almost always found in fast water. When it's ready to emerge, the nymph swims to shore or a partially exposed rock, crawls completely out of the water, sheds its nymphal skin, and flies to a nearby tree to rest. The method of emergence portrays one distinct disadvantage to imitating this mayfly: the emerging dun is usually not readily available to trout. After a day or two resting on a bush or tree, the dun sheds its skin and becomes the White-Gloved Howdy spinner.

As we just stated, few duns are normally on the water; however, on windy evenings or during periods of high water, many nymphs apparently don't swim to shore but emerge in the stream.

The spinner too can be important throughout the summer, and the imitation of it is effective. I've had more success with the Slate Drake or dun pattern, although I must confess I've used that imitation more than the White Gloved Howdy.

Several years ago when I first used the Slate Drake, I placed it in an inconspicuous compartment of my seldomly used patterns – and now it is one of the most important artificials I have.

THE YELLOW DRAKE EMERGES

We've all heard many success stories about the Green Drake, and probably even the Brown Drake. But who's ever apprised you of the Yellow Drake? If you haven't had the opportunity to fish during an emergence of this impressive mayfly, you're missing a lot of late-season sport.

The Yellow Drake is an important hatch from the angler's and trout's points of view for several reasons. *Ephemera varia* appears in late June and July, well after the last Coffin Fly has deposited its eggs. A full two or three weeks after the Green Drake has ended its annual appearance, the Yellow is just beginning its emergence. The species arrives in small numbers by June 20 – but within a couple days, enough duns are present to produce a fishable hatch.

The Drake is significant also because it emerges for a protracted period and because it's extremely common on many streams and rivers. The Yellow Drake is unusually common for a mayfly so neglected. I have seen hatches on large streams

The Yellow Drake artificial.

like the Beaverkill and the Loyalsock and on rivers like the Little Juniata, but also on small mountain creeks like Six Mile Run in north-central Pennsylvania. The hatch is atypical on the last stream, since most of its stretches are swift, and nymphs of *Ephemera varia* require less rapid stretches to endure. However, there are ample beaver dams and man-made impoundments on Six Mile Run to create the slow-water habitat needed by the nymph. The best hatches on other fast-water streams also seem to occur in sluggish areas.

Finally, the dun of the species commands attention because of its often sluggish takeoff when emerging. Because of this characteristic we gave the dun a rating of 3 on the Insect Emergence Chart in Chapter II. This quality, coupled with moderate size, universality, and appearance at dusk, can and does encourage large trout to capture emerging duns.

With so many advantages to fishing this hatch, you'd think many fly fishermen would plan trips to meet the Yellow Drake. Few anglers, however, do. In all my years of fly fishing, I have seen only a dozen or so anglers who actually fished while this hatch progressed. From these observations, and because this species is common, large, and lethargic, it is probably the most overlooked hatch of the season in the Eastern and Midwestern United States. I've often wondered why the Yellow Drake and other late-season species are neglected by most anglers. Probably low water, fewer trout, and less numerous hatches discourage many from fishing in July and August. Certainly, fishing while the Green Drake emerges is impressive, and meeting and fishing the Michigan Caddis (*Hexagenia limbata*) can be awe-inspiring, but we continue to disregard the Yellow Drake.

I first met this hatch on Mom's Pool on the same Fishing Creek I mentioned earlier. This pool is one of at least three artificial dams created many years ago for milling purposes. Fishing Creek, and especially Mom's Pool, has incredible hatches of *Ephemera varia*. My first visit to this stream was ten years ago on a hot July evening. Since it was an extremely warm day, I decided to cool off by wading in this exceptionally cool mountain water. Mid-July water temperatures barely reach 60 degrees, even during the hottest summer days. More times than I'd like to remember, I've had to back out of the pool during the height of a hatch and rest on the bank to warm up. Several times I've worn long underwear in the middle of the summer to keep warm while wading this water.

As I entered the water I saw only an occasional dun emerge – all were taken readily by one of a dozen or so barn swallows flying 2 or 3 feet above the surface in a swerving flight. As I watched, these acrobatic birds captured two duns still resting on the surface. About 8:00 p.m. three trout began working above me, so I waded upstream within casting distance of the lowest feeding fish. My first cast covered the lowest trout, about 2 feet above it. A bird – it looked like a cedar waxwing – swooped down from a nearby tree, grabbed the artificial, and flew away with it. There I was holding the fly rod in my right hand and looking at the other end of the line, now 10 to 15 feet in the air, propelled by an ambitious but disillusioned waxwing. I guess this is the ultimate in imitations: one so deceptive that it duped a keen-sighted insect-eating bird.

By 8:30 p.m. a major hatch had commenced and a large trout fed consistently on slow-moving duns directly across from me. The lunker rose just a foot or two from a high, rocky ledge on the far shore. My first cast caught a rock on the ledge, and I lost my Yellow Drake artificial. I quickly tied on another imitation, cast above the rising fish, and covered the rise. He struck almost immediately and I set the number 12 hook. The fight was on and the heavy trout ran downstream rapidly, taking out precious line from my reel. I waded through the chilled water downstream with the fish until it stopped, hesitated, then swam back upstream toward its lair under the rock ledge. I knew if it reached the jagged rocks I'd lose it, because there it could easily fray the 5X leader. I put as much pressure on the fragile leader as I could, and successfully turned the heavy trout toward me. It ultimately tired, and moved to the surface near me. I scooped the net under it, and triumphantly lifted an 18-inch golden brown trout out of the water. Now I really felt the chill of the water; besides, darkness had encompassed the stream, and the imitation was hopelessly soaked, so I decided to quit.

Tom Bean of Noxen, near Bowman's Creek in northeastern Pennsylvania, is one of those few fly fishermen who consistently plans his fishing trips around the Yellow Drake emergence. He visits nightly a section of Bowman's called Botnick's Pool. Here is an ideal stretch for the *Ephemera varia* nymph. Botnick's is about a quarter of a mile of very slow water formed by a 2-foot-high breast of stream-gathered rocks. Nightly, from late June until early August, Tom fishes this deep, slow water with much success.

Recently, Tom returned home one night and asked me to duplicate the dry fly he had in his hand. The only problem was that the imitation he showed me no longer had wings or hackle, but just a piece of yellow yarn. He had just caught several large trout on the artificial, and now the fly was mutilated beyond recognition. When Tom described the original dry fly and the hatch he had met I surmised that the fly was the Yellow Drake and the hatch was *Ephemera varia*.

I tied a few imitations for Tom, and accompanied him on his next trip to Botnick's Pool. When we climbed down the steep cliff leading to the stream, we saw a few Yellow Drakes already emerging. Several small trout seized some of the naturals, but Tom suggested we wait until some of the lunkers fed. In a few minutes a huge fish began gulping the yellow mayflies under a hemlock about 15 feet away from Tom. He immediately cast toward the rising trout. On the second attempt the trout rose to the artificial, seized it, and swam to the bottom of the pool. The fish stayed deep and headed downstream toward the breast. Tom waded along the shoreline, following the fighting trout. After fifteen minutes the huge brown trout lost much of its strength and now swam aimlessly near the surface. I quickly got in position with my net, lowered it into the water, and lifted up a 23-inch beauty.

Night after night Tom does well with the Yellow Drake imitation.

Spinner falls for this species occur about the same time or a little earlier than the dun. Since the spinner resembles the dun, one imitation will work double duty.

Don't overlook the Yellow Drake if you want some late-season action.

Chapter IX
Fishing the Un-Hatches

You've arrived at your favorite stream on a good average date to fish when a common mayfly species is supposed to emerge. Even though you've planned every detail thoroughly, and have followed the four rules for meeting and fishing the hatches, the expected hatch doesn't appear. Or the predicted hatch does emerge, but in very limited numbers. What do you do now? There are several options open to you. First, you might wait until dusk for a spinner fall. Second, you might use a dry fly imitating a species that recently emerged from the stream. Third, you might want to try an attractor pattern. Fourth, imitations of terrestrial insects like the ant, beetle, grasshopper, and cricket can be effective on these days of sparse hatches. Sure there are other alternatives – you could use a wet fly, streamer, or nymph – but suppose you want to rely on dry flies.

We'll exclude option 1, waiting for a spinner fall, and examine the latter three. Using an imitation of a species which possibly emerged the past couple days is a valid suggestion. If trout have been feeding on the Pale Evening Dun for the past couple weeks, then that pattern might be effective even though no naturals appear that night. Imitations of a species are often productive long after the hatch has ended.

The second option we'll examine is using an attractor pattern. What? You say it's sacrilegious to discuss attractor patterns in a text devoted to matching hatches with exact imitations? Not under these circumstances – not when a hatch is absent. Furthermore, attractor patterns are often very effective.

Attractors do not copy specific insects. Rather, they may or may not have the proper shape and form of a mayfly, stonefly, caddis fly, or another insect (or spider, etc.); and often the artificials are bizarre. The patterns might be so outlandish that they possibly irritate trout into striking – or they might even suggest an unusually juicy morsel.

Two attractors, especially the Wulff Royal Coachman and the Trout Fin, can be very productive dry flies during an un-hatch in the East and Midwest. These two patterns even succeed, sometimes unbelievably, during hatches.

Several years ago I fished while thousands of *Tricorythodes* spinners fell spent on Falling Springs. The imitation I used for the female spinner was virtually ineffective, even though it was difficult to distinguish it from the natural. In a frustrated moment during the spinner fall, I tied a size 16 Wulff Royal Coachman onto the tippet and cast the dry fly above trout rising to *Tricorythodes* naturals. These

Three good attractor patterns (from left to right): the Trout Fin, Goofus, and Royal Coachman.

naturals of course are appropriately duplicated by a size 24 Reverse Jenny Spinner. On many occasions trout approached the Coachman, nudged it or swirled under it, and returned to their feeding positions. Other trout followed the attractor on its drift downstream for 3 or 4 feet, and these too returned to their original feeding spots without touching the dry fly. But several trout followed the artificial for some distance and slowly gulped it in. Why in the world would a trout take an oversized pattern like a size 16 Coachman during a fantastic *Tricorythodes* spinner fall? Sometimes the Coachman works well during a hatch or spinner fall; but it and the Trout Fin also are effective during the un-hatches.

A few years ago I met a late-season angler, John Weaver, on Bowman's Creek. His creel bulged with trout, and I asked if I could see his catch. When he opened the wet creel, I saw four large browns.

"What are you using?"

"The Trout Fin – it's the only thing to use this late in the season," he said.

"Could I see one of the artificials?"

"Sure. The one I've been using is pretty ragged now," John said as he showed me the damaged dry fly attached to his leader.

It was an odd-looking pattern, one I had never seen before. It had white quill wings, furnace hackle, furnace hackle fibers for the tail, and a bright orange floss body.

With tongue in cheek I asked, "When does the mayfly that this dry fly imitates emerge?"

He looked at me for what seemed like a minute and said, "It doesn't imitate any insect, and besides, no mayflies are on the water tonight."

Before he left that evening, John gave me a couple Trout Fins and suggested that I use them on my next trip. I conveniently placed the artificials in the "seldom-used" section of my fly box and promptly forgot about them.

A week later, on the same stretch of water, I again met John with another heavy creel full of trout. He asked if I had tested the Trout Fin yet. When I indicated that I hadn't, he again urged me to try the dry fly during the late-season no-hatch time. I decided now I would test the Trout Fin on the next trip, which was planned for Penn's Creek the following weekend.

Several of us arrived at the Cherry Run section of Penn's Creek early Saturday morning. I was anxious to use the Trout Fin and had tied a dozen size 12s the night before. No insects were on the water and no trout rose – this was an ideal time to use the Trout Fin. I started fishing at the head of a long pool where fast water from the rapids above slowed into a moderate stretch of what looked like productive water. On the second cast a heavy trout cruised toward the artificial. The trout drifted with the floating fly, but a foot or two behind it. Finally, 5 feet downstream, the large brown sucked in the Trout Fin. This same type of success occurred all day, cast after cast, pool after pool. I caught more than twenty trout on that damned Trout Fin that day!

The un-hatch occurs more often than the hatch on many streams. Here's where an attractor pattern can be important. Look at small mountain streams. Have you seen any profuse hatches on many of these small brooks? Look also at marginal water – streams located just outside large metropolitan areas. These streams are stocked heavily early in the season only because of their proximity to many anglers. Many of these streams are almost void of nymphal life. Few hatches occur on many of these waters, and those that do appear do so in limited numbers.

In the West too the un-hatches are often more important than the hatches. On many occasions I've seen streams void of mayflies, caddis flies, and stoneflies. What patterns are effective on these trips?

Again, the Wulff Royal Coachman has produced some exciting fly fishing for me on Western streams. I entered the Madison River on the lower end of Yellowstone Park one hot July afternoon. No insects emerged and of course no trout surfaced. I immediately checked the water temperature and noted a 73-degree reading. At this point I almost backed out of the water and returned to the car. But this was only the second opportunity I had had to fish this productive section of water, so I decided to stay and try the Coachman. The Coachman I used had three stiff hackles – I recommend three rather than two when fishing many of the faster Western rivers.

The stretch of water I entered contained all moderate to fast water. During the first fifteen minutes I had no strikes, and again almost decided to retrace my steps back to my car. But before I did I wanted to cast over one more deep pocket of water upstream a few feet.

On the second cast over this deep pocket the artificial floated directly over a submerged boulder and promptly disappeared. I set the hook on the attractor, and for a few seconds didn't know whether I had hooked concealed debris or a fish. Suddenly the snag began to move downstream slowly – no rapid movement, but rather a planned retreat toward the rapids below. The heavy fish stayed deep, not once showing its color. Finally, I turned the trout upstream toward me, and urged

A Wulff Royal Coachman used on Western streams. Note the heavy body and dense hackle.

it to follow me to the shore with as much pressure as I felt the 4x tippet could withstand. I beached the 4-pound brown and gently unhooked the Coachman from its lower jaw.

On another occasion with the Wulff Royal Coachman I had phenomenal success. This occurred on the Buffalo River near Island Park, Idaho. During the first few hours of morning fishing I noted only a few *Epeorus albertae* spinners above the water – none of these touched the surface. Several large *Acroneuria* stoneflies fluttered to the surface to lay their eggs and were captured almost immediately by trout. I decided to stay with the Coachman and caught more than twenty trout in two hours of fishing.

Are there other attractor patterns which are productive on Western waters? The Goofus (also called the Goofus Bug and Humpy), Royal Humpy, and Renegade consistently take trout during the un-hatches.

Recently I watched a local fisherman use the Renegade on the Buffalo River, near Box Canyon. On almost every cast he caught a rainbow – some of them were 2 pounds and heavier. This pattern seems to work equally well as a wet or dry fly.

The Humpy or Goofus reminds me of a high-riding Coachman. The difference of course is the deer-hair back on the Goofus. Body colors on these dry flies vary from red to green to yellow, and all are effective patterns.

During the next un-hatch, whether you're fishing Eastern, Midwestern, or Western streams, you can use an imitation of a dun or spinner which recently emerged. Or you can try an attractor pattern like the Goofus or Wulff Royal Coachman.

Chapter X
Meeting the Western Hatches

In Chapter I we discussed the four rules to follow if you plan to meet any of the mayfly hatches. These four rules are to fish while a common mayfly (or caddis fly or stonefly) emerges, at an appropriate date and time for that species, and on a good stream where this species occurs. But to meet Western hatches other factors are important. These other factors are water temperature, altitude or elevation, water discharge, and weather.

If these are the only additional rules (or variables), and if we recognize and understand them, then why is meeting Western hatches risky? Mainly because the West, especially the Rocky Mountain area, is a land of contrasts. Water temperatures, stream elevations, and water flow vary considerably from river to river, and they can vary substantially from stretch to stretch on the same water. Of course, stream flow, water temperature, and weather affect Eastern and Midwestern hatches, but these regions often lack the extreme variability of the West. I will discuss water temperature, altitude, water flow, and weather, and attempt to demonstrate how diverse these factors are on Western streams, and how this diversity seems to affect the predictable appearance of many mayfly species. To put this another way, these factors (water temperature, altitude, etc.) may influence the dates and times a mayfly emerges, and the stream on which it emerges.

Steve Jensen in his excellent master's thesis, *Mayflies of Idaho,* suggests that some Western mayfly species often emerge within predictable temperature, elevation, and stream-flow limits. Many authors writing about Western hatches have indicated that *Epeorus longimanus* replaces *E. albertae* on higher elevations of the same stream. Others have mentioned that *Ephemerella coloradensis* replaces its sister species *E. flavilinea* on higher sections of the same streams.

If we take a closer look at the Blue-Winged Olive Dun, *Ephemerella flavilinea,* using all the variables, we'll more fully understand the ingredients necessary to meet the hatches. Jensen suggests that this species usually appears when the water temperature is between 45 and 65 degrees, on moderate stretches of water, at elevations ranging from 4,000 to 6,500 feet. When I first met this species, I did so on Henry's Fork near Island Park, Idaho. The altitude of Henry's Fork at this point is 6,150 feet, well within the prescribed range. During this initial meeting and at the beginning of the emergence, I recorded a water temperature of 59 degrees. What would have happened if I had been fishing a stream at an elevation below

The Blue River is an example of a high-altitude stream. The elevation of this Colorado stream at this area is 8,120 feet.

4,000 feet or in water warmer than 65 degrees? I might not have met the Blue-Winged Olive Dun.

Therefore, in addition to approximate time of day (usually in the evening for *Ephemerella flavilinea*), the time of year (late June or July), a good stream (Henry's Fork), and a common species, elevation and water temperature are also important.

But, just when we've pinpointed the variables necessary to meet the Western hatches, we're confronted with another problem – diversity. Water temperatures vary tremendously from stream to stream. To illustrate the latter, look at the Madison River. On the Madison in Yellowstone Park I recorded a temperature of 73 degrees at 4:00 p.m. one day. The next day, 20 miles below Hebgen Lake, on the same Madison River, I noted a 57-degree water temperature, again at 4:00 p.m. Why this difference? The upper Madison is influenced extensively by the geysers and thermal waters of Yellowstone Park, whereas the section below is fed continuously by melting snow and water from the bottom of Hebgen Lake.

Following is a further indication of this water-temperature variability. These are water temperatures recorded on various rivers from July 7 to July 12 – all recorded from 4:00 to 7:00 p.m.

Gallatin River, Specimen Creek area, July 11: 47 degrees
Bitterroot River, Florence, Montana, July 7: 54 degrees
South Fork of the Madison River, West Yellowstone area: 54 degrees
Yellowstone River, Corbin Springs area, July 9: 56 degrees
Henry's Fork, Island Park, Idaho, July 12: 60 degrees
Clark Fork, Deer Lodge, Montana, July 8: 64 degrees
Gibbon River (lower section), Yellowstone Park, July 10: 72 degrees
Madison River, Yellowstone Park, July 10: 73 degrees

This is diversity! In a matter of 25 miles in the West Yellowstone area we have the warm upper Madison River and the cold Gallatin River – the Gallatin River had afternoon temperatures in the middle to upper 40s, whereas the Madison registered 73 degrees.

Why does the water temperature vary so greatly? Melting snow affects many Western stream temperatures much of the summer. The Bitterroot is typical; every few miles another feeder stream pours in additional cold water from melting snow from the Bitterroot Range, just a few miles away. Temperatures on this stream remain cold throughout July. Any river flowing any distance without these colder feeder streams will often warm considerably; this is what happens to Clark Fork in northwestern Montana.

If mayfly species emerge at fairly specific water temperatures, and Western streams are highly diverse in these temperatures, then predicting emergence dates for many Western species is impossible. Wrong! Sure, it will be more of a hit-and-miss proposition than in the East and Midwest, but many hatches can be met with some degree of accuracy – especially hatches on the same stream from year to year. Other hatches, like *Tricorythodes* species and *Heptagenia solitaria* (Gray Fox), which appear over much of the season, are also fairly easy to meet.

But many Western species also exhibit a preference for fairly specific elevation ranges. *Callibaetis coloradensis* is usually found on lakes of streams with slow water above 5,000 feet, whereas *Callibaetis nigritus* is found on the same type of water, but below 4,500 feet.

Let's look at some typical Western streams and the elevations they attain at various locations.

Blue River, Dillon, Colorado: 8,760 feet
Colorado River, Kremmling, Colorado: 7,300 feet
Firehole River, Grand Loop Area, Yellowstone Park: 7,154 feet
Henry's Fork, Box Canyon area: 6,300 feet
Bitterroot River, Victor, Montana: 3,400 feet
Clark Fork River, Tarkio, Montana: 2,900 feet

Again we have extreme diversity. If many mayfly species inhabit only waters at specific elevations, then many streams will be void of many species, or contain them on only limited stretches. Over the years I've found altitude to be the least

A slow section of the Colorado River near Kremmling, Colorado. Good hatches of *Callibaetis nigritus*, *Tricorythodes minutus*, and *Heptagenia solitaria* occur here in early fall.

dependable variable. If all other conditions are appropriate for a given species, except for elevation, then a mayfly might be found at a higher or lower altitude than that listed in the Insect Emergence Chart in Chapter II.

Western streams also vary considerably in their velocity and discharge. Many waters are extremely fast, especially during spring and summer runoff. By mid-July most waters finally subside and become fishable (especially for the dry-fly fisherman). Again the West has contrast. Some of the streams in Yellowstone Park are fishable in April, May, and June. Streams also vary in velocity. Velocity seriously affects which mayfly species inhabit a stream. Flow varies from very slow, like portions of Henry's Fork in Idaho and the Colorado River in Colorado, to moderate-flowing rivers, like the Bitterroot River in Montana and the Blue River in Colorado, to rapid streams, a good example being the Gallatin River in southwestern Montana.

Of course another factor which affects hatching activity is weather. Again the West, especially the Rocky Mountains, has weather extremes. Weather too affects the predictability of meeting the hatches. Charlie Brooks of West Yellowstone tells me that he's fished in snowstorms in June, July, and August. This of course is not typical, since daytime temperatures often near 90 degrees in midsummer. A sudden cold snap, a heat wave, a cold rain, a late-summer snowstorm – all affect tremendously the fly fisherman's effort to meet the hatches.

Thus variations in water temperature, elevation, water discharge, and weather all make it difficult to meet the hatches. However, if we keep all the aforementioned cautions in mind, we can often meet and fish Western hatches – not always, but often. Since temperature, elevation (to a limited degree), and velocity affect the appearance of many mayfly species, we have listed them in the Insect Emergence Chart for Western species.

Because of the added variables, it's important to consult local fishermen for stream conditions, current hatches, hot spots, etc. Following is a list of reputable sporting-goods stores near Western streams. These stores, along with many others not mentioned, have competent personnel to keep you aware of needed information. Since hatches are not as predictable in the West as they are in the East and Midwest, I strongly urge you to stop in at one of these or any other to ascertain emergence activity.

Anglers All
5211 South Santa Fe Drive
Littleton, Colorado 80120

Streamside Anglers
1109 W. Broadway
Missoula, Montana 59801

Dan Bailey — Flies and Tackle
209 W. Park
Livingston, Montana 59047

Will's Fly Fishing Center
P.O. Box 68
Island Park, Idaho 83429

Bud Lilly's Trout Shop
West Yellowstone, Montana 59758

Let's look at three hatches I met recently, and compare the information on these variables with those listed in the Insect Emergence Chart.

Species	Date	Time	Water Temperature[1]	Elevation[2]	Flow[3]
Ephemerella flavilinea	July 10	8:00 p.m.	59	6150	
Chart data	June 15 and later	Evening	M&C	M&H	M
Paraleptophlebia memorialis	July 18	1:00 p.m.	64	3450	S
Chart data	July 1 and later	Morning and afternoon	M&C	A	A
Ephemerella grandis	July 6	11:30 a.m.	54	3450	M
Chart data	June 5 and later	Late morning and afternoon	M&C	L&M	M

[1] Water temperature: Cold (C) is below 55 degrees, moderate (M) is from 55 to 65.
[2] Elevation: Low (L) is below 4,000 feet, moderate (M) is from 4,000 to 7,000 feet, high (H) is above 7,000 feet; (A) means all elevations.
[3] Flow: (S) means slow, (M) means moderate.

These hatches and many, many more were major hatches, and all were met because emergence dates, times, water temperatures, elevations, and water flows were appropriate for the species.

One other ingredient we have not mentioned is the size of the stream. As we said in Chapter I, some species are found in small streams, others in larger streams, others in rivers, others in lakes and ponds, and a few species are found in all of these. This element too is important.

With all these cautions in mind for meeting the hatches, we'll look at fishing the Western hatches in the next three chapters. We'll look at the Red Quill and its effectiveness as an imitation in the morning, afternoon, and evening. Also we'll study the Western Green Drake through a story about morning fishing. Then we'll examine an afternoon emerger, the Little Dark Brown Dun. Finally we'll scrutinize evening hatches by looking at the downwings, and a story about an evening spinner fall on the Colorado.

Chapter XI

Fishing the Morning Hatches

(*Western*)

In the list below, (A) indicates that hatches or spinner falls also often occur in the afternoon, (E) that they often occur in the evening. Dates listed are very approximate; remember that Western dates are even less precise than Eastern and Midwestern.

Duns

Baetis tricaudatus (A & E) – Little Blue Dun; late morning, afternoon, and early evening; April to November[1]

Baetis intermedius (A & E) – Little Blue Dun; late morning, afternoon, and early evening; April to November[1]

Ephemerella inermis (A & E) – Pale Morning Dun[1]; late morning, afternoon, and early evening; May 25[1]

Cinygmula ramaleyi – Dark Red Quill; late morning; May 25

Pteronarcys californica (stonefly) – Salmon Fly; emergence often occurs in the morning, but egglaying can happen almost any time of the day or evening; May to August, depending on the stream

Acroneuria pacifica – Willow Stonefly; egglaying phase can occur almost any time of day or evening; June and July

Callibaetis nigritus (A) – Speckle-Winged Dun; late morning; June to October[1]

Baetis bicaudatus (A & E) – Pale Olive Dun; late morning, afternoon, and early evening; June through October[1]

Paraleptophlebia heteronea (A) – Dark Blue Quill; morning and afternoon, June 1

Ephemerella grandis (A) – Western Green Drake; late morning and afternoon; June 5 (hatches appear in mid-June on the Upper Madison and Henry's Fork)

Ephemerella tibialis (A) – Red Quill; late morning and afternoon; June 5

Callibaetis coloradensis (A) – Speckle-Winged Dun; late morning and early afternoon; June 12[1]

Epeorus longimanus (A) – Quill Gordon; late morning and early afternoon; June 12

Ephemerella flavilinea (E) – Blue-Winged Olive Dun; midmorning and evening (evening hatch seems to be more important); June 15

Ephemerella doddsi (A) – Western Green Drake; late morning and afternoon; June 15

[1] Hatches or spinner falls may occur for many days.
[2] Hatches or spinner falls may occur before date listed.
[3] Color varies and common name may be inappropriate.
[4] Not listed in Emergence Chart, but may be important.

Baetis parvus (A & E) – Dark Brown Dun; late morning, afternoon and early evening; June 20

Ephemerella infrequens (A) – Pale Morning Dun[1]; late morning and afternoon; July 1 (hatches occur until mid-August on colder streams)

Paraleptophlebia memorialis (A) – Dark Blue Quill; morning and afternoon; July 1

Rhithrogena futilis (A) – Quill Gordon; late morning and afternoon; July 1[2]

Cinygmula reticulata (A) – Pale Brown Dun; late morning and afternoon; July 5[2]

Paraleptophlebia vaciva (A) – Dark Blue Quill; morning and afternoon; July 5

Paraleptophlebia debilis (A) – Dark Blue Quill; morning and afternoon; July 5[1]

Siphlonurus occidentalis (A) – Gray Drake; late morning and afternoon; July 5 (hatches occur well into August)

Rhithrogena hageni (A) – Pale Brown Dun; late morning and afternoon; July 10

Ameletus cooki (A) – Dark Brown Dun; late morning and afternoon; July 10[2]

Rhithrogena undulata (A) – Quill Gordon[3]; morning and afternoon; July 10[2]

Tricorythodes minutus – Pale Olive Dun; morning (duns sometime appear as late as 11:00 a.m.); July 15[1]

Paraleptophlebia packii[4] (A) – Dark Blue Quill; morning and afternoon; July 20

Ephemerella coloradensis (A) – Dark Olive Dun[3]; midday; August 1

Paraleptophlebia bicornuta (A) – Dark Blue Quill; morning and afternoon; September 10[2]

Spinners

Baetis tricaudatus (E) – Light Rusty Spinner; early morning and evening (evening seems to have the larger spinner falls on many occasions – this goes for many of the *Baetis* species); April to November[1]

Baetis intermedius (E) – Dark Rusty Spinner; early morning and evening; April to November[1]

Ephemerella inermis (E) – Pale Morning Spinner; morning and evening; May 26[1]

Cinygmula ramaleyi (A) – Red Quill Spinner; late morning and early afternoon; May 28

Baetis bicaudatus (E) – Light Rusty Spinner; morning and evening; June through October[1]

Callibaetis nigritus (A) – Speckle-Winged Spinner; late morning; June to October[1]

Paraleptophlebia heteronea (A) – Dark Brown Spinner; morning and afternoon; June 2

Callibaetis coloradensis – Speckle-Winged Spinner; late morning; June 13[1]

Ephemerella flavilinea (E) – Dark Olive Spinner; morning and evening; June 16

Baetis parvus (E) – Dark Brown Spinner; morning and evening; June 21

Ephemerella infrequens (E) – Rusty Spinner[3]; morning and evening; July 2

Paraleptophlebia memorialis (A) – Dark Brown Spinner; morning and afternoon; July 2

Epeorus albertae (E) – Salmon Spinner (male is Light Cahill); morning and evening (morning spinner fall seems to be more protracted, but evening fall might be heavier); July 6

Cinygmula reticulata – Dark Rusty Spinner; early morning; July 6[2]

Heptagenia solitaria (E) – Ginger Quill Spinner; late morning and evening (evening seems to be heavier); July 6[1]

Paraleptophlebia debilis (A) – Dark Brown Spinner; morning and afternoon; July 6[1]

Siphlonurus occidentalis (E) – Brown Quill Spinner; morning and evening (evening seems to be heavier); July 6[1]

Rhithrogena hageni (E) – Dark Tan Spinner; morning and evening; July 11

Tricorythodes minutus – Reverse Jenny Spinner (female), Dark Brown Spinner (male); morning (can continue into early afternoon in September); July 15

Paraleptophlebia packii (A) – Dark Brown Spinner; morning and afternoon; July 21

Paraleptophlebia bicornuta (A) – Dark Brown Spinner; morning and afternoon; September 11[2]

Morning fishing in the West – the time of the Pale Morning Duns, the time of the Western Green Drake, the time of the Speckle Wings, and yes, the time of the Pale Olive Duns (*Tricorythodes*). Morning fishing, especially fly fishing, can be rewarding if you plan to meet and fish while one of the almost-endless early-day hatches occurs.

We meet some spectacular hatches in the morning, none probably more remarkable than the Western Green Drake (*Ephemerella grandis*). These mayflies, which are apt to appear on some streams as early as mid-June, begin their daily emergence as early as 10:00 a.m. These Drake duns always amaze me because they habitually emerge on moderate to fast stretches, still extremely high from spring runoff. The duns are awkward in their takeoff, and consistently rest on the surface for long distances. On many occasions I've noted hundreds of subimagos on the water, but none in the air. Most duns were either victims of the fast water or of rising trout. Even though rivers are high during the time they emerge, trout eagerly take the struggling duns.

The Western Green Drake with a hair wing.

At about the same time the Green Drake appears, so does *Rhithrogena futilis*. This moderate-sized mayfly is also slow in its takeoff from the water and can be important to meet and fish. I've dubbed the dun and spinner of this species Quill Gordons because they remind me so much of the Eastern species *Epeorus pleualis*. I've noted this dark gray dun on the water many days during late June and early July from 10:00 a.m. to 2:00 or 3:00 p.m.

The morning sector contains some other important hatches to meet and fish. In middle to late June *Ephemerella inermis* begins its annual appearance. This species is often called the Pale Morning Dun and usually initially appears daily about 10:00 a.m. On streams like Henry's Fork the Pale Morning Dun continues appearing until 7:00 p.m. Duns are on the water for many weeks and often, especially after late June, produce fishable hatches for hours. *Ephemerella inermis* is unbelievably variable in color, especially body color. I've seen tan, olive, reddish brown, and pale yellow mayflies – and all have been identified as members of this species.

Concomitant with *Ephemerella inermis* is its sister species *E. infrequens*. These subimagos too are commonly dubbed Pale Morning Duns. *E. infrequens* also varies tremendously in color. Body color of duns ranges from tan to pale yellow with an olive cast. Duns usually begin appearing around 11:00 a.m. in early July.

And the list of morning-emergers goes on and on. If you fish slow streams, lakes, or ponds you're apt to encounter one of the Speckle Wings that consistently appear around 11:00 a.m. *Callibaetis* species (Speckle Wings), many of which are multi-brooded, appear from mid-June through much of September. The Colorado, and to a lesser extent the Blue River, has respectable *Callibaetis* hatches.

Morning is also the time for the Dark Blue Quill to start its appearance. *Paraleptophlebia* species appear from late May until September or October, almost without interruption on many Western streams. *Paraleptophlebia heteronea* is one of the earliest of the Blue Quills to appear, often emerging in early June. The genus continues to appear in July with *P. debilis* and *P. memorialis* emerging, and on into September and October when *P. debilis* and *P. bicornuta* appear. Most species of this genus emerge from midmorning until midafternoon, and spinners are active at the same time.

Morning is also the time for several species to complete their life cycle by mating and laying eggs. On any morning in July you might encounter active spinners of *Epeorus albertae* (Salmon Spinner) or *Siphlonurus occidentalis* (Brown Quill Spinner). Both species also mate in the evening, and the latter time slot seems to harbor the heavier falls. There are other spinners that can be seen mating in the morning. *Ephemerella infrequens* and *E. flavilinea* can produce fishable morning spinner falls. *E. infrequens* is often imitated with the Rusty Spinner (because of color variation this common name might not be appropriate), and *E. flavilinea* with the Dark Olive Spinner. Spinners of *Heptagenia solitaria* also can be observed in the morning and evening. As with the Salmon Spinner and Brown Quill Spinner more Ginger Quills seem to fall in the evening.

Even into September many mayfly species emerge and fall in the morning. *Tricorythodes minutus*, which first appears in mid-July, continues well into September almost every morning on many of the slower, silted rivers in the West like the Colorado in central Colorado.

Want to fish while some excellent hatches appear? Then try morning fishing in the West. Almost any month of the season you can fish while morning hatches and spinner falls occur.

A DRY FLY FOR ALL DAY AND
ALL SUMMER IN THE WEST

There's an imitation which effectively matches many Western mayfly species. This dry fly duplicates mayflies which emerge in May, June, July, August, and September. This same dry fly copies species which appear in the morning, afternoon, and evening. Furthermore, this artificial is productive on many of the Western streams. It has provided success on the Bitterroot and Blackfoot in northwestern Montana, on the Box Canyon Area of Henry's Fork in Idaho, and on the Colorado, Blue, and Eagle in Colorado.

The same Red Quill so effective in the East and Midwest is also an effective Western pattern.

What dry fly is so effective, so many days of the year, on so many streams? It's the Red Quill. If this artificial imitates so many mayflies so closely, and is productive almost any time of day, on many streams, then the Red Quill should be an extensively used pattern on Western waters. But let me cite an experience I had in trying to obtain more Red Quills one day. A year before I had mutilated my last three Red Quills – or rather a few heavy trout did – and I visited two well-known sporting-goods stores to replenish my supply. Neither store had any Red Quills on hand; in fact, one of them said they never stocked the imitation. One salesman tried to sell me some Quill Gordons, urging me that they were very close to the Red Quill. In desperation, I returned to my motel room, unpacked my fly-tying supplies, and tied several of the red-bodied imitations. I needed them the next day for a planned fishing trip to the Bitterroot River.

As indicated before, the Red Quill is productive in the morning. One morning, around 10:00 a.m. in mid-July, I fished the Bitterroot River just south of Florence, Montana. I entered the tail of a long pool that had been formed by a huge, half-submerged pine tree. As I scanned the surface I noted four trout rising to a sporadic hatch. Although there were few naturals on the water, those that did appear rested a long time before taking off. I quickly captured several duns and saw that they had tannish red bodies and could be correctly imitated with a size 16 Red Quill. I tied a Red Quill onto the tippet and cast above one of the four fish now surfacing. Each trout rising to the naturals in that pool quickly seized the imitation. All four of the trout were heavy rainbows that had been feeding on that red-bodied morning hatch.

This productive morning mayfly was later identified as *Ephemerella inermis,* the Pale Morning Dun. As I have suggested many times before, members of this species vary considerably in body coloration.

The Red Quill is also effective in the afternoon. A few miles upstream from Florence I met an exciting prolific spinner fall one late-July afternoon, again on the Bitterroot. Little feeding occurred before 1:00 p.m. – a few Gray Dakes and Dark Blue Quills appeared on some slow water in a nearby sandbar, but no trout fed on these. Suddenly, several trout began feeding voraciously on spent spinners directly in front of me. I stood at the head of a pool where the fast water channeled into a narrow, but deep, fast stretch. I searched the eddy near the fast water, and observed a few, than a hundred or so bright red spinners spent on the surface. These red imagos (*Rhithrogena undulata*) too could be appropriately matched with the Red Quill.

I hurriedly tied on a size 14 imitation and cast directly upstream into the fast water in the channel. Five trout now freely fed on these red spinners, and quickly seized the imitation. But trout that I didn't see taking naturals also took the artificial. Spinners fell and trout fed until almost 3:00 p.m., when the last available spent female was captured near my feet by a small trout.

During that hot Montana afternoon, in the middle of the summer when fly fishing is supposed to be poorest, I had met and fished while a great spinner fall occurred. In the two-hour period of the spinner fall, I had hooked and released fifteen trout on a Red Quill. The Red Quill is an effective afternoon pattern, especially when a spinner fall occurs.

But the Red Quill is also an excellent choice for evening fishing. I remember an evening on the Blackfoot River near Potomac in Montana. When I arrived at the river in early July, I stood near a cliff overlooking a long fast stretch. I wondered what mayflies would inhabit this rapid section, but I did observe several trout already.

By the time I had climbed down to the stream, thousands of caddis flies had begun to abandon nearby bushes and trees and move toward the center of the river to lay their eggs. About 7:30 p.m. I noticed hundreds of *Rhithrogena undulata* spinners hovering near trees where they had recently shed their pellicle (subimagal skin). I captured several males and quickly concluded that these adults too

A section of the Blackfoot River in northwestern Montana. Hatches of *Rhithrogena undulata* are common on this stream.

(females may be lighter) could be copied with the Red Quill. The *Rhithrogena undulata* spinner on the Blackfoot is somewhat darker than the same species on the Bitterroot, but I felt confident that the same Red Quill which had proved to be so successful on the latter stream would suffice here on the Blackfoot.

A trout surfaced barely a foot from the shore. I covered it on the second cast and the foot-long rainbow hit immediately. Every tenth or fifteenth cast seemed to produce a trout on that fast section – and all this action happened with the effective, productive Red Quill. Although trout rose intermittently throughout the evening, I never noted one natural, especially one looking like the Red Quill, on the water.

I quit that evening on the Blackfoot about 9:00 p.m., but only after a dozen or more trout had seized that Red Quill dry fly.

The Red Quill is effective in August and September. I remember the first evening that I met the *Heptagenia solitaria* imago, on the Eagle River in Colorado. This spinner is better imitated with the Ginger Quill, but I didn't have any Ginger

Quills with me on that initial meeting. The Red Quill proved to be an excellent substitute.

Morning, afternoon, or evening – May, June, July, August, and even September – the Red Quill is an imitation which can be productive in the West. If the Slate Drake is an imitation for all summer in the East, the Red Quill is an imitation for all season in the West.

A MORNING ON THE BITTERROOT WITH THE WESTERN GREEN DRAKE

I arrived on the Bitterroot River one midmorning in late June. Spring runoff still created fast, extremely high water. The water temperature barely reached the 50-degree mark. Pine trees, uprooted by the tremendous force of the purging water, lay in the slower areas of the stream. The river appeared to be 3 or 4 feet above its normal late-summer flow. How in the world would I ever catch trout on dry flies under these circumstances?

Rather than fish I sat by the stream, mesmerized by the rapid, churning water. A good hatch of *Ephemerella infrequens* duns appeared shortly after I arrived. Nothing, however, rose for these moderate-sized mayflies, although the hatch became heavier. By 10:30 a.m. Quill Gordons (*Rhithrogena futilis*), a larger mayfly, joined the smaller *Ephemerella infrequens* (Pale Morning Dun). Both species rested on the surface for protracted periods before flying to nearby trees. But no trout rose to either species. At this point I seriously doubted that any trout would surface-feed under these adverse conditions.

Then, about 11:00 a.m., a much larger mayfly appeared. Two of these mayflies fluttered aimlessly in an eddy created by two uprooted trees. Then three of these large mayflies appeared, then four.

I stood below the uprooted trees to catch and identify these mayflies. While I waited for the duns to reach me, three separate trout surfaced for the duns before I could capture one of them. I soon did collect a couple male duns and assumed that from the dark grayish black coloration and green cast that these were Green Drakes (*Ephemerella grandis*).

Weren't these duns supposed to have bright green bodies? I knew that they lost the green cast rapidly, but I captured several and studied the duns within seconds of their appearance. These duns, as well as some duns I saw on the upper section of the Gibbon River, had a distinct greenish cast, but they were not green. Evidently, here's another example of the tremendous color variation the same species exhibits on various different Western streams (and probably to some extent on the same stream).

But I had only a bright green imitation with me that morning. I tied one on anyway, and cast above one of the three rising trout. On the first drift over one of the trout, I noticed a rapid movement directly beneath the artificial, but no strike. On the third or fourth cast that movement became a strike as a heavy rainbow sucked in the Green Drake imitation. The fish leaped out of the swollen water, then headed deep, and wound my leader around some submerged debris.

Four trout hit that Green Drake dry fly that morning before I decided to quit. No, that's not an unusually high number; but under the extremely poor early-summer stream conditions I was satisfied.

It was now 2:00 p.m. and I headed back to my car. As I did, an occasional trout still rose to the sporadic Green Drakes. Plenty of Pale Morning Duns and Quill Gordons still appeared, but not once did I see a trout take either.

I hurried back to my motel that afternoon – I had a lot of fly tying to complete before I fished again the next morning. I wanted to copy the Bitterroot version of the Western Green Drake more closely. I tied a half-dozen imitations which had bodies of dark grayish black polypropylene mixed with a small amount of the same material, but green. I ribbed each body with pale yellow thread. Now I was prepared to fish the hatch the next day. The question that went through my mind that evening was, would the hatch appear tomorrow, or was it finished for the year? Only a visit to the stream could tell.

The next morning proved to be even more successful on the Bitterroot. I arrived at the same pool, sat on the same bank, and waited for something to happen. Almost immediately, around 10:30 a.m., the first Green Drakes appeared. No sudden or heavy appearance – just a few duns emerging at the head of the pool every five or ten minutes. But almost every time one of these large mayflies attempted to leave the surface, the fluttering action attracted trout.

One trout rose near the head of the pool, two or three in the center, and one took laggards that had floated the length of the hole near the tail. This is great fly fishing. First, you know that even though the hatch is less than concentrated, the duns drift on the surface for an extended period, and this encourages fish to rise. Second, you realize that the species will probably continue to emerge well into the afternoon.

Methodically, I selected one trout, then another, and another, until I had covered, caught, and released most of the trout in that pool that had risen to the Green Drake naturals.

The Western Green Drake (*Ephemerella grandis*) continued to appear on the Bitterroot until the second week in July that year. As stream conditions improved, so did the success with an imitation of the Green Drake. *E. doddsi* is a very common sister species, and it also appears on many streams in the morning and afternoon, possibly a week or two later than *E. grandis*.

If you get the opportunity from mid-June to early July to fish while this large *Ephemerella* species appears you'll never forget it. Mornings, especially when fishing during a hatch of Western Green Drakes, can produce exciting, memorable fishing experiences.

Chapter XII

Fishing the Afternoon Hatches
(*Western*)

In the list below, (M) indicates that hatches or spinner falls also often occur in the morning, (E) that they often occur in the evening. Dates listed are very approximate; remember that Western dates are even less precise than their Eastern and Midwestern counterparts.

Duns

Baetis tricaudatus (M & E) – Little Blue Dun; late morning, afternoon, and early evening; April to November[1]

Baetis intermedius (M & E) – Little Blue Dun; late morning, afternoon, and early evening; April to November[1]

Ephemerella inermis (M & E) – Pale Morning Dun,[2] late morning, afternoon, and early evening; May 25[1]

Cinygmula ramaleyi (M) – Dark Red Quill; late morning (may continue into the afternoon); May 25

Baetis bicaudatus (M & E) – Pale Olive Dun; late morning, afternoon, and early evening; June through October[1]

Paraleptophlebia heteronea (M) – Dark Blue Quill; morning and afternoon; June 1

Ephemerella grandis (M) – Western Green Drake; late morning and afternoon (see Chapter XI for more information); June 5

Ephemerella tibialis (M) – Red Quill; late morning and afternoon; June 5

Callibaetis coloradensis (M) – Speckle-Winged Dun; late morning and early afternoon; June 12[1]

Epeorus longimanus (M) – Quill Gordon; late morning and early afternoon; June 12

Ephemerella doddsi (M) – Western Green Drake; late morning and afternoon; June 15

Heptagenia elegantula (E) – Pale Evening Dun; late afternoon and evening; June 20[1]

Baetis parvus (M & E) – Dark Brown Dun; late morning, afternoon, and early evening; June 20

Ephemerella infrequens (M) – Pale Morning Dun[2]; late morning and afternoon; July 1

Paraleptophlebia memorialis (M) – Dark Blue Quill; morning and afternoon; July 1

Rhithrogena futilis (M) – Quill Gordon; late morning and afternoon; July 1[3]

Cinygmula reticulata (M) – Pale Brown Dun; late morning and afternoon; July 5[3]

Paraleptophlebia vaciva (M) – Dark Blue Quill; morning and afternoon; July 5

Paraleptophlebia debilis (M) – Dark Blue Quill; morning and afternoon; July 5[1]

---

[1] Hatches or spinner falls may occur for many days.
[2] Color varies and common name may be inappropriate.
[3] Hatches or spinner falls may occur before date listed.
[4] Not listed in the Emergence Chart, but may be important.

Siphlonurus occidentalis (M) – Gray Drake; late morning and afternoon (heaviest hatches seem to occur around 3:00 p.m.); July 5 (hatches occur well into August, especially on colder streams)
Heptagenia solitaria (E) – Gray Fox; late afternoon and evening; July 5[1]
Rhithrogena hageni (M) – Pale Brown Dun; late morning and afternoon; July 10
Ameletus cooki (M) – Dark Brown Dun; late morning and afternoon; July 10[3]
Paraleptophlebia packii[4] (M) – Dark Blue Quill; morning and afternoon; July 20
Ephemerella coloradensis (M) – Dark Olive Dun[1]; midday; August 1
Paraleptophlebia bicornuta (M) – Dark Blue Quill; morning and afternoon; September 10[3]

Spinners

Cinygmula ramaleyi (M) – Red Quill Spinner; late morning and early afternoon; May 28
Paraleptophlebia heteronea (M) – Dark Brown Spinner; morning and afternoon; June 2
Epeorus longimanus (M) – Red Quill Spinner; late morning and early afternoon; June 16
Paraleptophlebia memorialis (M) – Dark Brown Spinner; morning and afternoon; July 2
Paraleptophlebia vaciva (M) – Dark Brown Spinner; morning and afternoon; July 6
Paraleptophlebia debilis (M) – Dark Brown Spinner; morning and afternoon; July 6[1]
Ameletus cooki – Dark Brown Spinner; early afternoon; July 11[3]
Rhithrogena undulata (E) – Red Quill or Dark Red Quill[2]; afternoon and evening; July 11[3]
Paraleptophlebia packii (M) – Dark Brown Spinner; morning and afternoon; July 21
Paraleptophlebia bicornuta (M) – Dark Brown Spinner; morning and afternoon; September 11[3]

As in the East and Midwest, afternoon fly fishing in the West can be the least rewarding time of day to fish. Afternoon is not the most propitious time to see free-ranging lunker trout feeding. But add an afternoon hatch or spinner fall to the picture and the fly fisherman can have an exciting experience – the waters can come alive with rising trout. Indeed, afternoon in the West is blessed with some excellent hatches and spinner falls.

We have many holdover subimagos in the afternoon. These are mayflies that initially appear in the morning, but continue into the afternoon, often in heavy numbers. The two species that make up the Western Green Drakes (*Ephemerella grandis* and *E. doddsi*), the Pale Morning Duns (*E. inermis* and *E. infrequens*), and the Red Quill (*E. tibialis*) are only a few of the *Ephemerella* species that appear in the morning and continue into the afternoon.

Baetis species, commonly imitated by the Little Blue Dun, also continue into the afternoon from the morning. With many species of this genus, the heaviest hatches often occur in the afternoon. *Baetis parvus* (Dark Brown Dun), *B. bicaudatus* (Pale Olive Dun), and *B. intermedius* (Little Blue Dun) are three *Baetis* species that can be important to meet and fish on many summer afternoons. As we'll see later, *B. parvus* is one of the most important hatches I have ever experienced in the West.

Members of another genus, *Paraleptophlebia*, so ably imitated by the Dark Blue Quill, are also holdovers from the morning. *Paraleptophlebia debilis* and *P. memorialis* can be productive many July afternoons, whereas *P. bicornuta* is important because it appears in early September.

The *Baetis parvus* dun is an important mayfly to meet on many Western streams.

The Dark Brown Dun on a size 20 hook is a productive imitation of the *Baetis parvus* dun.

Spinner falls also occur in the afternoon. Some of the best afternoon fishing I have experienced happened while spinners of *Ameletus cooki* (Dark Brown Spinner) and *Rhithrogena undulata* (Red Quill) fell.

Afternoon also is the time of the sporadic emerger the Gray Drake (*Siphlonurus occidentalis*). When you fish this hatch in late July and early August, if trout are feeding you can have an extremely productive afternoon.

Afternoon fishing in the West can be exciting – especially if you've prepared yourself to fish while one of the many hatches appears.

THAT GREAT AFTERNOON HATCH
ON HENRY'S FORK

It was my third trip to the fabled Henry's Fork in Idaho. On my previous trips I had seen many *Ephemerella inermis* (Pale Morning Dun) subimagos, and many trout rising to these mayflies. I saw many more *E. flavilinea* (Blue-Winged Olive Dun) duns, and correspondingly more fish feeding on these. Yes, I even met and fished while thousands of Blue Quills (*Paraleptophlebia debilis*) began their annual emergence. Also, I noted some precursory Gray Drakes (*Siphlonurus occidentalis*) emerge along the edges in midafternoon. But nobody ever told me that one of the greatest hatches I would ever experience – that includes the East, Midwest, and West – would be the diminutive Dark Brown Dun (*Baetis parvus*). Here on this stream noted for its great hatches, I experienced the Dark Brown Dun every afternoon for more than a week.

I had gone to Idaho in mid-July with plenty of imitations to match the Blue-Winged Olive Dun, Brown Drake, Blue Quill, and Western Green Drake. The Green Drake (*Ephemerella grandis*), however, had emerged around June 20 (and usually does so on this stretch); the Brown Drake (*Ephemera simulans*), which I had met earlier that year on Pine Creek in Pennsylvania, had appeared on the lower Railroad Ranch about June 25. I was afraid I had missed most of the major hatches by this mid-July meeting.

I planned to fish the section just above the Railroad Ranch, and arrived there about 9:00 a.m. At 10:00 a few Blue-Winged Olives (*Ephemerella flavilinea*) appeared, but not enough to create any frenzied surface feeding. An hour or so later a few Pale Morning Duns (*E. inermis*) emerged, but again few trout rose to this sparse hatch. I sat back on the shore next to the water and collected male duns of the six or so species sporadically emerging. As many writers have said before, this stream, and this section in particular, is a veritable insect factory. By noon I was convinced that no hatch would probably occur before evening – but I decided to remain and collect and photograph more insects.

Around 1:00 or 1:15 p.m., I noticed a few small dark brown mayflies emerging. I hoped the species wouldn't emerge in any great numbers, since I didn't have any imitation for it. The closest artificials I had with me to imitate this little mayfly were a size 18 Dark Blue Quill and Blue Dun. Things didn't work out the way I had planned. This was the hatch of the day – no, of the week! By 2:00 p.m. literally millions of these dazed duns floated past me – and not one took flight. Trout that had been inactive quickly became active. Fish moved out of the weed beds into feeding channels in the stream, and a major afternoon hatch was underway. In a 100-yard section more than a hundred trout rose to these small duns. All of this action occurred in the middle of a hot Idaho afternoon.

Great, but I had no imitation which I felt adequately matched the hatch. I quickly tied on the size 18 Dark Blue Quill and started casting over ten rising fish.

Ten casts, twenty casts – still no success. Too many trout rose to the naturals, and I found myself covering three, four, and even five trout on one cast. Finally a large fish swirled at the imitation, and then a second and third trout did the same thing. I was confused, frustrated, and angry – why hadn't someone told me about this important Western hatch?

Accepting defeat for the moment, I headed back to my car 100 yards away. I had my fly-tying gear in the car, and decided to tie several Dark Brown Duns on size 20 hooks. While I was tying these diminutive imitations, wind gusts scattered some of my feathers yards away, and I spent precious time retrieving them. I did not dare look back at the water I had just fished – I was fearful that the hatch would end by the time I had completed tying three imitations.

The hatch had not ended. Thousands and thousands of motionless Dark Brown Duns still drifted on the surface, and more than a hundred trout still methodically fed, as I reentered the area I had left twenty minutes before. Now, with much more confidence, I was prepared to meet and fish the hatch. I cast to the first rising trout just a few feet from shore. After ten or more casts the feeding trout finally seized my artificial rather than a natural. The foot-long rainbow leaped several times to show its displeasure before I netted and released it. Then a second trout, a third trout, and on and on until I caught more than fifty fish during that afternoon hatch.

From 2:00 to 4:00 p.m. there were so many duns on the water that there was hardly any chance for a trout to take the imitation. But by 4:00 p.m. the hatch had diminished just enough that catching rising trout became easier. Trout still fed and duns still appeared at 5:00 p.m. The hatch had continued without interruption for more than four hours.

Certainly this was an outstanding afternoon hatch – one which emerged in heavy numbers, occurred all afternoon, encouraged hundreds of trout to rise, and in turn, produced many rises to appropriate imitations. The hatch appeared from July 12 through July 15 (and probably before and after those dates), and always began between 1:00 and 1:30 p.m. On each of these days thousands of duns emerged and hundreds of trout fed on them.

Interspersed with the Dark Brown Duns were many Pale Olive Duns (*Baetis bicaudatus*). Enough of these subimagos appeared on the water every afternoon to produce rising trout.

Want to meet and fish while an excellent hatch appears? Then try Henry's Fork when the Dark Brown Dun emerges.

Chapter XIII
Fishing the Evening Hatches
(Western)

In the list below, (M) indicates that hatches or spinner falls also often occur in the morning, (A) that they often occur in the afternoon. Dates listed are very approximate; remember that western dates are even less precise than Eastern and Midwestern.

Duns

Ephemerella inermis (M & A) – Pale Morning Dun[1]; late morning, afternoon, and early evening; May 25[2]

Ephemera simulans – Brown Drake; evening; May 25 (appears on Henry's Fork, Idaho, in late June)

Hexagenia limbata[3] – Michigan Caddis; late evening; June 12

Ephemerella flavilinea (M) – Blue-Winged Olive Dun; morning and evening (evening seems to be heavier); June 15

Heptagenia elegantula (A) – Pale Evening Dun; late afternoon and evening; June 20[2]

Heptagenia solitaria (A) – Gray Fox; late afternoon and evening; July 5[2]

Epeorus albertae – Pink Lady (male can be imitated by the Light Cahill); evening; July 5

Cinygma dimicki – Light Cahill; evening; July 5[4]

Ephemerella hecuba – Great Red Quill; evening; July 5

Ephoron album – White Mayfly; evening; August 15

Spinners

Baetis tricaudatus (M) – Light Rusty Spinner; early morning and evening; April to November[2]

Baetis intermedius (M) – Dark Rusty Spinner; early morning and evening; April to November[2]

Ephemera simulans – Brown Drake; evening; May 26 (usually later than date listed)

Ephemerella inermis (M) – Pale Morning Spinner; morning and evening; May 26

Baetis bicaudatus (M) – Light Rusty Spinner; morning and evening; June through October[2]

Ephemerella grandis – Great Red Spinner; evening; June 6 (usually later than date listed)

[1] Color may vary and common name may be inappropriate.
[2] Hatches or spinner falls may occur for many days.
[3] Generally considered a Midwestern species, but may be locally important in the East and West.
[4] Hatches or spinner falls may occur before date listed.
[5] Name taken from *Isonychia* spinner.

Ephemerella tibialis – White-Gloved Howdy[5]; evening; June 6
Hexagenia limbata – Michigan Spinner; dusk; June 13
Ephemerella doddsi – Great Red Spinner; evening; June 16
Baetis parvus (M) – Dark Brown Spinner; early morning and evening; June 21
Heptagenia elegantula – Pale Evening Spinner; evening; June 21[2]
Rhithrogena futilis – Quill Gordon; evening; July 2[4]
Ephemerella infrequens (M) – Rusty Spinner[1]; morning and evening; July 2
Epeorus albertae (M) – Salmon Spinner (male can be imitated by the Light Cahill); morning and evening; July 6
Ephemerella hecuba – Great Brown Spinner; evening; July 6
Cinygma dimicki – Light Cahill; evening; July 6[4]
Siphlonurus occidentalis (M) – Brown Quill Spinner; morning and evening; July 6
Heptagenia solitaria (M) – Ginger Quill Spinner; morning and evening; July 6
Rhithrogena hageni (M) – Dark Tan Spinner; morning and evening; July 11
Rhithrogena undulata (A) – Red Quill or Dark Red Quill; afternoon and evening; July 11[4]
Ephemerella coloradensis – Dark Brown Spinner; evening; August 2
Ephoron album – White Mayfly; evening; August 15

When I think of evening fishing I remember vividly one of my trips to the Bitterroot River in Montana. It was an early July evening, and for the two hours that I had scanned the stream, not one trout surfaced. I doubted whether this would be a good evening to meet and fish while any hatch or spinner fall occurred.

At 8:00 p.m. several *Cinygma dimicki* duns emerged from slow water just upstream from where I stood. A few minutes later spinners of the same species met over the water. But still no trout fed.

Now it was almost dark and several trout took up feeding positions in fast water noticeably slowed by a partially submerged evergreen. Soon the several trout became twenty hungry, feeding fish.

I noticed hundreds of *Rhithrogena futilis* now mating, and tied on a Quill Gordon to match the spinner. Rainbow after rainbow took the Quill Gordon imitation before I quit that evening.

But that's not the only memorable fishing experience in the evening – I recall meeting and fishing while thousands of *Ephemerella flavilinea* duns appeared one late June evening on Henry's Fork, and while *E. inermis* continued to appear in the Box Canyon Area of Henry's Fork.

Among the most productive evenings is the one I spent on the Yellowstone River when I fished while thousands of downwinged caddis flies and stoneflies returned to that river to lay their eggs. And that too was the evening I was to meet and fish at the time when the huge stonefly the Salmon Fly (*Pteronarcys californica*) reappeared.

There are many other evening hatches and spinner falls that can engender memorable fishing experiences. Both *Epeorus albertae* duns and spinners are on the water many summer evenings. *Heptagenia* species like *H. elegantula* (Pale Evening Spinner) and *H. solitaria* remind me of many Western trips that were successful because I fished while spinners of these species fell. The latter adult is appropriately imitated by the Ginger Quill.

A SEPTEMBER EVENING ON THE
COLORADO RIVER

It was early September. I had an unexpected opportunity to fish several streams in Colorado. But what about the hatches? Would I encounter any? Would any of these hatches be heavy enough to produce rising trout?

I stayed overnight in Kremmling, Colorado, and awoke to a light frost and a temperature of 29 degrees. I arrived on the Colorado River around 10:00 a.m. and scanned the surface for emerging duns, falling spinners, and feeding trout. There were plenty of mayflies in the air and a few on the water. *Tricorythodes minutus* spinners that had emerged not much more than an hour before already fell spent onto the water. *Callibaetis* and *Paraleptophlebia bicornuta* duns and spinners dotted the surface. The former are imitated by the Speckle-Winged Dun or Spinner, and the latter by the Dark Blue Quill and Dark Brown Spinner. Although there were many species on the water none appeared (except for *Tricorythodes*) in heavy enough numbers to encourage trout to rise.

I did little fishing that morning, but sat back on the shore much of the time watching the hatching characteristics of the various mayfly species. Around 10:30 a.m. hundreds of Ginger Quill Spinners (*Heptagenia solitaria*) took positions a few inches above the surface. Little did I realize that this same species would create one of the greatest evening spinner falls that I have ever witnessed.

A *Heptagenia solitaria* female spinner. This species produces excellent spinner falls on many Western streams during August and early September.

At 2:00 p.m. I still sat there by the Colorado searching the water and the air for signs of new mayfly species. I bent over my reflex camera and took several shots of *Callibaetis* duns and spinners. A state fish warden came by and asked how I had done fishing. I told him I had done little fishing and seen very few trout rise. He urged me to try the Gore Gorge section of the Colorado a few miles below Kremmling. So at 4:00 p.m. I traveled to that section of the river.

Above the gorge, the Colorado is a slow, silted, meandering river; but as it enters the gorge, it becomes a rapid rampaging torrent with long fast stretches and short, deep holes. As I entered the gorge area I noted *Baetis* spinners already mating. But I also noted a fairly sizable (10 to 12 mm) dun emerging in good numbers. Trout near the far shore fed freely on subimagos that waited too long before taking flight. I captured several duns and assumed that they were *Heptagenia solitaria* subimagos from their yellowish tan coloration (and of course because I had seen spinners of this species upstream in the morning).

By 6:30 p.m. thousands of tan spinners appeared a few inches above the water. These spinners were the same species as the emerging duns, and had probably emerged the night before.

Few trout rose to the duns or spinners – at least any that I could easily reach. I was ready to quit for the day, and moved upstream through the gorge to the first large pool above it. Here thousands of Ginger Quill spinners hovered inches above the surface. Occasionally trout jumped completely out of the water to capture one of the fluttering adults. Now hundreds of male and female imagos drifted on the surface, and more than twenty trout rose to the newly found food supply.

The Ginger Quill is an excellent imitation for the *Heptagenia solitaria* spinner, so I quickly tied on a size 12 pattern and cast above a large trout feeding not more than 10 feet from me. On the first cast the trout hit and I set the hook. Without ever jumping once, the heavy fish headed downstream toward the first fast stretch entering the gorge. I turned the trout and it headed back upstream. I netted the 18-inch rainbow, released it, and cast above another fish rising to imagos. That trout too took the imitation on the first pass. Now on to another rising trout, then another, and so on until I had caught and released more than twenty trout in less than an hour during that spinner fall.

As is often the case in the East and Midwest, no other fishermen were there to meet and fish the spinner fall. Again, as with so many Western species, no one had prepared me for this important mayfly. No one had emphasized that *Heptagenia solitaria* is extremely important to meet and fish. No one had prepared me for that evening spinner fall on the Colorado River in September.

The next morning I headed for the Eagle River, 50 miles to the south. I spent the entire morning locating ranchers who owned land adjacent to the Eagle River and asking their permission to fish on their property. This brings up an important point to remember when fishing Western waters: Much of the good water is on private land. The ranchers who own this land jealously guard their legal right to private property. I've discovered that most ranchers will allow you to fish if you ask. Always ask for permission, especially in the West.

I was fortunate that morning – I located a rancher who owned a 5-mile section of the Eagle River. He indicated that I could fish any part of the stream he owned. I thanked him and traveled to the stream.

When I arrived at the river around 3:00 p.m. I noted hundreds of *Baetis* duns emerging along the edges of a large pool. No trout, however, rose to these diminutive mayflies. Since the Ginger Quill had worked so well on the Colorado River the night before, I decided to try it on the Eagle. On my second or third cast in a large deep hole, a heavy trout sucked in the imitation and promptly broke the 5X tippet.

I tied on a second Ginger Quill imitation and cast above a trout which had surfaced just a minute before. This fish hit on the first pass, and I netted and released a 15-inch cutthroat.

I waded downstream 200 feet to the next good pocket of water. Here too, many *Baetis* duns emerged, but again no trout rose to these Little Blue Duns. Within a half-hour six trout took the Ginger Quill in this second pool. All this action occurred on a hot September afternoon while few trout rose to naturals.

It was now 6:30 p.m. *Baetis* and *Ephemerella* spinners became active, but so did another spinner, *Heptagenia solitaria*. Now I understood why trout had so readily taken the Ginger Quill. The spinners which are so effectively imitated by the Ginger Quill had been on the Eagle for a number of days, and these hungry trout fed even when few *Heptagenia* naturals were apparent, and even in the middle of the afternoon.

More than ten trout now fed on spent spinners, and by 7:00 p.m. I had caught more than twenty trout. Fifteen of these trout were 15 or more inches long.

Do you have time in September to spend an evening on the Colorado – or for that matter, many other Western streams? Then fish in the evening while Ginger Quills effectively copy the mating spinners of *Heptagenia solitaria*.

DOWNWINGS ARE FOR THE WEST – ESPECIALLY IN THE EVENING

On many occasions when I have fished Western waters I have encountered more emerging and egglaying caddis flies and stoneflies than mayflies. One evening in early July on the Yellowstone River, just below Corwin Springs, I noted only three mayflies emerge. During that same six-hour episode I saw thousands of downwings perform their egglaying flight. Each downwing species seemed to take its turn over the water – first a pale yellow stonefly; then a dark brown caddis; then the huge Willow Fly (*Acronurea pacifica*); and last, the giant of giants, the Salmon Fly (*Pteronarcys californica*).

As is common in early July, the Yellowstone River was high and discolored from melting snows in nearby Yellowstone Park. The river was impossible to wade and no trout surfaced. John Bailey had warned me earlier that day that the river was high – certainly no place to use dry flies. As I walked along the shore I

The Salmon Fly tied by Al Troth

saw thousands of mating Salmon Flies clinging firmly to the willow trees. Wind gusts of 30 or more miles per hour were common during that hot day in the canyon. Occasionally, the breeze dislodged several stoneflies from their resting place and forced them prematurely to the water. A few trout fed on these occasional visitors. Other dislocated Salmon Flies landed on my hat, face, or fishing vest in an attempt to escape the winds. I noticed some Willow Flies also in the air and on the trees. If things went well I might be on this highly productive river while one of these species landed in numbers on the water and became available as food for hungry trout. I hoped that one of these unpredictable females chose tonight to lay their eggs.

It was now 9:15 p.m. I had stayed for six hours at the water – still no movement by the female *Pteronarcys*. I was ready to return to the motel; I had not fished during the six-hour stay, but patiently waited for the return of the Salmon Fly.

About 9:20 p.m. one, then two, then a hundred, then several thousand females decided to fly toward the river to deposit their eggs. They flew almost 100 feet above the water, then down toward and onto the surface. As these huge fluttering orange-bodied stoneflies floated on the surface, large trout everywhere seized them – many fed within inches of the bank. I cast that awful-looking dry fly above what I thought was a heavy trout. The imitation had barely hit the cloudy water when a heavy fish sucked it in. Now the fight was on – the trout headed for the center of the river and I couldn't turn it with my 4X tippet. Within seconds the leader snapped and I found myself hurriedly tying another Salmon Fly onto the tippet. Ten trout took that unsightly imitation that night before I quit. When I left the river, trout were still feeding on the spent females, but darkness had made fishing impossible. The six-hour wait had been worthwhile, for I had finally experienced an egglaying episode of the Salmon Fly.

If you ever get the opportunity to fish while *Pteronarcys californica* returns to the water, you'll never forget the action. Carry several imitations of the giant Willow Fly also, for this imitates a stonefly species which also can be important in June and July.

As we have mentioned many times before, the time to fish the downwings is when they return to the water to lay their eggs. Local authorities state that *Pteronarcys* females can return almost any time of day, but sometimes noon is preferred – I was successful in meeting and fishing the stonefly at dusk.

Imitations of the Salmon Fly are extremely difficult to tie; I recommend you buy imitations rather than tie them. Probably the best Salmon Fly pattern I have ever seen is the one tied by Al Troth of Dillon, Montana. He uses buoyant elk hair dyed orange to duplicate the body of this large stonefly. This imitation floats better than any other pattern I have tested, and I have heard many stories of success with it.

Pteronarcys californica is found on many Western waters. Emergence of this species often occurs in the morning, and the hatch normally moves upstream daily, like to the Green Drake on Penn's Creek in the East. Bud Lilly lists the following streams as having good *Pteronarcys* hatches. The Salmon Fly usually appears first on Henry's Fork in May or early June. Shortly thereafter, it emerges on Rock Creek in northwestern Montana, then Clark Fork, the Blackfoot, and the Madison. Hatches occur on the latter two waters in middle to late June, or early July. One of the last waters for this large stonefly to appear is the Yellowstone River. It often occurs on the Yellowstone in early to middle July. Water temperatures are often in the high 40s and low 50s and streams are often discolored when this species appears. Both conditions prevent, or at least inhibit, dry-fly fishing.

Earlier I said I tied my Eastern and Midwestern caddis and stonefly patterns with deer hair and no hackle. I strongly recommend including two hackles on each Western downwing pattern. Eastern patterns usually do not float well on the faster Western streams. However, my Eastern pattern did work well one evening on Clark Fork, near Deer Lodge, Montana. This water is much slower in its upper reaches than it is 20 miles below.

Here again, no mayflies appeared. About 8:00 p.m. thousands of caddis flies (Family Philopotamidae) skittered on the water. Since color, especially body color, of caddis flies is very misleading in the air, it's important to capture a natural and duplicate it with an appropriate imitation. Always carry sizes from 12 to 20 with cream, olive, tan, brown, gray, dark brown, green, and black bodies. The species laying eggs that evening on Clark Fork could be appropriately copied with a size 16 Dark Brown Caddis. Twenty heavy brown trout took that caddis pattern that evening on this highly productive stream.

Many of the Trude patterns (Black, Blonde, etc.), Sofa Pillow, and others with downwings effectively imitate many stonefly and caddis-fly species.

On many occasions, especially evenings, I have encountered downwings on

Western waters when no mayflies emerged. If you want to meet and fish while some dramatic, spectacular surface feeding occurs, then use downwing imitations – downwings indeed are made for the West.

Chapter XIV
A Plea to All Fishermen

Every time I cast a dry fly on Hendrickson's Pool on the Beaverkill, I am amazed at the number of trout this and every other pool on these sacred waters contain. Try being on these stretches almost any evening around dusk – the rises during a spinner fall are difficult for the mind to comprehend. I find myself many times during these emergences or falls casting over not one rising trout, but rather twenty or thirty. As Guthrie Conyngham and his brother Jack have said many times, these rises at dusk remind them of Pennsylvania's Lehigh River and how it used to be thirty years ago.

But let's look at the Beaverkill in midmorning during late July or August. The Beaverkill has a fairly adequate *Tricorythodes* emergence and associated spinner fall occurring from 7:00–11:00 a.m. On Barnhart's Pool during the fall, fifty or sixty trout might be feeding freely on the spent imagos.

Falling Springs in south-central Pennsylvania is similar to the Beaverkill, although much smaller. Try to arrive on this highly fertile limestone stream around 8:00 a.m. in August. You'll see *Tricorythodes* duns already appearing in great numbers. By 9:00–9:30 a.m. the spinner fall commences, and even though the pools in this stream are extremely small, you'll see twenty or thirty trout feeding in almost every one.

Now let's look at the Loyalsock Creek in north-central Pennsylvania. The Loyalsock is an excellent freestone stream – not quite as large as the Beaverkill nor as fertile as Falling Springs. Still, the Loyalsock is noted for some fantastic hatches, and excellent trout fishing. Again, the Loyalsock, in its middle section at least, has an adequate *Tricorythodes* hatch. The species is not as dense as on Falling Springs, but is still heavy enough to encourage trout to surface-feed. However, on a good day you'll see only five or ten trout rising to the spinner fall in the long pool just below Hillsgrove. Why this discrepancy in numbers of rising trout when compared with the previous two streams? This area of the "Sock" is open water where all kinds of hardware and bait can be used. The legal limit on this stream is eight, and most anglers will remain until they kill their limit (if they're lucky). Areas of the Beaverkill and Falling Springs described earlier are so-called "no kill areas" where trout caught must be promptly returned to the water. What I'm saying is that stretches or streams where trout must be released contain more trout later in the season – more trout to catch, release, and enjoy many times by many fishermen.

If we want better fishing, then we have to encourage fishermen to release trout so they can be enjoyed another time. But before we encourage anglers to release more, we must be ready to answer compelling questions. Here's part of the rationale some fishermen use for keeping fish.

1. The trout will die anyway, so why should I release them?

Several years ago I discovered the Little Juniata River in central Pennsylvania as a fabulous trout stream. I fished the water daily for weeks after a friend had told me about the huge native browns in the stream. After a few weeks of these solitary trips, I decided to invite another friend to experience the success which is so frequent on this stream. We had no success that evening and I apologized time and time again to the friend I had invited. I should have known better; on the way to the stream I was bragging about the number and size of the trout, and it seems every time I do this I have no success.

I revisited the Little Juniata River a week later, and as I hiked to a pool a half-mile downstream from the Espy Farm, I saw the friend whom I had invited to the stream a week earlier. With him were four other anglers he had invited. When I asked if they had had any success, two of them opened their creels and displayed eight heavy browns that ranged from 15 to 18 inches long and must have weighed 2 to 3 pounds each. My mouth dropped in disgust and dismay when I viewed these large trout, now killed, never to challenge another angler.

"Why didn't you release them?" I said rather angrily.

"Oh, we caught others and released them, but these would have died."

They were using soft-shelled crabs and they were probably correct. Trout often take live bait voraciously and swallow bait and hook. Usually with flies, trout can be released unharmed. I guess this is why I rely on artificials. This is also a good reason for all of us to encourage others to take up fly fishing. I can recall catching the same unusual-looking brook trout on Bowman's Creek three times within a two-week span. How many other fishermen also had the pleasure of hooking this same trout?

2. Who'd believe that I caught all these trout if I released them?

Most sportsmen believe keeping trout, not releasing them, is the proper thing to do. This is a way to display to all your fishing expertise. It'll be difficult to release trout the first couple times – maybe others won't believe you – but give it a try. Besides, releasing trout can be contagious among your peers.

John Hagan, Lloyd Williams, and Dick Mills guard jealously the trout in the "fly fishing only" area of Bowman's Creek. They've seen many incidents of greed on this stretch when fishing is good. One day, after the state released some trout, they saw one "sportsman" catch and keep two limits. When he caught his first limit the angler furtively walked back to his car, emptied the contents of his creel into his trunk, and calmly reentered the stream and started fishing again. By the time he had caught a second limit of six trout, John Hagan had had enough and waded over to the fisherman and asked him to stop. The angler ceased only after three fishermen converged on him. This man probably went home that evening and bragged to his friends about his expertise, when almost anyone could have done as well.

3. I promised the trout to a friend.

I say let the friend go catch his own fish. He doesn't fish? Let him buy some at the local fish market. I can't really argue with anyone who really enjoys trout and takes a few for his own benefit.

Certainly, there are some times when you can and should keep trout: late in the season on a marginal stream; large lunkers which take many small trout; and artificial situations, such as private streams which are overstocked with trout.

As your fly fishing progresses from beginner to expert, I hope an incredible metamorphosis will occur. Your attitude toward your prey will become one of deep respect. I say "I hope" because as you advance through the stages you'll probably experience more and more success and fewer and fewer failures – from few trout to many trout. Somewhere along the way evolves admiration for the quarry as a highly selective creature so revered that the mere thought of killing one after successfully enticing it to the dry fly is revolting. Returning the trout to its native haunt becomes the natural thing to do, and keeping an occasional trout hooked too deeply or the rare lunker is the exceptional bonus.

Index

Acroneuria pacifica (Willow Stonefly), 102, 182, 183, 184
Altitude. *See* Stream elevation
Ameletus mayflies, 56–57
  A. cooki (Dark Brown Dun and Spinner), 57, 99, 175
American March Brown, 22, 67, 76, 85, 130, 135
Anatomy (mayflies), 47, 49–50, 52–60, 67, 68, 69, 72
Animal Kingdom, 45, 47
Ants, 18, 88
Aquatic beetles, life cycle of, 19
Aquatic insects, 17, 113
  classification system for, 45, 47
Aquatic Insects of California (Usinger), 19
Arthropoda Phylum, 45, 47
Artificials. *See* Imitations
Attractor patterns, 154–157

Baetidae Family, 22, 54–56
Baetis mayflies, 3, 23, 24, 55, 59, 81, 83, 84, 90, 92, 93, 95, 124, 125, 174, 181, 182
  B. bicaudatus (Pale Olive Dun), 55, 95, 174, 177
  B. intermedius (Blue Dun), 55, 90, 174
  B. levitans, 55
  B. parvus (Dark Brown Dun), 55, 92, 93, 174, 176, 177
  B. quebecensis, 55
  B. tricaudatus (Blue Dun), 55, 90
  B. vagans (Little Blue Dun), 55, 70
Bald Eagle Creeks (Pennsylvania), 5, 61, 63, 64, 118, 134
Beaverkill River (New York), 7, 52, 81, 120, 127, 136, 144, 147, 151, 186
Beetles, 18, 19, 87
Bicolor group (*Ephemerella* mayflies), 53, 124
Big Fishing Creek (Pennsylvania), 6, 7, 115, 144
Big Slate Drake (*Hexagenia atrocaudata*), 5, 12, 16, 50, 85, 143
Bitterroot River (Montana), 27, 91, 95, 160, 161, 168, 169, 171, 172, 179
Blackfoot River (Montana), 100, 168, 170, 184

Black Quill (*Leptophlebia* mayflies), 24, 54, 60, 73
Blue Dun, 55, 58, 90, 91, 92
Blue Quill (*Paraleptophlebia* mayflies), 9, 54, 91, 114–116, 124, 167
Blue River (Colorado), 94
Blue-Winged Olive Duns (*Ephemerella* mayflies), 10, 53–54, 81, 83, 94, 114, 116–118, 144, 158, 159, 162, 167
Body color. *See* Coloration
Bowman's Creek (Pennsylvania), 18, 117, 120, 127, 129, 149, 152, 187
Brachycentrus fuliginosus (Grannom), 17, 22, 67, 86, 130
Brook trout, 14, 18
Brown Drake, 45, 47, 49, 78, 143
Brown Quill Spinner, 97, 167
Brown trout, 14, 128, 133
Buffalo River (Idaho), 97, 157

Caddis flies (Tricoptera order), 14, 22, 25, 114, 123, 125, 142, 143, 182–185
  classification system for, 45, 47
  emergence time of, 10, 23
  habitats of, 3–6
  imitations, 67, 86–87, 128–130
  life cycle of, 17
  nomenclature, 20
  and stream selection, 8
Caenidae Family, 52
Caenis mayflies (Angler's Curses), 15, 52, 60, 118
  C. anceps, 52
  C. simulans, 52
Cahills. *See* individual Cahills
Callibaetis mayflies (Speckle-Winged Duns), 23, 54, 55–56, 59, 94, 167, 180, 181
  C. coloradensis, 56, 94, 160
  C. ferrugineus, 56
  C. fluctuans, 56
  C. nigritus, 56, 160
Cedar Run Creek (Pennsylvania), 10, 116, 118, 127
Chimarrha caddis flies, 17
  C. atterima (Little Black Caddis), 67, 86

Chocolate Duns (*Ephemerella* mayflies), 53–
54, 81, 124
Cinygma mayflies, 58, 59
  C. dimicki (Light Cahill), 58, 96
Cinygmula mayflies, 58, 59, 90, 92
  C. ramaleyi (Dark Red Quill), 58, 90
  C. reticulata (Pale Brown Dun), 58, 96
Classification. *See* Caddis flies; Mayflies;
  Stoneflies
Coffin Fly, 79
Coleoptera order (aquatic beetles), 19
Colorado River (Colorado), 52, 91, 161, 180,
  181
Coloration (mayflies), 47, 49–50, 52–58, 67,
  68, 69, 70–85, 89–102, 114, 127
Commercial imitations, 70–85, 90–102
Common and fishable species, 3–6, 10, 11
Common names (mayflies), inaccuracy of,
  20, 45
Cream Cahill, 82
Cream Drake, 52
Cream duns, 3, 130–140
Crickets, 18, 87

Dark Blue Quill, 54, 71, 91, 174, 180
Dark Blue Sedge (*Psilotreta frontalis*), 17,
  86, 143
Dark Brown Dun, 92, 93, 99, 174, 176, 177
Dark Brown Spinner (*Paraleptophlebia* may-
  flies), 54, 71, 91, 100, 114, 121, 175
Dark Cahill, 85, 94, 96
Dark Green Drake, 16, 50, 77
Dark Olive Dun, 53, 101
Dark Olive Quill, 81, 118
Dark Olive Spinner, 83
Dark Red Quill, 58, 90, 99, 100
Dark Rusty Spinner, 85
Dark Tan Spinner, 98
"Decennial Census of the United States
  Climate—Heating Degree Day Normals"
  (U.S. Department of Commerce), 20
Downwing patterns, 129–130, 182, 184, 185
Dry-fly patterns
  Eastern, 70–88
  Western, 89–102
DuBois, Donald, 67, 149
Duns (mayfly subimagos), 3, 5, 14–15, 16
  cream, 3, 130–140
  Eastern and Midwestern, 110–153
    afternoon, 122–140
    evening, 141–153
    morning, 114–121
  emergence characteristics of, 11, 61, 62, 64,
    65, 110
  Ephemeridae, 47, 49–50, 52–58
  imitation procedures for (Eastern), 70–86,
    88
  imitation procedures for (Western), 89–102
  rating of (Eastern), 24, 25, 28–35
  rating of (Western), 27, 36–43
  Western, 164–185
    afternoon, 173–177

evening, 178–185
morning, 164–172

Eagle River (Colorado), 181, 182
Early Brown Spinner (*Leptophlebia* mayflies),
  54, 73
Early Brown Stonefly (*Taeniopteryx faciata*),
  67, 87
Egglaying (mayflies), 11, 50, 83, 85–86, 102–
  103, 143, 144, 182, 183, 184
  methods of, 14, 16, 24–25
Elk Creek (Pennsylvania), 3, 6, 116
Emergence
  afternoon (Eastern and Midwestern), 122–
    140
  afternoon (Western), 173–177
  characteristics of, 3–11, 20–27, 61–65
  date, 6–7, 10–11, 20–21, 25, 26, 62, 63, 65,
    73, 75, 77, 78, 82–85, 90, 94–98, 101, 158,
    160
  length of, 23–24
  peak, 61, 62, 64, 65
  stream elevation, 25, 26, 64, 158, 160–161,
    162
  time, 9–10, 11, 21–22, 64–65, 74, 77, 82,
    83, 90, 91, 94, 96, 97, 99, 100, 101, 147
  water temperature, 25, 26–27, 61–63, 64,
    90, 116, 158, 159–160, 162
  chart for (Eastern), 28–35
  chart for (Western), 36–43
  evening (Eastern and Midwestern), 141–153
  evening (Western), 178–185
  morning (Eastern and Midwestern), 110–
    121
  morning (Western), 164–172
Epeorus mayflies, 4, 24, 58, 59
  E. albertae (Salmon Spinner), 58, 97, 167,
    179
  E. deceptivus, 58
  E. grandis, 58
  E. longimanus (Blue Dun), 58, 91–92
  E. nitidus, 58
  E. pleuralis (Quill Gordon), 6, 14–15, 21,
    58, 71, 125, 126, 127
  E. vitreus (Cahills), 58, 79–80
Ephemera mayflies, 3, 49, 60
  E. compar, 49
  E. guttulata (Green Drake), 2, 15, 16, 22,
    49, 79, 143, 145, 147
  E. simulans (Brown Drake), 45, 47, 49, 78,
    143
  E. varia (Yellow Drake), 15, 22, 49, 61–65,
    136, 143, 150–153
Ephemerella mayflies, 24, 53–54, 60, 80–81,
  102, 103, 114, 116–117, 118, 124, 125,
  144, 171–172, 174
  E. attenuata (Blue-Winged Olive Dun), 53,
    81
  E. bicolor, 124
  E. coloradensis (Dark Olive Dun), 53, 101
  E. cornuta (Blue-Winged Olive Dun), 10,
    53, 83, 118

E. deficiens, 53, 116
E. doddsi (Western Green Drake), 53, 95, 172, 174
E. dorothea (Pale Evening Dun), 53, 80–81, 130
E. flavilinea (Blue-Winged Olive Dun), 53, 94, 158, 159, 162, 167
E. funeralis, 53
E. grandis (Western Green Drake), 53, 89, 95, 162, 166, 171–172, 174, 176
E. hecuba (Great Red Quill), 100
E. inermis (Pale Morning Dun), 27, 53, 90–91, 166, 167, 169, 174
E. infrequens (Pale Morning Dun), 53, 98, 167, 174
E. invaria (Pale Evening Dun), 53, 80, 125, 130, 134, 136, 139
E. lata, 53
E. longicornis, 53
E. margarita, 54
E. needhami (Chocolate Dun), 54, 81, 124
E. rotunda (Pale Evening Dun), 4–5, 54, 74, 125, 130
E. septentrionalis (Pale Evening Dun), 54, 74, 139
E. subvaria (Hendrickson), 6, 10, 11, 21–22, 53, 54, 72, 73, 125, 126, 127, 128
E. tibialis (Red Quill), 54, 92, 174
E. walkeri, 54
Ephemerellidae Family, 53–54
Ephemeridae Family, 3, 14, 22, 47, 49–50
Ephemeroptera order (mayflies), 14, 47, 49–50, 52–58
  Baetidae Family, 22, 54–56
  Caenidae Family, 52
  Ephemerellidae Family, 53–54
  Ephemeridae Family, 47, 49–50
  Heptageniidae Family, 57–58
  Leptophlebiidae Family, 54
  naturals and imitations, 70–86, 89–102
  Polymitarcidae Family, 50
  Potamanthidae Family, 50, 52
  Siphlonuridae Family, 56–57
  Tricorythidae Family, 52–53
Ephoron mayflies, 15, 50
  E. album (White Wulff), 50, 101, 102
  E. leukon (White Mayfly), 50, 85, 143

Falling Springs (Pennsylvania), 186
Fisherman's Handbook of Trout Flies, The (DuBois), 67, 149
Fishing Creek (Pennsylvania), 62, 151
Fly patterns, 5, 15, 16, 184, 185
  Eastern, 70–89
  variations in, 66–69
  Western, 89–104
Fly-tying
  caddis flies, 86–87, 130
  Eastern mayflies, 69–86
  stoneflies, 87, 102, 130
  terrestrials, 87–88
  Western mayflies, 89–102

Gallatin River (Montana), 25, 96, 160, 161
Ginger Quill, 75, 98, 135, 179, 180, 181, 182
Ginger Quill Spinner, 11, 143
Golden Drakes (*Potamanthus* mayflies), 52
"Good stream," characteristics of, 7–9, 11, 22
Goofus (attractor), 157
Grannom (*Brachycentrus fuliginosus*), 17, 22, 67, 86, 130
Grasshoppers, 18, 87
Gray Drake (*Siphlonurus* mayflies), 26, 56, 97, 175
Gray Fox, 22, 26, 57, 66, 67, 75, 97, 98, 130, 134, 135, 143, 147, 160
Great Red Quill (*Ephemerella hecuba*), 100
Great Red Spinner, 45, 76, 95, 136
Green Caddis (*Rhyacophila lobifera*), 17, 22, 86, 125, 128, 132, 143
Green Drake, 2, 6, 7, 15, 16, 22, 49, 67, 79, 113, 114, 143, 146–147

Hatches
  advantages of meeting, 1, 2
  Eastern and Midwestern, 110–140
    afternoon, 122–140
    evening, 141–153
    morning, 110–121
  and emergence, 61–65
  entomology of, 44–45, 47, 49–50, 52–58
  fishing without, 154–157
  and imitation, 66–104
  recording, 11–12
  rules for meeting, 3–11
  Western, 158–185
    afternoon, 173–177
    evening, 178–185
    morning, 164–172
Hendrickson (*Ephemerella subvaria*), 6, 10, 11, 21–22, 23, 53, 54, 72, 73, 125, 126, 127, 128
Henry's Fork (Idaho), 27, 91, 96, 97, 158, 159, 167, 168, 176, 179, 184
Heptagenia mayflies, 5, 24, 57, 59, 75, 179
  H. aphrodite (Pale Evening Dun), 57, 75, 139
  H. diabusia, 57
  H. elegantula (Pale Evening Dun), 57, 93, 94, 179
  H. hebe, 57
  H. pulla, 57
  H. solitaria (Gray Fox), 26, 57, 97, 98, 160, 167, 170, 179, 180, 181, 182
  H. walshi (Pale Evening Dun), 57, 75
Heptageniidae Family, 4, 22, 57–58
Hexagenia mayflies, 3, 12, 50, 59
  H. atrocaudata (Big Slate Drake), 5, 12, 16, 50, 85, 143
  H. limbata (Michigan caddis), 50, 93
  H. munda, 50
Hoaglands Branch (Pennsylvania), 3
Hook size, 22
  caddis fly, 86–87
  mayfly, 70–86, 89–102

Hook size (*Continued*)
  stonefly, 87, 102
  terrestrials, 87–88
Hydropsyche caddis flies, 17
H. slossanae (Spotted Sedge), 86

Imagos. *See* Spinners
Imitations
  caddis fly, 86–87, 128–130
  and fishable species, 5
  and insect nomenclature, 20
  mayfly (Eastern), 70–86, 88, 148, 149
  mayfly (Western), 89–102
  size of, 22
  stonefly, 87, 102
  and takeoff from water, 16
  terrestrials, 18, 87–88
  variations in pattern of, 66, 67, 68–69
Impala, 89
Insecta class, 45
Isonychia mayflies (Slate Drake), 3, 25, 56, 59, 147–150
  I. bicolor, 56, 78, 117, 147
  I. harperi, 56, 78, 147
  I. sadleri, 56, 78, 147
Isoperla signata (Light Stonefly), 23, 87, 129, 130

Jenny Spinner, 54, 69, 71, 84
Jensen, Steven, 26, 158

Keuffel and Esser Weatherproof Level Book, 12

Larva (caddis fly), 17
Leadwing Coachman (*Isonychia* mayflies), 78, 147–148
Leafhoppers, 18
Lehigh River (Pennsylvania), 127
Leptophlebia mayflies (Black Quill), 24, 54, 60, 73
  L. cupida, 54, 73
  L. gravestella, 54
  L. johnsoni, 54
  L. nebulosa, 54
Leptophlebiidae Family, 54
Light Cahills, 3, 4–5, 22, 69, 76, 77, 79, 80, 82, 83, 94, 96, 130, 136, 139, 140, 143
Light Rusty Spinner, 95
Light Stonefly (*Isoperla signata*), 23, 87, 129, 130
Lilly, Bud, 184
Litobrancha recurvata (Dark Green or Brown Drake), 16, 50, 77
Little Black Caddis (*Chimarrha atterima*), 67, 86
Little Blue Dun (*Baetis* mayflies), 70, 83, 84, 124, 174
Little Juniata River (Pennsylvania), 5, 128, 132, 151, 187
Little Marryat, 81
Loyalsock Creek (Pennsylvania), 11, 52, 126, 127, 149, 151, 186
Lunker trout, 133, 143, 144, 147

Madison River (Yellowstone Park, Wyoming and Montana), 97, 99, 156, 159, 160, 184
Mallard-quill sections, 69, 72, 89
March Browns, 66, 67
Marinaro, Vince, 118
Matching the Hatch (Schwiebert), 148
Mating ritual, 12, 44, 77, 115, 117, 144, 146
Mayflies (*Ephemeroptera* order), 17. *See also* Duns; Nymphs; Spinners
  classification system for, 45, 47, 49–50, 52–58
  Eastern and Midwestern, 110–153
    afternoon, 122–127, 130–140
    evening, 141–153
    morning, 110–121
  emergence characteristics of, 7–11, 20–27, 61–65
  habitats of, 3–6
  identification of, 58–60
  imitation procedures for (Eastern), 66–86
  imitation procedures for (Western), 89–102
  life cycle of, 14–16
  nomenclature, 20
  Western, 158–185
    afternoon, 173–177
    evening, 178–185
    morning, 164–172
Mayflies of Idaho, The (Jensen), 26, 158
Mayflies of Michigan Trout Streams (Leonard and Leonard), 69
Michigan Caddis (*Hexagenia limbata*), 93

Needham, James G., 74
Needham, Paul, 14, 18
Nymphs (mayfly), 3–4, 7, 14, 16, 17, 22, 47, 49–50, 145, 150

Ocelli, 52, 59
Olive Cahill Spinner, 82

Pale Brown Dun, 96, 98, 99
Pale Evening Duns, 4–5, 22, 53–54, 57, 74, 75, 80–81, 93, 94, 125, 130, 132, 133, 134, 136, 139, 179
Pale Evening Spinner, 74, 179
Pale Morning Duns, 27, 53–54, 90–91, 98, 166, 167, 169, 174
Pale Olive Duns, 9, 84, 95, 100, 114, 167, 174, 177
Pale Sulphur Dun, 84
Paraleptophlebia mayflies (Blue Quills), 25, 54, 60, 71, 91, 114, 124, 167, 174, 180
  P. adoptiva, 54, 71, 114, 115, 124
  P. bicornuta (Dark Blue Quill), 54, 91, 174, 180
  P. debilis (Dark Blue Quill), 54, 91, 174
  P. guttata, 9, 54, 71, 114, 115
  P. heteronea (Dark Blue Quill), 54, 91
  P. memorialis (Dark Blue Quill), 54, 91, 162, 174
  P. mollis, 54, 71, 114, 115, 124
  P. packii, 54
  P. strigula, 54, 114, 115
  P. vaciva (Dark Blue Quill), 91

Peak emergence, 61, 62, 64
Penn's Creek (Pennsylvania), 2, 3, 6, 7, 9,
    12, 16, 18, 22, 44, 68, 144, 146, 147
Perhach, John, 72, 79
Photography, and fly imitation, 67
Pine Creek (Pennsylvania), 7, 44, 45, 124
Pink Cahill, 79, 80
Pink Lady, 97
Plecoptera order (stoneflies), 14, 87, 102
Pollution
  and caddis flies, 17
  and common and fishable species, 4–5
  and "good streams," 7
Polymitarcidae Family, 50
Potamanthidae Family, 50, 52
Potamanthus mayflies (Golden or Cream and
    Green Drakes), 50, 52, 60
  P. distinctus, 52
  P. rufous, 52
  P. verticus, 52
Pseudocloeon mayflies (Olive Duns), 54, 55, 59
  P. anoka, 55
  P. carolina, 55
  P. futile, 55
Psilotreta frontalis (Dark Blue Sedge), 17, 86
Pteronarcys californica (Salmon stonefly),
    102, 179, 182, 183, 184
Pupal stage (caddis fly), 17

Quill Gordon, 6, 14–15, 21, 58, 71, 91, 92,
    99, 125, 126, 127, 166

Rainbow trout, 14
Red Quill, 10, 21–22, 54, 71, 72, 73, 90, 92,
    99, 100, 127, 168–171, 174, 175
Red Quill Spinner, 72, 92, 127
Renegade (attractor), 157
Reverse Jenny Spinner, 9, 84, 100, 120
Rhithrogena mayflies, 58, 92
  R. futilis (Quill Gordon), 58, 99, 166
  R. hageni (Pale Brown Dun), 58, 98, 99
  R. undulata (Red Quill), 58, 99–100, 169,
    170, 175
Rhyacophila lobifera (Green Caddis), 17, 22,
    86, 125, 128, 132, 143
Royal Humpy (attractor), 157
Rusty Spinner, 55, 70, 84, 98

Salmon Spinner, 77, 80, 97, 167, 179
Salmon Stonefly, 102, 179, 182, 183, 184
Schwiebert, Ernest, 148
Siphlonuridae Family, 56–57
Siphlonurus mayflies, 56, 59
  S. alternatus, 56
  S. occidentalis (Gray Drake), 25, 26, 56, 97,
    167, 175
  S. quebecensis, 56
  S. rapidus, 56
Six Mile Run (Pennsylvania), 63, 151
Slate Drake, 56, 78, 114, 117, 147–150
Speckle-Winged Duns, 23, 94, 160, 167, 180,
    181

Spinners (mayfly imagos), 11, 14, 16, 65
  Eastern and Midwestern, 110–153
    afternoon, 122–140
    evening, 141–153
    morning, 114–121
  Ephemeridae, 47, 49–50, 52–58
  falls, 11, 16, 24, 25, 44, 45, 118, 135, 142,
    143, 147, 153, 154, 155, 157, 169, 181,
    186
  imitation procedures for (Eastern), 70–86
  imitation procedures for (Western), 89–102
  rating of (Eastern), 24, 25, 28–35
  rating of (Western), 27, 36–43
  Western, 164–185
    afternoon, 173–177
    evening, 178–185
    morning, 164–172
Sporadic species, 16, 21, 22, 24
Sporting-goods centers, 162
Spotted Sedge (*Hydropsyche slossanae*), 86,
    129, 130
Spring Creek (Pennsylvania), 5, 138
Stenacron interpunctatum mayflies (Light Ca-
    hills), 57, 77, 139
  Stenacron interpunctatum canadense, 4–5,
    22, 57, 69, 76, 77, 130, 136, 139, 140
  Stenacron interpunctatum heterotarsale, 57
  Stenacron interpunctatum interpunctatum,
    57
Stenonema mayflies, 3, 22, 24, 57, 59, 75–76,
    143
  S. fuscum (Gray Fox), 11, 22, 25, 57, 66,
    67, 75, 98, 130, 134, 135, 143, 179, 180,
    181, 182
  S. ithaca, 57
  S. luteum (Light Cahill), 25, 57, 82, 83, 96
  S. pulchellum (Cream Cahill), 57, 82
  S. vicarium (American March Brown and
    Great Red Spinner), 45, 57, 76, 95, 130,
    135, 136
Stoneflies (Plecoptera order), 14, 25, 123,
    129, 182–185
  classification system for, 45, 47
  habitats of, 3–6
  imitations, 67, 87, 102
  nomenclature, 20
Stream elevation, 25, 26, 64, 158, 160–161,
    162
Stream selection. *See* "Good stream"
Subimagos. *See* Duns

Taeniopteryx faciata (Early Brown Stonefly),
    67, 87
Temperature
  air, 6, 20, 21
  water, 8, 9, 25, 26–27, 61–63, 64, 90, 116,
    158, 159–160, 162
Terrestrials, 17–18, 87–88
Tricoptera order (caddis flies), 14, 86–87
Tricorythidae Family, 52–53
Tricorythodes mayflies, 15, 23, 24, 52–53, 60,
    68, 114, 118, 120, 121, 160, 186
  T. attratus, 53

Tricorythodes mayflies (*Continued*)
  T. minutus (Pale Olive Dun), 53, 100–101,
    167, 180
  T. stygiatus (Pale Olive Dun), 9, 22, 23, 53,
    69, 84
Trout, 12, 115
  diet of, 14, 16, 17, 18, 19
  and "good streams," 9
  and mayfly emergence, 61, 62, 63, 65
  release of, 186–188
Trout Fin, 154, 155, 156
Trout Streams (Paul Needham), 14, 18
True burrowers (Ephemeridae), 47, 50, 52
Two-winged flies, 18

Un-hatches, 154–157
Upper Madison River (Montana), 25

Water discharge, 158, 161
"Water pennies" (*Psephenus herrick*), 19

Water temperature, 8, 9, 25, 26–27, 61–63,
  64, 90, 116, 158, 159–160, 162
Weather, 6, 123, 126, 127, 158, 161–162. *See
  also* Temperature
Western Green Drake, 53, 89, 95, 162, 166,
  171–172, 174, 176
White Deer Creek (Pennsylvania), 22, 127,
  149
White-Gloved Howdy, 78, 92, 150
White Mayfly, 85, 143
White Wulff, 50, 79, 82, 85, 101, 102
Willowemoc River (New York), 149
Willow Stonefly (*Acroneuria pacifica*), 102,
  182, 183, 184
Wulff Royal Coachman, 154, 155, 156, 157

Yellow Drake (*Ephemera varia*), 15, 22, 49,
  61–65, 136, 143, 150–153
Yellowstone River (Montana and Wyoming),
  26, 107, 179, 182, 184